# HOW TO DEVELOP A SUCCESSFUL HIGH SCHOOL PASSING ATTACK

PRENTICE-HALL, INC., Englewood Cliffs, N.J.

# HOW TO DEVELOP A SUCCESSFUL HIGH SCHOOL PASSING ATTACK

by Noel Reebenacker
Head Football Coach
Marblehead (Mass.) High School

# DEDICATION

To Charley O'Rourke

*The finest coach a passer could have*

*How to Develop a Successful High School Passing Attack,*
by Noel Reebenacker



LIBRARY OF CONGRESS
CATALOG CARD NUMBER: 65–16593

Third Printing.....February, 1968

PRINTED IN THE UNITED STATES OF AMERICA

40532–BC

# BUILDING THE ATTACK

While the primary method of attack for most high school football teams is the running game, the influence exerted by the professional teams upon the college and in turn upon the high-school game will cause this trend to change somewhat. The fact that many of our nation's outstanding college teams boast strong passing attacks indicates the trend toward a more wide-open style of offensive attack.

Because the key to a successful passing attack is a good passer, most of this book is devoted to the development of an outstanding passer. My first objective is to show the coaching procedure involved in developing the boy who is raw material in the lower grades into an outstanding passer in his last two years in high school. If you wait for the boy with all the natural talent to come along, your great passers will be few and far between, or nonexistent.

To have a successful passing team, there are many other fundamental areas a coach must work on diligently. Capable receivers must also be developed to complement the passer, and pass protection blockers must be properly trained to make the passing game strictly a team effort. Only when you have developed the fundamental skills of the passing game may you turn your attention to the task of incorporating these skills into an over-all passing attack.

The second major objective of this book is to show how a successful passing attack may be incorporated into any offensive game. I show how we do it at Marblehead and how the reader can incorporate passing into his attack.

A high-school coach should not be afraid to make extensive use of the passing game. Tom Manning, our quarterback several seasons ago, threw a total of 25 touchdown passes in nine games which now stands as a state record. High-school teams can pass successfully and there are many outstanding teams that rely chiefly on the forward pass. There are some who say that a passing team is a lazy team directed by a lazy coach. This is not true. A great deal of hard work and determination must be contributed by both the coach and player in order to develop an outstanding passing attack. The effort is great but the reward is greater.

# CONTENTS

1. SELECTING YOUR PASSER . . . . . . . . . 1

Our Football Organization . . 1
Consider the Age of the Boy . . 2
Develop a Depth of Passers . . 3
Passing Potential . . 4
*Size . Throwing ability*
Intelligence and Eligibility . . 6
*Know-how*
Leadership . . 8
Speed . . 8

2. THE THROWING MOTION AND THE SET POSITION . . . . . . . . . . 9

Individual Instruction . . 9
Group Instruction . . 10
Passers Working on Their Own . . 10
Teach the Basic Skills First . . 11
Moving Back to Pass . . 12
Feet Position and Body Weight . . 13
The Grip . . 14
The Overhand Throw . . 15
*Positioning the ball to throw . Drawing the ball back . Bringing the ball forward . Releasing the ball . The follow-through*
A Caution to the Coach . . 20
The Four Sources of Power . . 20
*The wrist . The arm . Shoulders . Back*

Stepping Up to Throw . . 23
*Stepping up into the pocket . Stepping forward for greater distance*
Warming Up . . 24
Control and Accuracy . . 26
*Keep your eye on the target*
Leading Your Receiver . . 27
Changing the Direction of Throw . . 28
Timing Your Release . . 30
Our Best Method to Improve Timing . . 34
Throwing from the Set Position . . 35

3. THROWING FROM MOVING OR OFF-BALANCE POSITIONS . . . . . . . 36

Practice Off-Balance Throwing . . 36
Use the Right Foot as a Base . . 37
The "Right-Handed" Factor . . 37
Passing While Running Right . . 38
Passing While Running Left . . 39
Passing While Running Forward . . 42
Passing While Moving Backwards . . 43
Running Pass Drills . . 44
*Drill 1 . Drill 2 . Drill 3*
Pass-or-Run Option . . 46
Teaching Pass-or-Run Skills . . 47
*Use your films*
Two Pass-or-Run Situations . . 48

4. STRIVE FOR PERFECTION . . . . . . . . . 49

Work on Passing Year Round . . 49
*The winter months . Spring workouts . The spring practice . The summer months*
Poor Timing . . 52

Loss of Accuracy . . 52
*Underthrown pass . Loss of Lateral accuracy*
Loss of Spiral . . 54
Throwing a Hard Pass . . 54
The "Gun Shy" Passer . . 55
Perfection Is Your Goal . . 56

5. THE RECEIVER . . . . . . . . . . . . . . 57

Qualities of a Good Receiver . . 57
*Good hands . Good movement . Speed and size*
Improving a Poor Pass Receiver . . 59
Techniques for Catching a Football . . 60
*Loose hands . The hands and arms of the receiver . "Giving" with the ball . Concentration*
Some Boys Never Develop . . 62
Individual Faking Moves . . 63
*The wrinkle fake . The double wrinkle fake . Z-in and Z-out . The hook . The hook-go fake . The fake block . Change of pace . Change of direction*
Breaking Down a Pass Defense . . 73
Working with Receivers and Passers Together . . 73

6. A PASSING OFFENSE . . . . . . . . . . . 75

Advantages of Standard Pass Play . . 75
Disadvantages of Standard Pass Play . . 75
Terminology . . 76
Our Offensive Set-up . . 78
Standard Pass Patterns . . 79
*Trail-out pass . Trail-in pass . Hook-go pass . Deep cross pass*

Miscellaneous Standard Passes . . 86
*Fall-off pass . Pro pass*
Screen Passes . . 89
*Executing a screen pass . Halfback technique on the screen pass*
The Individual Pass Pattern . . 93
*Rolling out on an individual pass pattern . The stay pass . Individual pass moves*
Our Offensive System . . 96
*Our cross series*
Off-Tackle Run . . 97
The Off-Tackle Pass . . 98
*27–0 pass against an overshifted defense*
Weak Side Off-Tackle Run and Pass . . 100
*The run, 46–0 . The 46–0 pass*
Defensive Adjustments and Variations . . 102
*Loosening the end . Covering the flat with an inside linebacker . Safety man covering the flat . The defense may run with you . The defense may overshift*
Series Action Passes . . 105
*The cross series . Cross series passes . The fan series . The 19–60 fan pass*
Slot "T" Line-up Compared to
Pro "T" Line-up . . 109
The Short Pass versus the Long Pass . . 110
Summary . . 111

7. PROTECTING THE PASSER . . . . . . . . 113

Rushing the Passer . . 113
The Time Element . . 114
Normal Blocking for Linemen . . 115
*Lineman with the defensive man head on . Withdrawing pressure . An uncovered blocker*

Aggressive Blocking for Linemen . . 117

*Aggressive techniques . The uncovered blocker*

The Waiting Block . . 118

A One-on-One Drill for Pass Protection . . 120

Normal Backfield Blocking—
Pocket Protection . . 120

Situations Faced by Protecting Back . . 121

*Blocking the end who rushes from the outside . Halfback block of end on inside path . Halfback blocking the tough end . The non-rushing end*

Blocking an Outstanding Defensive End . . 124

Aggressive Backfield Blocking . . 124

Backfield Pass Blocking Drill . . 125

*Dummy drill . Semi-live drill . Live drill . Aggressive drill*

Pocket Protection . . 128

*Pocket protection blocking rules . The tight linebacker*

Handling Stunting and
Red Dogging Defenses . . 130

*The stunting defense . The shooting linebacker*

The Concentrated Rush . . 132

*Holding in one receiver to block . Throwing a short quick pass . Rolling out*

Protecting for the Rollout . . 134

*Blocking the on side . Blocking the off side*

Rollout Right Pass . . 136

*Left tackle . Left guard . Center . Right guard . Right tackle*

Backfield Blocking . . 138

*Fullback . Halfback*

Expect a Determined Rush . . 139

8. COMPILING AND KEEPING RECORDS . . . 141

Be Realistic in Your Record Keeping . . 142

Our Record Keeping Organization . . 143

Game-by-Game Record . . 144

*The scouting report*

Game Film Analysis . . 145

*Offensive game film review . Analysis of opponent. Keeping of statistics*

Seasonal Summary . . 151

*General seasonal passing summary . Summary of individual pass plays*

Balance Your Attack . . 155

9. INTEGRATING A PASSING ATTACK INTO ANY OFFENSE . . . . . . . . . . . 156

Evaluate Your Present Passing Game . . 156

*Diagram present pass plays . Place your passes in categories . Test your memory . Use of your game films . The film study*

Determine Your Passing Needs . . 162

*The element of surprise*

Collect Your Findings . . 164

10. INTEGRATING NEW TRENDS AND IDEAS INTO YOUR ATTACK . . . . 166

Be a Student of the Game . . 166

*Books, periodicals, articles as sources . Attendance at coaching clinics . Learn from your assistants . Learn from your opponents . Learn from losing*

The Sprint Series . . 170

*Initial experience with the sprint pass . Difficulties encountered in sprint series*

The Rollout versus the Pocket Pass . . 175

*The passer is the key*

Influence of the College Game . . 177
Influence of the Professionals . . 178
*Personnel problems created by the pro attack*
The Tandem Backs . . 180

11. ATTACKING PASS DEFENSES . . . . . . . 181

Difficulties of Pass Defense . . 181
Pass Defense Alternatives . . 182
Rushing the Passer . . 182
*Protect your passer . Passes to use when rushed . Tight-covering halfbacks . The rush from one end*
Holding up the Receivers . . 184
*Overcoming the delaying of receivers*
Complete Downfield Coverage . . 186
*Passing against full coverage . Type of pass*
Defeating Man-to-Man Coverage . . 189
*Type of pass*
Zone Coverage . . 190
*Weakness of zone defense . Advantages of zone defense . Normal zone coverage*
Defeating a Zone Pass Defense . . 193
*Force some man-to-man coverage . Flooding zones . Pass into "in-between" areas . The passer is the key*
Perfect Your Own Pass Defense . . 196
*Become a pass defense expert*

12. THE WEEK OF THE GAME . . . . . . . . 197

Be Prepared for Anything . . 198
Combating Various Offensive Formations . . 198
Combating Various Defenses . . 199

Knowledge of the Rules . . 201
Game Week Preparation—
Coaches Meetings . . 202
*Preparing your defense . Preparing your offense*
Introducing Your Plans at Practice . . 206
*Offensive plans . Defensive plans*
A Practice Schedule . . 208

13. CONDUCTING THE GAME . . . . . . . . 211

Believe You Can Win . . 212
Your Written Preparation . . 213
*Personnel charts . Offensive plans . Defensive alignments*
Role of the Assistant Coaches . . 214
*Work of the assistant coach . Work of the line coach*
Coaching Teamwork Is Required . . 217
The Job of the Head Coach . . 217
*Substitution . Observe backs and ends*
Defensive Strategy . . 219
Offensive Strategy . . 219
*Uncover defensive weaknesses . Stay with success*
Fooling the Defense . . 222
Making Your Passing Game Go . . 222
*Your passer will be rushed . Breaking down downfield coverage . Example of exploiting a pass defense*
Originating Plays . . 226
*Halftime opportunity*
Making the Big Play . . 226
Be Predictably Unpredictable . . 227
Passing Strategy . . 228
Conclusion . . 229

INDEX . . . . . . . . . . . . . . . 231

ONE

# SELECTING YOUR PASSER

Many college coaches feel that the natural instincts of a great passer are inborn. These coaches concern themselves with searching for a "natural" passer and recruiting him. Other coaches feel that a natural athlete can be made into a great passer and have been quite successful in proving this. I subscribe to the second belief: The potential talent must be present but often good coaching is necessary to bring it out.

At the high school level, we cannot go out and recruit a ready-made passer. There will be few, if any, boys who come along in a coach's career who are natural-born passers. If we wish to have an outstanding passer in high school we have to develop one. From the boys who will be in your football program from the early grades until they graduate as seniors, you must select the one who is to be your passer.

## Our Football Organization

Organized football in Marblehead begins at the fifth and sixth grade level with our midget football program that is conducted by a small group of dedicated townspeople. The junior high-school program provides football for the seventh and eighth graders. At the high-school level we have a separate ninth grade team, a junior varsity team, and our varsity team.

A boy in Marblehead has an opportunity to play in an organized football program from the fifth grade until he graduates. This program gives us the chance to begin looking for our future passers among the boys in the younger age groups.

However, our football situation is far from being ideal. I have a full teaching load, which makes lack of time a serious limiting factor in the conduct of the program. The other limiting factor is the poor physical set-up, both inside and outside. We are the only team in our conference that is compelled by lack of space to practice on our game field. If you get nothing else from this text, I hope to convince you that you can be a consistent winner even though your circumstances are far from the best. Live with your shortcomings and be determined to be a winner in spite of them.

Our school population is about average for our conference, which comprises eight teams. For some reason we seem to consistently field one of the lightest teams in the league. Because of the small size of our players, the passing game is the only style of offense that permits us to be consistent scorers.

## Consider the Age of the Boy

There is a direct relationship between the age of the boy when he starts as a quarterback and the stage of development he is able to reach by his senior year in high school. The younger you start him, the more proficient he will become.

The best time to make the selection is when he is about to enter eighth grade. This is often difficult to do because you may not be able to find the time due to teaching duties to go to another school to evaluate and make a judgment.

In our school, the ninth grade is a part of the high school. As a result the teams practice in the same area and it is easier to find an opportunity to visit the ninth grade team at practice. Our selection is made by the ninth grade season or during that next spring practice.

A capable athlete selected for the position of quarterback

by the end of the ninth grade should be a playing quarterback as a junior and be a starter as a senior. This is an ideal situation and often a sophomore or junior may win the starting assignment from a senior. It is much easier to switch a senior quarterback to another position than it would be to switch a halfback to quarterback for his senior year.

Converting a boy from another position to quarterback in the tenth grade or later will result in your getting only one useful season (as a senior) from him as an effective signal caller. Switching a senior to quarterback in an emergency situation, will result in only an adequate job. If a boy does well in making such a change, then there is little question that he would have been even more effective in his original position.

## Develop a Depth of Passers

My objective is to select at least one boy from each class and then work with him to develop him into a passer. This means that an abundance of good athletes may be quarterbacks while the rest of the backfield starves. It is simple enough to switch one or more of your quarterbacks into other backfield positions once he has begun to develop a passing ability. Because he has been trained as a quarterback, it will be easy for him to play the quarterback position in a emergency. By operating in this manner, you will always have good quarterback depth for your ball games and good quarterbacks returning for the next year.

Our passer returning next year for his senior season is possibly an even greater passer than Tom Manning. Unfortunately his receivers won't be as capable as Manning's. This boy can throw for any distance from any body position, and he is one of the best running backs I've coached. Our junior passer will play a halfback post but will continue to receive work at the quarterback position.

The boy who will be our sophomore quarterback has great speed and will, I feel, develop into a very fine passer. In fact, this boy in all probability will be a starting quarterback in his junior year. He is a fine athlete and could possibly break into our starting lineup next season, perhaps as a defensive half-back. No matter how much or little he plays on Saturday, he will be the offensive quarterback in the junior varsity game on Monday. He won't play defense on the junior varsity but the offensive experience is an absolute necessity.

There are several promising boys who are coming up to the ninth grade from whom a selection is yet to be made. The criteria used in making the selection are basically as follows, in order of importance:

1. Potential as a passer
2. Intelligence
3. Leadership
4. Speed.

### Passing Potential

At the beginning of each fall, I visit the ninth grade team at practice. Prior to the visit I have talked with the eighth and ninth grade coaches and have the names of boys they feel could be developed into quarterbacks. The visit is made during the second or third week of practice so that the ninth grade coach has had some opportunity to observe his squad.

I first take out each boy I wish to look at, one at a time. I don't interrupt their practice to do this. The boy and I will go over to the side and I'll throw with him for about five minutes. Then I call out the next boy. In addition to the names on the list, any other boy who looks worthy will also be called over. There are several basic things that I look for.

*Size.* Does he have height? He may not have it now but do you feel he will eventually? Big hands and feet are often indications of this. Does he have big hands? A boy will throw better if he can get more "hand" on the ball. Will he have reasonable weight? A "skinny" quarterback may be more subject to injury and would be less effective as a runner.

Any or all of these physical characteristics may be lacking and yet his other qualities may be such that you would still select him. The best quarterback we've ever had was five feet ten inches, 135 pounds, having average-sized hands, and only possessing average speed. His sense of timing, *releasing the ball at just the right moment,* turned out to be his biggest asset. We also have had a boy with all of these desirable assets. He stood six feet, weighed 170 pounds, had very large hands, good speed and was a real heady runner. He developed his passing technique until he could throw a distance of nearly 70 yards in the air. Also he threw very well while running both left and right. He was extremely dangerous on the rollout and ran for as many scores as he threw for. If you have a quarterback who in addition to being a good passer can really move, you have the finest offensive weapon in football.

*Throwing Ability.* Any boy who has ever played football has thrown the ball often. In watching the movements of a boy, you should not make any corrections at first. But these are the things you should look for:

1. Does he throw overhand rather than sidearm?
2. Does he throw with any degree of accuracy?
3. Are the movements of his arm, body, eyes and feet all coordinated?
4. How far can he throw?
5. Does the ball have a reasonable spiral?
6. Is he coachable?

After a few minutes, make a few corrections. Correct his grip, change his follow through, or make other changes you feel would be helpful. Observe whether he responds quickly to your instructions. A slight improvement should be noticed immediately.

There are many boys you could teach to be good passers if you had sufficient time. Since you don't have much time, you try to choose a boy who already has some of the attributes of a good passer. For example, a great deal of time is needed to teach a sidearmer to throw overhand. A boy who throws overhand at the beginning can be developed a great deal faster, so look for a boy who can throw overhand at the start.

You will find that you will not spend the five minutes with each boy. After just a few throws, you will be convinced that some boys will not be good quarterbacks. There are certainly many factors involved, but remember this one thing: *your quarterback must be a good passer.* Therefore, passing potential must be placed at the top of the list.

## Intelligence and Eligibility

It would certainly be unfortunate for a coach to spend a great deal of time with a boy only to have him become ineligible to play because of poor or failing grades. So before choosing a boy, be certain that he is capable of passing the courses he is enrolled in. A check of his scholastic record will tell you whether he is. It is not necessary that he be a "brain." Attaining passing grades is sufficient.

*Know-how.* Now that we have found an eligible boy, let's concern ourselves with the type of intelligence he must have to be a good quarterback. It is implicit in the phrase—"football know-how." Because high-school football is a game for boys and not for coaches, most of the plays should be called by the quarterback. Therefore, he must be able to call plays: he must have "football know-how."

Since it is difficult to recognize the ability to call plays in a boy, only through intimate contact with him will you be able to spot it. But by then it may be too late. Your junior high-school coaches, men in the town who have worked with the boy in Little League Baseball, YMCA, Midget Football, etc. can often give you a great deal of information about him. You may hear them say he is very mature, a natural leader, quick thinker, etc. I'm sure you can properly evaluate these remarks.

Should you find later on that your quarterback lacks this football "thinking ability," you can compensate for it. You may find that you have to call many more of the plays than you would like to but sometimes this has to be done. There are also ways you can help a boy develop this play-calling ability that will be discussed later. Of course, the run or pass play requires thinking while running and only by practicing this art will a boy show improvement.

## Leadership

There seem to be two types of leadership displayed on the football field. First there is leadership by encouraging, pushing, cajoling, nagging, threatening others to make a greater effort. Then there is leadership by example: returning in the fall in the best condition or being first in line to form up for a tackling drill.

Your quarterback should be a leader by example. But he also needs to show leadership by encouraging others. Both these traits are very easy to observe and can easily be developed. A check with his previous coaches can give you information about his leadership ability.

In addition, a boy who has self-confidence in his ability and displays this feeling to others will certainly be more effective. The team should have confidence in him and should turn to him for leadership when the going gets tough. I'm not talking about a boy whose confidence is displayed in boasting and conceit, but a boy with the quiet, cool confidence of knowing he can and will lead when called upon. Keeping a boy's confidence at the right level, not too little and not too much, almost requires a master psychologist. You must see that he is self-confident rather than self-satisfied.

If the boy does well, praise him, but have helpful suggestions how he could do something better. A passer should always strive to do better and is always capable of at least a slight improvement. He should set his goals high but not out of reach.

Should a boy perform poorly, encourage him. Point out what he did well, as well as his errors. The worst thing a coach can do is to tear his quarterback apart before the squad. His self-confidence would be shaken and the entire squad's confidence would suffer. Don't baby him, but don't continually blast him. Depending on the temperament of the boy, a course somewhere between these two extremes should be followed.

## Speed

Every coach would like to have speed in all backfield positions, at the ends and often at the guards. Unfortunately, there just aren't that many boys in one high school with real speed. On your football squad you may (if you're lucky) have one boy that can really move. If he were a good runner as well it would be wasteful to use him as a quarterback because you must have one halfback who is a break-away threat.

There will be three or four boys with good speed and maybe just as many who can run better than average. It would be most helpful if one of these boys were your quarterback. The requirement of speed is often the most difficult to fill after the others have been considered. But speed is the frosting on the cake. A passer who can and will run is the most dangerous offensive weapon in the game of football today.

This brings up an interesting situation we have facing us next season. Our senior passer is not only a fine passer but an outstanding runner as well. There is another senior quarterback who is also an excellent passer but who is very slow. I have been severely criticized for not moving the runner back to halfback so that both these fine athletes would be able to play. To my way of thinking there is no decision to be made. In football today, the running quarterback is the difference between a good offensive attack and a great offensive attack.

In conclusion, selecting the right boy involves four basic considerations—passing potential, intelligence, leadership and speed. Try your best to fulfill all four requirements. Now that we have selected the boy, let's go to work.

TWO

# THE THROWING MOTION AND THE SET POSITION

Teaching a boy to become a good passer is time consuming. The scheduled practice time will not be sufficient to provide the individual instruction that is needed. Before going into the actual techniques of coaching a passer, it is necessary for us to plan ahead as far as time requirements are concerned. There are three different types of coaching situations.

## Individual Instruction

This involves having a coach give individual instruction to one passer or a few passers at the most.

1. Passers are required to stay out 15 minutes after practice every day to receive individual instruction.
2. Sometimes during a practice session there might be an opportunity to send a coach and some passers to a separate area for some work. This is seldom possible because these boys usually play defense and are busy the entire practice session.
3. The passer with the right attitude is usually out early for practice and we do spend a few minutes at that time.

4. During spring football practice, I spend a great deal of practice time giving individual instructions.

## Group Instruction

This area includes any instructions you are able to give your passer while you are working with large groups. For example, you may be able to run pass patterns against your own pass defense. There are many times in a practice session when you can coach the passer even though you are working with many boys.

1. Our practice is two hours long and is usually broken up into one hour of individual group practice and one hour of team practice. During a session of two hours, there is always at least one half hour devoted to some phase of the passing game. When we are practicing our own pass defense, we are also working with our passers. I'm sure that if someone were to total the minutes of a session that our passers are throwing he would find that on some days they had at least 60 minutes of passing practice.
2. Spring practice is devoted mainly to the passing game. Our conference rules do not permit us to wear pads in the spring. During this period, I work almost exclusively with the passers and receivers. This is when a great amount of my passing instruction is given.

## Passers Working on Their Own

There are many ways a boy can improve his ability by practicing on his own. In fact, a good passer must spend a great deal of his time, year round, practicing to perfect his techniques.

We are no different than any other school in that time

seems to be the determining factor of anything we do. There never seems to be enough time to do everything one wishes to do. By planning ahead, we provide the necessary time for coaching the passer without harm to our over-all coaching plan.

1. During practice there are times when the passers can go off on their own for a few minutes passing. I try to keep aware of this, and any time they are standing for a few minutes, I make them throw.
2. Every passer has a football at home. I point out to each passer the importance of throwing every chance he has. I assume that the boy I have selected likes to pass and has the necessary drive to practice on his own.
3. A passer is given a carefully prepared plan for scheduling his passing workouts during the all-important summer months. This plan includes the minimum time that he should work out, which will be presented in Chapter 4. Also, all of the passing drills that are given in the book are diagramed and the boy who wants to practice year-round should have a list of drills such as these for reference. He should have performed all of them under your guidance during spring practice so he will know the proper techniques.

## Teach the Basic Skills First

In teaching a boy to become a good passer, it is essential to start at the very beginning. You should spend the first few days in the fall working on the fundamentals of the game almost exclusively. You should do the same when working with your passer. These fundamentals must become so ingrained that they are performed automatically every time the boy passes. In the heat of a ball game you can be sure that grip or the follow-through is the furthest thing from his mind when he is moving back to pass.

## Moving Back to Pass

Our snap from center is very orthodox. The quarterback has his right hand well under, exerting pressure. His left wrist is locked to his right one with his left fingers pointing toward the ground and back so as not to be jammed. The ball is twisted as it is brought back so that the quarterback receives the ball with the fingers of his passing hand across the laces.

**Plate 1**

*Photos by Sam Harris*

The quarterback stands with his feet parallel, weight on the balls of his feet, his back reasonably straight (see Plate 1). He does his bending at the knees. Be sure he does not start leaning back as he is about to go back to pass. This is a sure tip to the defense. His hands stay with the center, who is beginning to move on the snap of the ball, until he gets the ball. He pivots to the right on his left foot, turns his body and steps right, left, right, and then a bounce on his right foot. As he comes back he fingers for his grip, is straightening up, and brings the ball up to his ear. These steps 1, 2, 3 bounce, will bring him back five and one half yards. When he lands on his right foot at the end he will be in the set position.

## Feet Position and Body Weight

Passing from the set position will bring about the greatest accuracy. If a boy is moving and has the time to set, he should do so before throwing. The feet are positioned about shoulder width, the left foot being toed out somewhat. The body weight is back on the right (rear) foot, little weight is placed on the forward foot. The right foot is positioned nearly perpendicular to the direction of throw, while the left foot is compromised between side and front. As the ball is brought forward, the left foot steps toward the target and a transfer of weight takes place from the back foot to the forward foot. When almost all the weight is on the left foot, the right foot will naturally twist to a forward position and will be dragged forward somewhat. Do not allow the passer to keep his right leg stiff as if throwing a fast ball. It should bend naturally as it begins to drag on his right toe. After the ball is thrown, the passer brings his right foot forward one step to a good position from which to defend himself.

Two of the errors encountered with the set position are overstriding with the left foot and stepping back right after the ball is released. After the ball is thrown, the hands, feet, and the entire body should all point in the direction of the throw.

## The Grip

It has already been mentioned that large hands are a great asset for a passer. The proper fingering of the ball, getting a lot of "hand" on it, has a direct effect on control and accuracy. Throwing with a poor grip is like firing a small caliber bullet out of a large caliber rifle.

We teach the boy to grip the ball in the following manner. His two small fingers overlap the strings. The large knuckle of his middle finger butts against the end of the strings while his forefinger is slightly spread (see Plate 2). His palm is not flat against the ball. You should be able to slide a pencil or your little finger up between his hand and the ball.

**Plate 2**

This grip will probably not lead to a spiral at first. The forefinger is the key to the spiral. As the ball leaves the hand, the forefinger is the last to break contact. This finger imparts the spin to the ball. By adjusting the placement of the forefinger, usually back towards the end of the ball, you can find the spot where the boy will start throwing a spiral. He should almost feel a "click" as he "wipes" his forefinger on the ball at the moment of release.

The strength with which he grips the ball will vary somewhat with each boy. A firm grip would be the best way to describe it. A light grip will cause a loss in both control and accuracy. A light grip should only be used on a wet day, or on a muddy field. If he grips the ball too hard, a boy will find that he is unable to release the ball at the proper moment and that he loses accuracy and control. Naturally if a boy is throwing well with his present grip, do not change it. There are many ways to grip properly.

## The Overhand Throw

When selecting a potential passer, you should always look for a boy who can throw overhand because the capacity to throw overhand is the most important ability a passer can possess. There are great passers in the game today who throw sidearm but they are exceptions to the rule. The average athlete must be taught to throw with an overhand motion if he is to realize his full potential as a passer.

The overhand throw results in a much more accurate throw. If the passer releases the ball at the wrong instant in his motion, the ball will be either underthrown or overthrown. This is much preferable to the sidearm throw, which if improperly timed will go to the right or left of the target as well as being underthrown or overthrown. Another distinct advantage to throwing overhand is that the upraised hands of the rushing linemen will be less of a problem. Perhaps the best argument for the overhand throw is that it is the more natural body motion.

In the following discussions, techniques are presented for the right-handed passer. You need only reverse the procedure to make the discussion relative to the left-handed passer. Just because a boy is left-handed, it doesn't mean that he should have any problems that a right-handed boy wouldn't have.

*Positioning the Ball to Throw.* To be certain of getting maximum control of the ball, the passer must hold the ball in both hands before beginning any throwing motion. The ball is so positioned that the knuckle of the left forefinger is next to the right cheekbone (see Plate 3). In this starting position, the point of the ball is pointing toward the target.

One very common error that many passers make is that they "hitch" the ball just as they start their throwing motion. A hitch is almost a nervous reaction, the ball being jerked forward or down or both before it starts back. When the brain says throw, the quicker the ball is released the better the pass will be. If when the brain says throw, you hitch and then start your motion, valuable time is lost. When the throw command is given with the ball positioned at the ear, the passer's first movement should be to draw the ball back. Some passers will always have a hitch but you may be able to get them to cut down on the size of it.

*Drawing the Ball Back.* When drawing the ball back, the passer keeps his left hand with the ball as long as he can comfortably do so. The left hand, when it is free of the ball will naturally return to a forward position (see Plate 4). Once the left hand is removed from the ball, the right hand continues to draw the ball back and now begins to raise it higher.

Tell your passer to lock his wrist against any twisting motion. The ball should be able to move only in a backward and forward direction. As the ball is drawn back, the wrist is cocked back. The shoulders are also twisted backward during the movement. "Cocking" the shoulders will cause the point of the ball to point away from the target, but when the shoulders are rotated forward, the point of the ball will return to the proper position. Let me repeat this caution: *do not allow the wrist to twist in this movement; lock the wrist.* If the ball should flutter, wobble sideways, or give the appearance of being scaled, you know immediately the wrist has been twisted.

If the ball is to be thrown long, one can get additional distance by twisting the trunk at the waist, the amount of this twist depending upon the distance the ball is to be thrown. At the instant the ball stops its rearward motion to begin the trip forward, the wrist, the shoulders and the trunk are all like coiled springs that when released will supply the power to the throw. The ball in this rearward position is held high and behind the head so as to insure an overhand throw (see Plate 4).

*Bringing the Ball Forward.* As the ball is brought forward, the trunk is twisted forward. When the trunk begins to untwist the shoulders are snapped forward to add their power to the ball. The wrist is snapped forward at the moment the ball is released. The body is twisted forward before the ball is released. In fact, the arm carrying the ball is the last part to begin its journey forward.

The elbow of the throwing arm leads the ball as it is brought forward, and the ball travels on a higher course than it did when it was brought back. When the forward movement is at about the halfway point, the power of the arm is released, and the arm is extended to a high overhand position just prior to releasing the ball. As the right hand moves forward, it should follow a path directly above the course it followed when drawn back. However, you may find that it is possible for a passer to cock his arm in one way and release it in another, and still be successful. I have had at least one boy who drew the ball back sidearm and brought it forward overhand. I didn't change his method because the forward overhand movement is more important than the backward movement.

*Releasing the Ball.* At the moment of release, the arm is extended upward and the ball is released high and in front of

Plate 3

Plate 4

the head. At this precise moment the wrist is snapped forward (see Plate 5). When releasing from this point, the boy has the feeling of throwing an overhand fast ball down to a batter. We have a beginner exaggerate this high release, instructing him to extend his hand upward even higher than is natural just to acquaint him with the feeling. Constant practice at releasing the ball is necessary to insure perfect timing because the position of the ball at the moment of release determines the height of the pass. If the ball is released too soon, the pass will be overthrown. If the release is late, the pass will be underthrown.

*The Follow-Through.* By watching a boy's follow-through, you can determine whether he throws overhand properly. When the ball is released, the arm continues its natural down-

Plate 5

Plate 6

ward movement diagonally across the body (see Plate 6). If the hand is touching the left front pocket at the end of the follow-through, the overhand throw has been properly executed. Tell your passer to keep that arm moving as though he were going to take a dollar bill out of his left pocket after he has released the ball.

During the entire overhand throwing process, the arm movements must correspond with the movement of the feet and the proper control of body weight as described earlier. The reason for discussing the overhand throw separately is that the footwork and body weight considerations differ when the ball is thrown from a moving or off-balance position. The arm movements of the overhand throw are the same regardless of whether the passer is in a set position or in any other position.

## A Caution to the Coach

One thing we coaches must avoid is overcoaching. This text is very specific as to how a boy should grip the ball, or as to how he should follow through. If we insist that a boy perform each step perfectly, we may find that he does each part very well but ends up throwing a poor pass. By becoming too involved in technique a boy may forget his primary objective—a completed pass. At practice, when a player begins to press and is throwing poorly, I often remark: "There he is, throw him the ball."

## The Four Sources of Power

The power that a passer is able to impart to the ball can be broken down into four major components. These are the forces that result from the action of his wrist, his arm, his shoulders, and his back. The short, quick pass depends mostly upon the wrist for its power and the long pass requires the use of all four sources blended smoothly together to get the maximum power behind the ball. But whether throwing long or short, the passing motion is always the same. Throwing a long or medium pass requires the same action of the wrist that a short pass demands.

*The Wrist.* A passer's wrist is his primary source of power and he must make proper use of it. By using wrist strength only, he should be able to snap the ball 15 yards and can release a short pass very quickly and accurately. For a short pass the ball is not brought back very far and is released by snapping the wrist forward.

The development of a strong wrist should therefore be an objective for every passer. There are many exercises that use either isometrics or weights to strengthen the wrist. A good drill for developing wrist strength is to have two passers in their normal passing stance stand 10 or 15 yards apart, facing each other. When the boy without the ball shouts "fire," the passer must release the ball as quickly as possible with a quick snap of the wrist. Frequent practice of this drill will strengthen the wrist and give the boy additional practice in passing. All of your drills for your passer should involve passing whenever possible. Only by continually throwing can a boy perfect his passing ability.

*The Arm.* The arm is of course the second source of power. When both arm and wrist are used, a ball can be released rather quickly and to distances of 25 yards. Naturally, movements of the wrist and arm blend into one continuous action. The corresponding body movements have been discussed, but it must be remembered that *all* of the movements are blended into one smooth continuous action.

An excellent drill for strengthening the arm is one we use for a warm-up every day. Have two passers stand 10 yards apart, feet spread shoulder width, squared off facing each other. The feet remain in place so the ball can only be thrown by using the arm and wrist. Once they are warmed up, move them 15 yards, then 20, and finally 25 yards apart. To throw 25 yards from such a facing-forward, feet parallel position is very difficult and requires a strong arm. Moreover, this drill not only strengthens a passer's arm; it is the best drill to develop the entire overhand throwing motion that is so important. Whenever throwing in this or any other drill, a boy should *always* throw at a target. Tell your passer to hit his man *right between the eyes.*

*Shoulders.* When throwing a greater distance as in the preceding drill, a passer can develop the third source of strength. A passer can add to power of the arm and wrist by proper movement of the shoulders while throwing medium and long distances. There are many ways to strengthen the shoulders that you are familiar with: Weight lifting, push-ups and pull-ups can strengthen shoulders. Let me repeat: when the power of the shoulders is added to that of the arm and wrist, *all of the movements must blend in one smooth, continuous action.*

*Back.* When throwing for long distances, the passer must bring the strength of the back into play. Twisting the shoulders will naturally cause some twisting in the trunk. In long-distance throwing, the trunk is twisted back and on the forward motion is snapped forward, so that the passer finishes with the weight on his front foot, his body inclined forward. The power of the back is integrated with the three other forces to supply a maximum amount of controlled power to the ball.

"Throw the same way every time." These are words you should caution your passer with continually. Whether he is on balance, moving laterally, or off balance, the movement of the passer's wrist, arm, shoulder and back will be the same. The throwing motion is the same for *all* passes, regardless of distance. For longer distances, more power is merely brought into play. The wrist snaps the same way on a long pass as it does on a short pass. A passer will employ these sources of power: 1; 1, 2; 1, 2, 3; or 1, 2, 3, 4. But he is really developing just one technique of passing. An excellent drill to help a boy develop this single technique while passing various distances is shown in Figure 1.

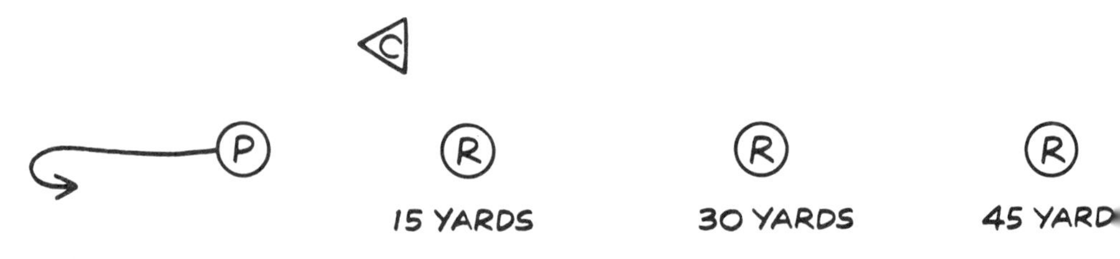


**Figure 1**

On a command from the coach, the passer fades back and sets up. When the coach shouts "short," "middle" or "long," the passer throws to the designated receiver. We often use passers instead of receivers, which makes it easier to rotate so that all will have a turn. One passer is worked for three or four minutes and then we switch to another. Make the passer hustle during this drill. When a boy begins to sweat he starts to pass better. We also introduce a sudden change in command. For example, the coach shouts "long" and as the boy starts to throw, the coach shouts "short." The passer must recover his balance and throw short.

I teach a passer to stop in the middle of his motion, recover and then throw elsewhere because of a personal experience as a player. During a game I was in the process of throwing to a receiver in the left flat when he stumbled and fell. Although my arm was moving forward, I was able to hold onto the ball, and recover. I changed direction slightly, threw a greater distance, and hit another receiver in the middle of the field for a touchdown. I am convinced that a passer can be taught to recover and throw to another spot. Indeed, my high-school passers have done this on several occasions.

## Stepping Up to Throw

Many coaches require their passers to step forward as they throw. One reason for this is that by stepping up into the protective pocket, they give the blocking halfbacks a better blocking angle on the rushing ends. Moreover, the forward momentum adds more power to the throw. Also stepping forward helps passers who have accuracy problems in learning to line up in the direction they are to throw. The major disadvantage of stepping forward is that it requires a longer time to complete the throwing motion. This can cause a passer to have trouble with his timing.

*Stepping Up Into the Pocket.* If a passer takes a few quick steps forward, he does not disturb the set position and the throwing motion. By taking the steps, he merely goes from a set position to a new set position, from which he immediately throws. He makes a quick forward jab with his left foot and follows it immediately with a short forward movement of his right foot. His feet are again in the proper position and he can continue his natural throwing motion from this second set position. You may find that some boys always step forward as they pass because of a nervous reaction. You need only teach these boys how to control the tendency to step forward.

It is a good idea to have boys who are not particularly good passers step forward to throw. The forward motion will add both power and accuracy to their passes. Of course, their timing will suffer and they will be unable to change the direction of their throw suddenly. Because quick release and ability to change direction are important to us, we do not teach our passers to step forward when they throw short and medium distances.

*Stepping Forward for Greater Distance.* In order to throw the greatest distance from a set position, the passer must step forward as he throws the ball. For extra power on long passes, we like to have our passer step up as he throws. In the step forward for extra power, the footwork is a little bit different from the step into the pocket. The first step is the same short forward jab with the left foot. However, the second step is a large step forward, with the right foot moving behind the left foot, passing and landing in front of the left foot. The next forward movement of the left foot begins the basic throwing motion. The large step with the right foot will provide additional power to the ball. If a passer is having trouble throwing a sideline pattern, this technique may give his pass the strength so necessary for this pass.

## Warming Up

Whenever a boy starts to throw, he should warm up properly, first throwing for short distances and then gradually throwing for longer distances. Throwing for distance before properly warming up may result in a serious injury which might sideline your passer for some time. Pushing a sore arm will only make it worse. Should you ever catch your quarterback throwing long without warming up, you should severely reprimand him. All squad members should be aware of the

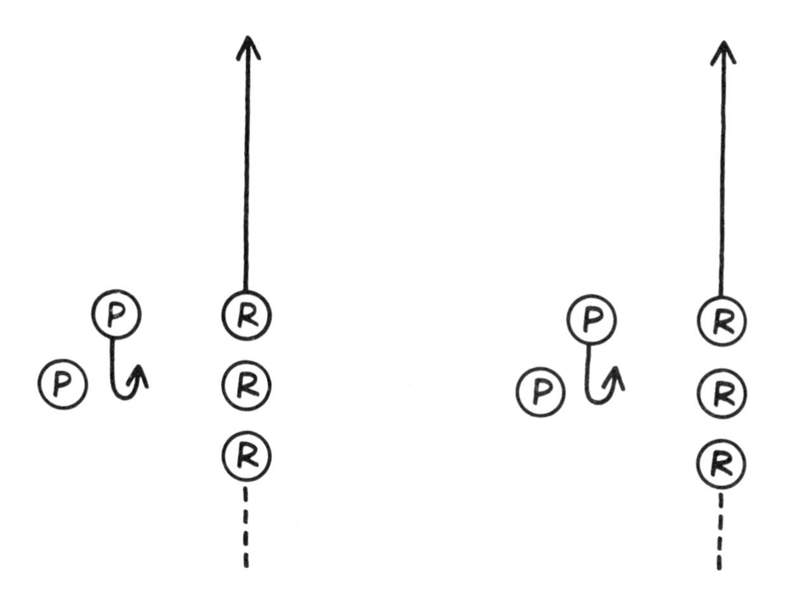


**Figure 2**

danger of not warming up or they may encourage the passer to throw long in pre-practice warming up.

Our passers warm up before the start of practice by using a very simple set up. A passer stands right beside a receiver who is in his three point stance (Figure 2). On the command "set go" the passer straightens up from a stance behind an imaginary center and "pops" the ball at the receiver's near shoulder at a distance of five or ten yards. By using extra balls and no centers, you can throw a tremendous number of quick, short passes in a short period of time. Not only are your passers being warmed up but your receivers are getting some necessary work on the quick reaction needed to catch a short pass.

Don't have your passer throw for very long periods of time, particularly at the beginning of the season. Try to plan your practice so that there will be several well-spaced periods of passing drill. It is easy enough to spot a tired or sore arm merely by watching the body movement and facial expression of the passer, and the flight of the ball. If a boy's arm is bothering him, stop him!

## Control and Accuracy

When he is throwing to a stationary target, we tell our passer to "hit him between the eyes." Whenever he throws, a passer should select a target; he should not just throw in the general direction of his receiver. Have your quarterback throw at different body parts of a standing receiver, i.e. between the eyes, either shoulder, either knee, stomach, high or low on either side. This *drill* helps not only your passers coordination but helps your receiver as well because he has to react quickly to catch a ball aimed at an unknown spot.

We make a little game out of this drill and have some fun with it. We pair off our passers for an accuracy contest and have them throw at a stationary target. Every time a passer hits his target between the eyes he gets a point. The first to get a certain number of points wins. The game can be played at any distance. We play this game frequently, often with a coach competing against a boy, and it stimulates the boys' desire to develop accuracy.

Control of the ball is, of course, a must for accuracy. Keeping two hands on the ball, locking the wrist, releasing high in front and wiping the forefinger across the ball help the control. In fact, all of the actions necessary to control are embodied in the technique previously described, the smooth flowing action in which all body movements are coordinated.

*Keep Your Eyes on the Target.* We cannot talk about accuracy without stressing the importance of teaching your passers that they must keep their eyes on their receivers. The passer must be looking at his receiver before he starts his throwing motion, and he must have his body correctly positioned in relation to his receiver before he throws. The important coaching point here is that you must teach your passer to keep his eye on the receiver even while the ball is in the air. Throwing a pass can easily be compared with bowling. A good bowler keeps his eye on the target pin even after he has thrown the ball, and the ball comes into his vision as it approaches the pin. If his eyes shift from the pin to the moving ball, he loses his accuracy. A passer should not see the ball for about half the distance it travels (except on a short pass). If his eyes remain on target he will first see the ball in the high front area of his peripheral vision, and it will come into his direct vision as it approaches the receiver.

This is a teaching point. Generally a boy will move his eyes from the target to the ball. The later this change of vision takes place, the more accurate will be the throw. You must teach him to keep his eyes on target.

There is another reason for keeping the eyes on the target: often a passer will not see the pass caught. As a player, I have been hit just as the ball was released and never saw the ball in the air; yet the films show the ball was thrown to the right spot. If one were able to develop accuracy only by watching the ball in flight, he would be effective only in dummy scrimmage. To help him keep his eyes on target, have the passer wear a baseball cap so that he can see only the receiver. Then it will be very easy to see if he looks up. Remember to emphasize, "You must keep your eyes on the target all the way."

## Leading Your Receiver

Giving a moving target the proper lead seems to be something that can best be developed only by throwing at moving targets. There are many ways to set up such drills. I use the set-up shown in Figure 3 only because more passes can be thrown in a shorter time.

In this drill each passer has a ball and recovers his own ball from the receiver. The receivers run across the field on a yard line to catch the pass and then line up on the other side. Once the passers have warmed up we deepen the angle of the receiver. We really hustle all the boys in this drill and a tremendous number of passes can be thrown in a very short time.

Again the passer must look at the moving target. He should not look for a point in front of the receiver and throw

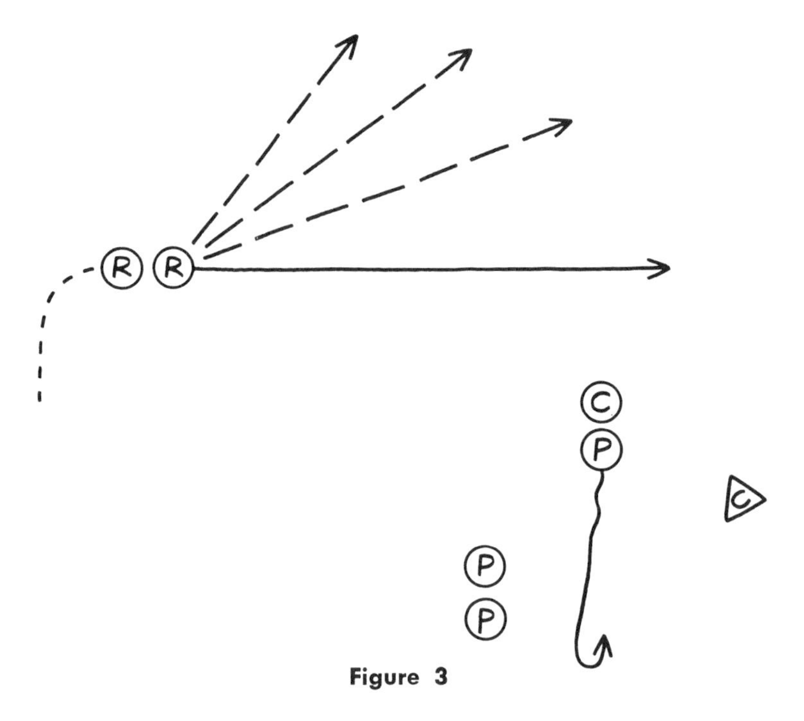


Figure 3

at that because throwing at a point is too mechanical and he will never get the "feel" of the right lead. He should look at the target and throw in front of it. He must judge how far in front because there are so many variables: the angle, the distance from the receiver, the speed of the pass and the speed of the receiver, to name a few. Only through continual practice will a passer develop this ability. One more coaching point, and a very important one, is that he should step toward the point he intends to hit. Although he keeps his eye on the target, he steps toward and follows through to the point where the ball and the receiver will meet.

## Changing the Direction of Throw

Once your passer begins to develop, it is wise to start training him to look in another direction, and even to fake, before looking at his receiver. Pass defenders are taught to look at the quarterback's eyes. As soon as he starts his throwing motion, they move toward the spot he is looking at. In high-school football, the passer who does not look at his receiver all the way is indeed a rarity. This is all the more reason why you should emphasize the necessity of looking away from the receiver.

If a passer is not looking toward and lined up in the direction of his receiver, he must first turn to the throwing direction and then pass. His weight will be on the rear foot, so it will be merely a matter of swinging the left foot around to the spot where he will be correctly lined up. Then he steps with the left foot as he throws. To swing that forward foot and step to throw at the same time requires skill that few boys will acquire. A change in direction requires a passer to set-up for the new direction ahead of time. With practice, a good passer will be able to do this in a fraction of a second.

An even more effective fake than just looking is to go through with the throwing motion. Have your passer take a step with the forward foot, bring the ball forward and slap it into his left hand. To recover, he brings his left foot back to where it was and throws his weight back onto his rear foot. Then he swings his body to the new direction and proceeds as just described.

One of the best passing drills we have does an excellent job of developing the ability of setting in the right direction, or faking in one direction and throwing to another. You can work with four passers in this drill (see Figure 4).

**Figure 4**

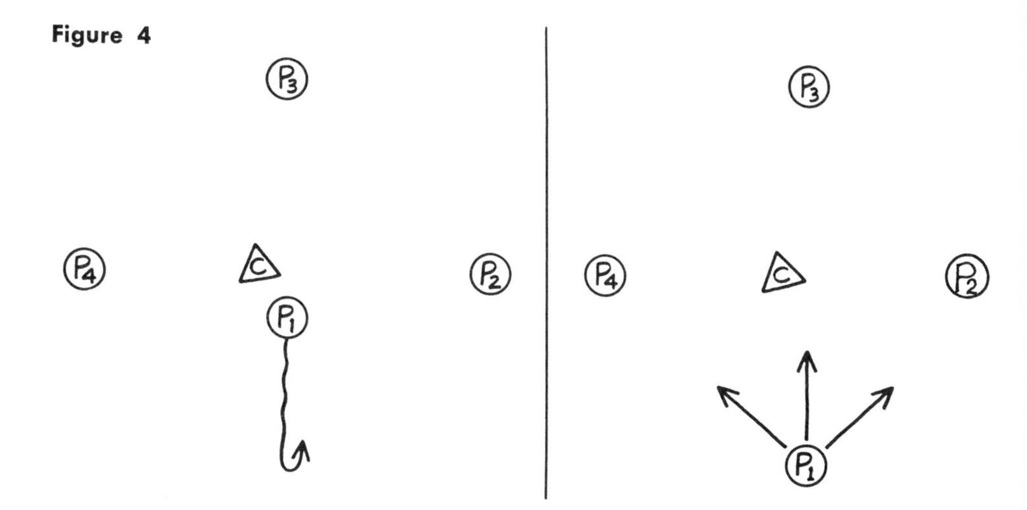

Let us start with passer number 1 who has the ball. He comes up to the coach, stands with his feet parallel as though he is under the center. The coach shouts "go" and the boy moves back to his set position as fast as possible and sets up looking at the coach. Once the boy is set, the coach yells "left" or "right" or "middle." The boy then changes his direction of throw (if not "middle") and throws to the spot designated by the coach. Now all four men are at the corners of a square again, and the man who has received the ball hustles up to the coach for his turn to throw.

Once the boys are warmed up this drill is varied, the coach giving direction changes. For example, the coach shouts "left" and the boy turns to the left and starts to throw. At this moment the coach shouts "right." The boy must slap the ball into his left hand, return to the set, then spin to the right, set and throw. This action must be performed quickly. It is good practice for the passer who at the last minute in a game sees a receiver is covered and must recover himself to throw elsewhere. Intersperse your single commands with double and, occasionally, triple commands so that the boy doesn't know if there's going to be a change.

Since they are throwing to stationary targets in this drill, they should be hitting their target right between the eyes. Make your passers really hustle in this drill. They should all break sweat. Once a boy begins to perspire, he will work much harder to develop his coordination. A passer who is sweating and heated up will be much more accurate. Passing is hard work and requires a positive attitude.

## Timing Your Release

The one thing that will make a good passer great is a fine sense of timing. Most high-school boys wait too long before releasing the ball. Some boys who are timid or nervous release too early because of their anxiety.

Most of the receivers we have are not very fast. The ball

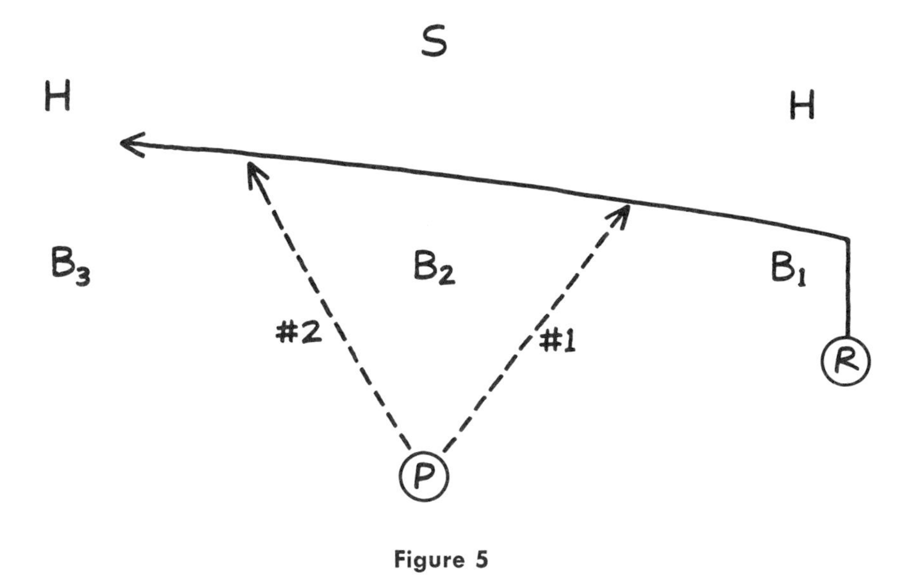


**Figure 5**

*must arrive* when they are open because they do not stay clear very long. It stands to reason, therefore, that the release time is dictated by the moment of arrival to the receiver. This can best be illustrated by some examples.

To throw to this receiver against the zone defense illustrated in Figure 5, the passer should throw the ball along path one or path two. For path one, the throwing motion must be started when the receiver is behind $B_1$ so that the ball and the receiver both arrive in the clear at the same time. If the passer started to throw when the receiver was first open, the ball would reach the receiver at the spot occupied by $B_2$. It follows, then, that to throw along path two, the throwing motion must begin when the receiver is behind $B_2$. The general rule is: *Throw the ball as the receiver is coming into the clear; do not wait until he is there.*

In Figure 6, let us assume H is faster than R. R should be able to fake and get two steps on H. Then H will recover and close quickly. The ball should be released as soon as R has his two step lead. Our quarterbacks have the tendency to wait for R to get a bigger lead which he never will.

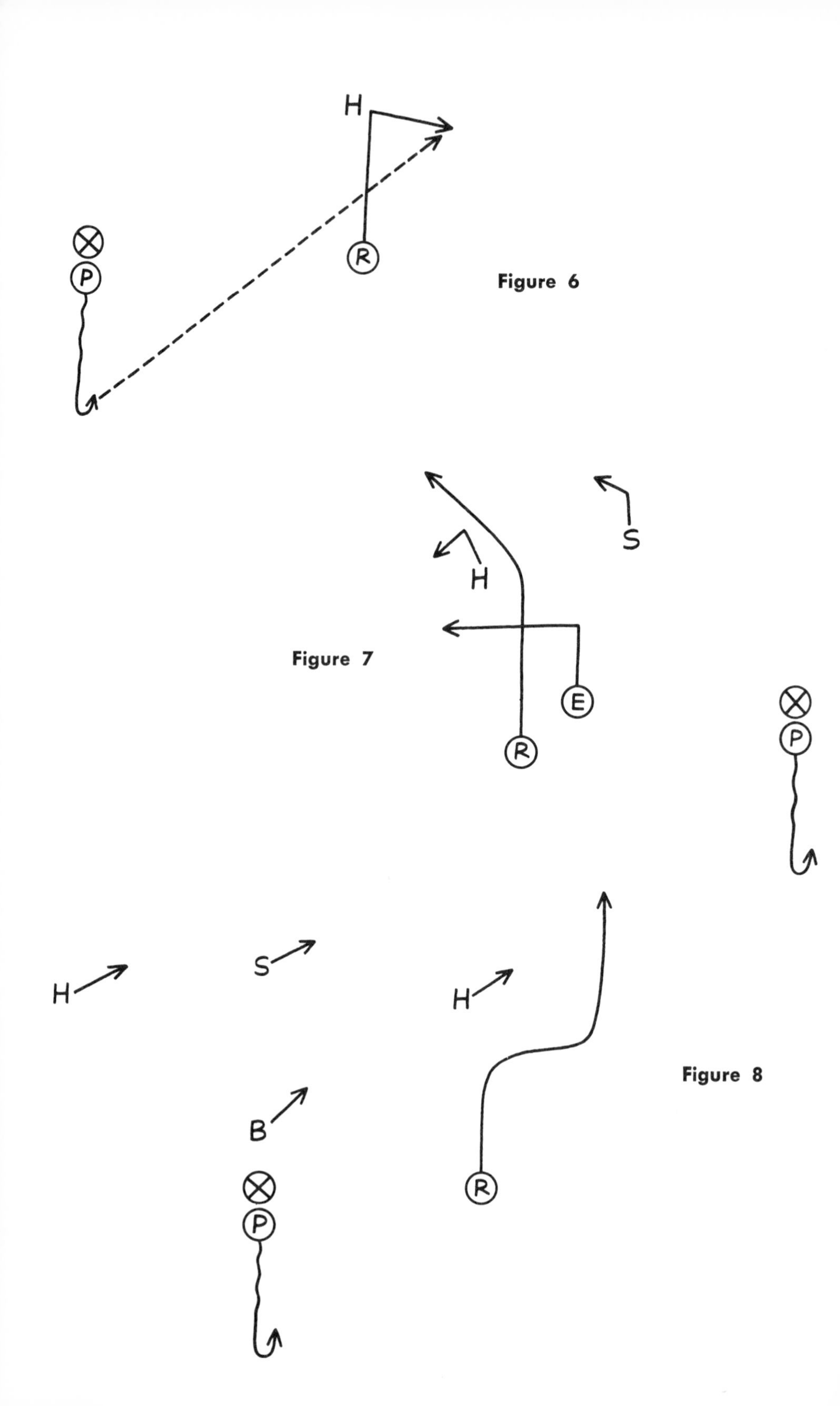

Figure 6

Figure 7

Figure 8

In example 3, as the defensive men drop back, they are looking to see what will develop. If H should leave R to cover E who has come into his zone, R will be open. The ball should be thrown as soon as R is open because S will be closing fast. In addition, the longer the passer waits, the greater the distance to throw becomes. The longer the ball is in the air, the better the chance a defensive man has of recovering.

Figure 8 illustrates that the longer the time the ball is in the air, the more time other defensive men will have to move into the area, and points up the fact that timing and knowledge of individual receivers go hand-in-hand. If the receiver is really fast, the passer often can and will wait for him to get a bigger lead.

One year our most successful pass pattern was our 19–60 fan pass. By having the slot back come back to fake the reverse, we attempt to freeze the safety man momentarily so that he will be late in helping to cover our right end (see Figure 9). The right end selects a deep or shallow pattern, depending on the defensive halfback. Our quarterback Tom Manning had a *terrific sense* of timing for this play, and continually bailed us out of trouble with it. The very next season we did not even

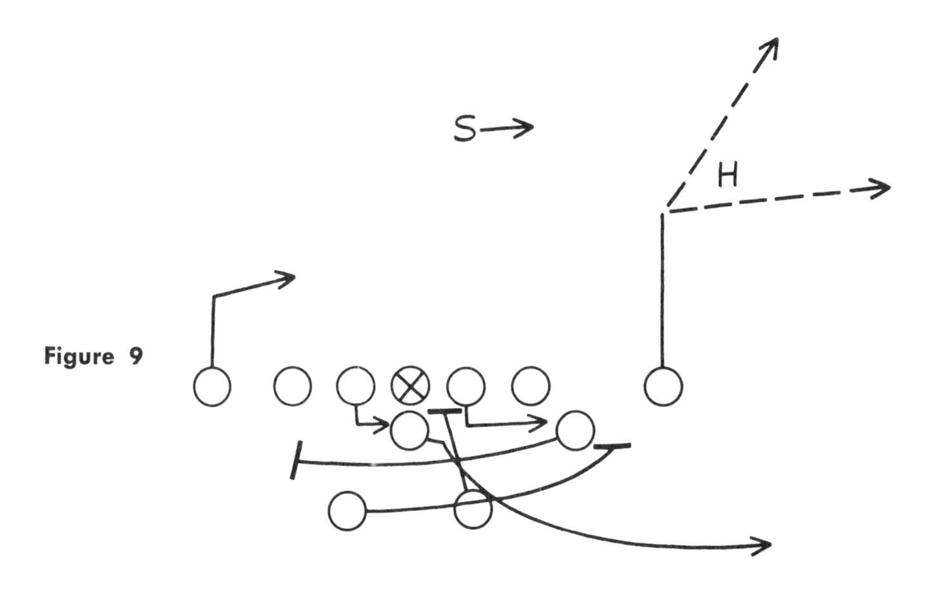

**Figure 9**

complete this pass once. The quarterbacks were waiting too long before throwing, giving the safety man time to come over to double team the right end.

### Our Best Method to Improve Timing

There is a very effective way of teaching the right time for release. You can use it in a one on one drill (receiver versus defender), dummy scrimmage (your ends and backfield against defensive backs and linebackers), or in a normal scrimmage.

The coach stands behind the spot where the passer will set. The coach shouts "FIRE" to the passer at the precise time the ball must be thrown. I presume that you will know the precise time you want the ball to be released. Through constant continual repetition, the boy should begin to think as you do because you both have the same view of the receiver. The amount of drill necessary will vary with each boy. After a while, position yourself in the same place, but tell your passer to throw when he feels he should. Tell him to think the word "FIRE" when he decides he should throw. Also, you will find that occasionally during the season a boy will go a little off timing, and you will need to return to this procedure to bring him back.

During one season, we were not able to pass effectively in the first few games. A study of the films showed that our passers were waiting too long. Our receivers were only of average speed, so that they were not clear for very long. (Incidentally, your films are very helpful in uncovering this weakness.) To improve his timing, I stood behind the quarterback and continually harassed him with the command "FIRE" and criticized him severely when he waited too long. The boy became very angry and started to really fire the ball. His timing showed immediate improvement. After a dismal start that year, we won our last five games and were conference champions. By getting this timing matter corrected and making more effective use of our play-passes, our passing game carried us to a successful season.

## Throwing from the Set Position

This chapter has been devoted to the throwing of a pass from the set position. If he has time, a quarterback should always throw from the "set." In a ball game, the passer will find that he is seldom able to come back to five and one-half yards, set and then step back up into the pocket. He will find that he will often be forced into different footwork. The important thing is that he should land on his right foot so that nearly all his weight is there when he starts to throw. It doesn't matter how he is moving; all he needs to do is get that right foot planted underneath him in order to throw.

If a passer is rolling right or left, he must stop and set-up quickly in order to have the most accurate pass result. There are only two times when he must throw while moving. First, if he is being rushed or chased and cannot set-up without being hit. Second, if the release time is reached before he is set. *Proper release time is vital to successful passing.*

We teach our passers that they must throw from the set whenever possible. Most of our practice time is spent throwing from the set position. Yet in our games, our passers are forced to throw over half their passes while moving. The next chapter may seem to contradict this chapter and should be read with it to get a complete picture. I think you will agree that there is no contradiction after all. We must teach, practice, and stress throwing from the set position because this maneuver is the basis of throwing while on the move. Throwing from the set is as basic to a passer as dummy scrimmage is to live scrimmage.

# THREE

# THROWING FROM MOVING OR OFF-BALANCE POSITIONS

All the basic skills of throwing presented in the past chapter are used while throwing from any moving position. I am referring to the grip, overhand motion, release and follow-through.

## Practice Off-Balance Throwing

We all realize that a passer will sometimes be forced to throw from an off-balance position. If you were asked how often this happens to your passer, your immediate answer would probably be "not very often." I would have said the same thing until, when analyzing the films taken during Tom Manning's senior year, I discovered that Tom was off-balance on 120 of the 172 passes that he threw. He had about the same completion rate for throwing from an off-balance position as from a set position. This means he threw 70 per cent of his passes that season from an off-balance position. If you were to analyze your own films, I think you would also be quite surprised at the number of positions that your passers throw from.

Because a great many passes are thrown while moving, it is only logical that the skills involved should be taught and practiced a great deal. If you teach your passer to throw from a set position, your job is about half done. He must also develop the ability to use these skills while throwing on the run or from an off-balance position.

## Use the Right Foot as a Base

The right foot must always be planted just before or at the start of the throwing motion. To try to throw without setting the right foot would be similar to trying to hit a golf ball while standing on ice. Once the right foot is planted, you may throw any distance effectively. I don't mean the right foot stays in that spot, because if it did, a boy who was moving would fall down. As he is throwing, the weight is on the right foot. If he is running to the right, the weight will be on the right foot for only a moment, but he must time his throw for that precise moment.

## The "Right-Handed" Factor

During my first year as a high-school coach, I came up with what I thought was an ingenious idea. (I'm sure that it has been tried before.) We would line up winged left, place our best lineman on the left and our best back at right half-back, and run the majority of our plays to the left.

The advantage gained was supposed to be that the defense would have to shift their best men to the side of our strength. According to my theory, these men should not have been as effective in their new spots as in the old. This sounds good in theory but in practice it doesn't work because of one factor that was overlooked. Every team is right-handed.

We lined up strong to the left and ended up running most of the time to the right. After a while, teams would not line up as strongly to our left and we began to have trouble moving the ball.

No matter how much you practice your offense to the left. or how you make charts to keep track of where you run, you will find that you run mostly to the right because you run best to the right. You should keep track of it and try to keep your left-handed game in constant use or else you will become too right-handed and easier to defend against. The ideal would be right 60 per cent, left 40 per cent, but may vary up to 75–25. This ratio is rather large and should definitely be the limit.

In the season previously mentioned, the passer threw 74 per cent of our rollout passes while running to the right. The small number thrown while rolling left had a high degree of success because the defense would tend to shift to our strength. If you are successful to the left even on a limited basis, your opponents hesitate to move too much to your strength. If they overshift on you, you can be very successful to the left, particularly in the left flat. If they play a balanced defense against you, you should be quite successful to the right. This has been our experience.

## Passing While Running Right

The quarterback who can pass and run is the greatest weapon in football. Since we all tend to be right-handed in our attack, in varying degrees, it behooves us to train our quarterbacks to pass while running right. Faking a pass or run while moving is discussed later in this chapter. Naturally we want the quarterback to set but he is usually unable to. There is a much greater need for him to set for the long pass than for the short pass. A passer should be able to throw short and medium passes with a great degree of accuracy while rolling right.

Remember, short and medium passes use the first three sources of power. While moving to the right a man cannot put the power of his back behind the ball. This means he will not be able to throw as far. In fact, you may feel fortunate if your passer is able to throw not less than 10 yards shy of his maximum distance from the set.

Just before he is about to throw, the passer cocks the ball up by his ear. As the right foot hits, he draws the ball back and continues his throwing motion. The ball should be released by the time the left foot comes down and begins taking his weight. The twisting back of the shoulders is exaggerated because this twist is the greatest source of power when running to the right.

His follow-through will naturally not bring his right hand to his left hip because of his movement. Tell him to "throw his hand along with the ball." He should feel that, if his hand were not connected to his arm, it would be thrown as accurately as the ball. This means that after the ball is released, the hand will have the tendency to follow and the arm will be well extended in the direction of the target.

With this pass no lead is necessary. The ball should be thrown directly at the receiver. The passer's lateral movement automatically causes the ball to lead the receiver. This is not an absolute rule because speed and direction are factors that certainly vary. As long as your passer is aware that lateral movement will, in effect, put a "lead" on the ball, he will learn to adjust properly. Again the only way to teach a boy to lead properly is to continually set up situations which force the passer to lead his target. You will find drills for leading later in this chapter.

## Passing While Running Left

Many coaches think it is very difficult for a right-handed passer to throw while running to the left. If you think this maneuver is too difficult, it may be best not to run a play that requires it. To overcome the difficulty, many coaches try to find a left-handed right halfback so that the left sweep can have the threat of pass and run. Most coaches would agree that your offense will be more effective if you have a good running pass play to the left as well as to the right.

First of all, it is not difficult to throw on the run while moving to the left provided your passer has developed the technique for doing so. My own experience as a passer convinced me that it is easier to pass when running left than when running right. I was more accurate and could throw farther. When rolling to the left, we were working our best end (the left end) against the poorer defensive halfback, and the play ran toward the weaker personnel. As a college passer, I had great success in rolling out left, and as a high-school coach, I can recall many times when such a maneuver contributed directly to a win.

First you must convince a boy that it is easier to throw while moving left. A demonstration by you, another coach, or perhaps a former player will go a long way toward convincing him. The technique involved is one of the most difficult to learn, but once it becomes second nature you have actually doubled the threat of your running quarterback.

There is body movement involved along with footwork. Before starting any passing movement, the ball must be cocked, both hands at the right side of the head. The body and foot movements are the same as if a boy running forward spins half way around in a clockwise manner and stumbles backwards.

In Figure 10, the ball is cocked ready to throw, 1. The next step with the left foot begins the turning movement. Turn on the left foot so that the right foot goes behind and beyond. Now you are facing the place from which you started. Actually you are running backwards momentarily. As the right foot lands (a basic rule), 3, the throwing motion begins.

Figure 10

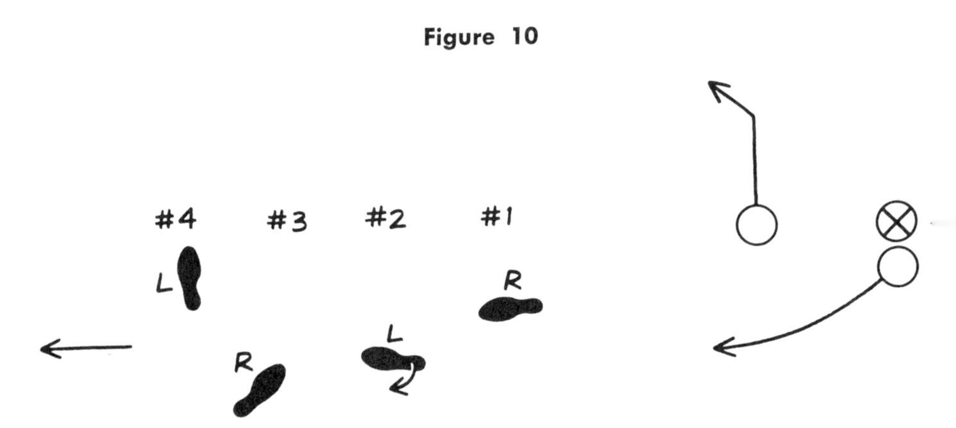

Momentum forces the left foot to swing from position 2 to 4. Sometime during this swing, the left foot is pointed at the receiver: at this instant the ball should be released. Notice that there is a natural tendency for the arm to follow through diagonally across the body to the left hip. At the moment of release, the body, eyes etc.—all have smoothly completed the operation of throwing a pass. The next instant the body becomes very awkward because the momentum is now forcing it to stumble backwards. An experienced passer stumbles and regains his balance. Trying it for the first time a boy may very well stumble and fall over backwards, but this makes no difference as long as everything was under perfect control at the moment of release.

It seems natural that it would be wisest to teach this movement by having your passer start running slowly and increase speed as his proficiency increases. Your quarterbacks can practice the footwork by running down a white line. Start them running forward. When you blow the whistle they are to take a half turn clockwise and run backwards, signal again and they run forward, and so forth. When he becomes proficient, your passer should be able to run at nearly full speed and turn and throw.

You will be quite surprised to see your passer throw for longer distances running left than he does even from a set position. When the ball is brought forward, the complete power of the back can be added to the pass and the momentum of running gives an additional snap to the entire body. Our strongest passer could throw from 45 to 50 yards while running right, from 50 to more than 55 yards from the set, and I actually saw him throw a 67 yard toss while running to the left. A passer can put tremendous power behind a ball if he uses the technique properly.

Leading a receiver properly while running to the left involves the same principle as lateral movement to the right. Just keep in mind that moving laterally affects the lead and that only by continuous practice can a passer learn automatically to make the adjustment. One thing you may notice is that the pass thrown while moving left will be thrown harder and arrive perhaps a little sooner because more strength is put behind it.

The short pass rolling left can be thrown even faster, but only by a very experienced passer. The ball is cocked before he starts his movement but all the action is from the waist up. His feet continue moving straight. He violently twists his upper body to get the power coming back and releases the ball as if he were throwing a dart. The follow-through is the same as if he were running right; that is, he should "throw" his hand as well as the ball. The passer feels very awkward when using this method because the move is not a natural one. There will be a strong tendency to overlead and a great deal of agility is needed. In high school Tom Manning threw by making the turning movement. As a college passer he has become very adept at the shorter pass without the halfturn. We have had no one yet at the high school level who has been able to throw accurately without the turn.

### Passing While Running Forward

We actually spend time practicing throwing to a receiver while running directly at him. This may sound odd because it would rarely be done in a game. If it happens once in a coaching lifetime and wins a game for you, then it has been worthwhile to spend some time on it. Late in the fourth quarter of a game tied at 14–14, Tom went back to pass and the crashing ends forced him to run straight up the middle. As he approached the line of scrimmage, he spotted a receiver with just about a two yard lead. The film showed that he released the ball at the spot where he had taken it from the center and that he was moving nearly full speed ahead at the moment the ball was released. The pass was completed for a touchdown and won the ball game. This is sufficient reason for me to spend some time with all my passers on this technique. Often a passer is moving slightly forward at the end of his rollout. In addition, practicing any phase of passing will help a boy's over-all passing ability.

Actually, it is easy to throw while running straight at your receiver. The body is twisted from the waist up and the full power of the shoulders can be utilized. When your passer first tries this pass, you will find that he overthrows and throws too hard. The forward movement adds momentum to the ball, so he must learn to throw a softer pass. But he must use *the same passing motion*, merely softening it a little. He will also have to be conscious of the distance and will actually have to feel as if he is underthrowing. The throw is started as the right foot hits the ground, and the ball is released as the left foot begins taking the weight. A little time spent on this move may very well pay you big dividends later.

## Passing While Moving Backwards

Passing while moving backwards can really be dangerous. If a boy stumbling backwards throws, chances are that he will throw soft and short. A soft, short pass is extremely vulnerable to interception. Perhaps the wisest thing to do is to caution your passer never to throw while stumbling backwards unless he is throwing a screen pass. However, I tell my passers to throw regardless of what direction they are moving in if there is a receiver moving into the clear.

There are several limitations to passing while moving backwards. The passer will not be able to get zip behind the ball and will lose distance. If he throws very hard and releases the ball high, he will be able to put some of the strength of his back behind the throw and increase his power. No matter how much he is stumbling or how far off-balance he may be, if he lands with his right foot behind him he has a momentary base from which to throw.

The ball should be cocked in both hands as he lands on his right foot. He twists his body and brings the ball back normally, but he must snap forward violently to get maximum power. You will find that if a rushing lineman forces your passer to stumble backward, he will usually be able to drift to one side or the other. He must learn to eat the ball if high hands blind him.

There are disadvantages to working with this movement. Your quarterback may start to drift back when he is not being forced. He will not be as accurate. Also when he rolls out he may start drifting too deep and thus lose the threat of the run. If he can start to turn up-field, the rollout actually becomes much more difficult to stop. Because of these disadvantages you may decide not to work on this technique.

Since a large percentage of our passes are thrown with the passer moving, I prefer to teach my quarterback the proper "feel" of throwing while moving in any direction. You will find that you will devote less time to developing these moves than you think you will. There are many drills the boys can work on by themselves, and using them can save you time.

## Running Pass Drills

### Drill 1

You need only two passers for drill 1. They start at one end of the field about 15 yards apart and jog toward the other end (Figure 11), passing to each other as they run. You will notice that one boy throws while running to his right and the other throws while running to his left. You may let them stop at the other end and throw a few passes from the set while

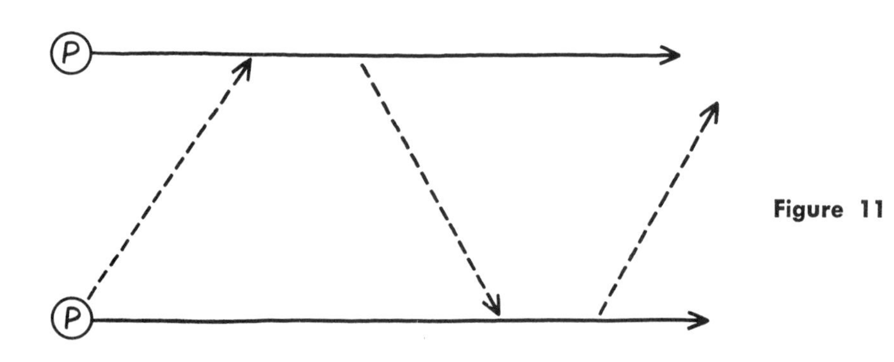


Figure 11

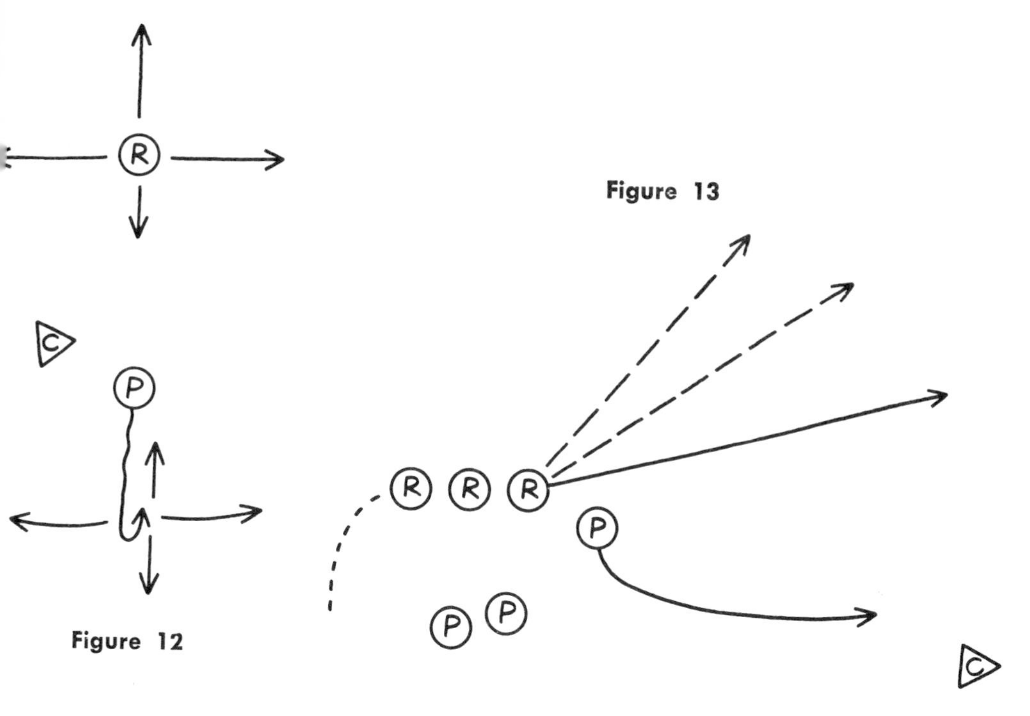

Figure 12

Figure 13

catching their breath. They return along the same paths, but their positions are reversed and they throw in the opposite direction. You may wish to increase distance or speed.

**Drill 2**

In drill 2 you can use two passers or a passer and a receiver (Figure 12). The passer fades back to a set position. The coach gives the commands, "right," "left," "forward" or "back." The passer moves in the proper direction and throws to the receiver who moves in the same direction.

**Drill 3**

We use drill 3 often because it involves the use of all our receivers and passers. Have your receivers line up on a yard stripe on one side of the field (Figure 13). At the snap of the ball they both move. The receiver then lines up on the opposite side of the field. To avoid wasting time, give each quarterback a ball and make him retrieve it. When every receiver is on the other side, the passers move over there and start the same drill but now run to the left. Have the receivers run a shallow pattern at first. Then you can deepen the pattern and change the angles if you wish. This is also an excellent conditioning drill because everybody runs a great deal, particularly the quarterbacks. They should break sweat and be made to work very hard.

## Pass-or-Run Option

While watching the Rose Bowl Game on TV one season, I was amazed at the moves made by the Wisconsin quarterback in a run-pass situation. He had moved his team down to the 20-yard line and was moving back to pass. He started to run and at several different times brought up the ball as if to pass. What amazed me was that he made this fake even after he was across the line of scrimmage. In fact, when he reached the 10-yard line he brought the ball up to fake a pass. He was already ten yards beyond the line of scrimmage. His move caused a defensive halfback to hesitate a moment, enabling him to run for the score. Defense halfbacks are taught to react instinctively to a passing move and in this case the halfback's instinct betrayed him. The success of this fake shows how profitable it can be to keep the halfback from knowing whether you will pass or run.

This run-or-pass technique is one of the most difficult things to teach a high-school boy. Once he is forced out of his pocket and has to start running, high-school quarterbacks will rarely think of looking for a receiver. They run because they feel they have to and must be taught not to. Receivers also need to be taught not to stop running their pattern.

Tom Manning had unusual pass-or-run ability. He would be forced to run and from the way he was moving there was no doubt that he was fully committed to running. But suddenly the ball would be in the air. Although Tom was not really a running threat, the defensive halfback would still come up and leave the receiver wide open. You would think that because he was such a terrific passer, the defensive halfbacks would stay back, but the instinct to come up fast on a runner would often betray them.

## Teaching Pass-or-Run Skills

The big question now is, how do you teach this skill? I have yet to see an adequate dummy scrimmage drill. Live scrimmage is far and away the best way to work on this skill. This past season we had nine scrimmages with outside teams besides our own intra-squad scrimmages—the most we've ever had. Surprisingly enough, it was the best season we've had with respect to injuries.

Remember that your quarterback represents a tremendous investment in teaching and training. To expose him needlessly to injury would be very foolish of any coach. In outside scrimmages both teams agree to stop on the whistle and I insist upon strict adherence to the rule. If my quarterback is running downfield or is hopelessly trapped I blow that whistle—not always because he must get used to being hit, but I do not permit him to be hit too hard or too often. He is too valuable not to take care of.

Since you stand behind your offense during scrimmage, you are in a good position to yell at him when the pass-or-run situation comes up. Take a moment after this play to discuss it with your quarterback. The more often this situation develops during scrimmage, the sooner he will develop a feel for it. It is easy enough for you to see that it comes up frequently. You can put in a pair of poorer guards so that he will be forced out of his pocket. Also run your action-passes frequently.

*Use Your Films.* Your films are an excellent teaching device and can be very helpful to you in going over pass-or-run situations with your quarterback. Take some old films and splice together a series of plays of the pass-run-pass variety. We have some excellent film of Tom Manning and it helps our quarterbacks a great deal when we go over these. Also, game films are very helpful in teaching a boy because he can see himself performing.

## Two Pass-or-Run Situations

There are two items that merit discussion here. First, if a passer has plenty of room to run and a receiver is in the open, what should he do? Run for the sure first down or throw for the possible touchdown? Score, down, field position, ability of the receiver, and other factors will directly affect the decision. Generally speaking though, the ball should be thrown. A wide-open receiver appears too seldom in a game to waste the opportunity. You are playing for the touchdown, so go for it.

Secondly, if the passer is moving forward and is not certain if he is over the line of scrimmage or not, should he throw? If there is a receiver open, he should throw. The fact that possible gain outweighs the possible loss by penalty makes it well worth the risk. Even if he were wrong 50% of the time you would still have an over-all gain. Chances are that he will seldom be over when he throws. Even if he is over, he can still fake a pass to keep the defenders back and give himself more running room. We have already seen how successful this can be.

In this chapter a great deal of discussion has been devoted to throwing while on the move. Yet the axiom of "throw the same way every time" still holds. Whether long or short, soft or hard, on- or off-balance, set or moving, the passing motion is still the same.

To summarize briefly, passes thrown while running right or moving backwards require more power for less distance. Passes thrown while moving left or forward require less power and go greater distances. Finally, the passer that has developed a pass-or-run option technique is the greatest weapon in modern football.

# FOUR

# STRIVE FOR PERFECTION

Practice makes perfect is an axiom for success in any athletic activity. Constant practice is certainly necessary in the development of an outstanding passer. A boy who throws a football only during the football season will never realize his passing potential. The outstanding passer must work on his skills the entire 12 months of the year.

## Work on Passing Year Round

The fact that football is restricted to certain periods of the year creates a problem for the coach who is developing a passer. Thus during the authorized practice period, you must actually teach the boy how to practice on his own during the off-season. You are not violating any ethics in doing this; after all, a basketball player on his own can go shoot baskets any time he feels the urge.

Immediately at the close of the season you should see that all of next season's passers have a football at home. The boys you select to be passers must want to practice at every opportunity. They should be boys who will be outdoors throwing the day after the season ends if the weather permits. On a warm winter day, I have gone outdoors to throw in an area that was cleared of snow.

*The Winter Months.* During the winter months, in New

England, a boy is restricted in the amount of passing he can do. But he has the opportunity to spend a few minutes a day on body building exercises, with particular emphasis on shoulder, arm and wrist development.

He should find some way to throw at least twice a week, for at least half an hour. He may be able to practice outdoors or at the local YMCA gym. Some school gyms are opened during the winter for periods of general play, and he may be able to use them. There is always some place to practice. Tom Manning played catch with his little brother in the cellar, even though he was forced to kneel so that the ball would not hit the ceiling. An interesting sidelight to this is that Tom's brother has developed into a fine little passer as a result and will be coming along in the next few years.

*Spring Workouts.* Once the weather improves enough to get outside in the spring, body-building work can be cut down and passing practice increased. During spring a boy should pass three times a week for at least a half-hour period each time. Notice that in all these cases I give the minimum. A boy needs to do at least this much but a boy with a great desire can and will do more. A passer can never practice throwing enough.

Quite a few of these boys will play other sports. This does not mean that they cannot devote a small amount of their time to passing. Frequently other sports will help them develop some of the qualities you desire. A passer who plays basketball gets plenty of practice in coordinating hands and eyes. The hockey player gets the same kind of practice and builds up the arm and wrist. If your passers cannot practice enough because of these sports and their studies, at least they are not standing still. Again, if the boy wants badly enough to be a passer, he will somehow fit in his work on the passing game.

*The Spring Practice.* When a passer reports for the two weeks of spring practice, his arm is well conditioned for throwing if he has worked during the winter. I spend nearly all of this period working with the passers and receivers. We start right in with the fundamentals of the grip and work right through the skills of throwing from an off-balance position. These boys throw plenty of passes during spring sessions and their arms must be in good shape. We keep a sharp lookout for sore arms and never push a boy with a sore arm. Only time and patience will cure a sore arm.

At the end of spring practice, each passer is given a copy of our passing drills. Warm-up procedure, practicing in pairs and in groups, practicing various skills, all are spelled out for him. He has performed all of these drills in spring practice. He knows the purpose of each one and how it is set up. We also tell him the minimum amount of passing he should do over the summer. Once the spring session is over, you are through coaching your passers until fall. If they are worth their salt, they will want to practice during the summer and it is up to you to prepare a guide for them.

*The Summer Months.* In one season we completed 13 touchdown passes to one receiver, our right end Bob Radcliffe. Bob and his quarterback were inseparable the entire summer before this season, and it would be impossible to count the number of passes that were thrown between them. It seems reasonable, then, that an ideal practice set-up would be to have a receiver or two work out with each quarterback during the off-season. In this manner not only are your receivers working but your passers have someone to throw to. As a bonus, the boys get used to working with each other.

During the summer, a passer must virtually live with a football. The number of practice sessions, three a week during the spring, should gradually increase until during the month of August a passer practices for at least one half hour every day. Many boys workout and hold a summer job; they have little time for anything else. Some boys will throw as much as four hours in one day. The devoted boy will often spend this much time.

When they report back in the fall, you'll know immediately who has worked hardest during the summer and who has not worked at all.

Let me offer you one caution in regard to summer practice. We all want our teams to report back in condition in the fall and therefore issue instructions for conditioning. This is a fine and natural thing to do. However, do not order your captains to organize team practice during the summer. If a boy is injured during an illegal workout indirectly organized by you, then you may find yourself in big trouble.

Once your season has begun, you will find that your passing instructions will be confined primarily to correcting passer weakness. Some weaknesses may not be picked up until you look at the game films. When you become familiar with the fundamentals of passing, however, you will easily be able to spot them and to work out ways to correct them.

## Poor Timing

At times your passing attack may not be clicking and you may not be able to determine the trouble. If this is the case, you should suspect that poor timing is the culprit. I have found that whether our passer is experienced or not, we have to work on timing every year. A young passer seems naturally to wait too long before he throws.

Your films will quickly show whether your passer's timing is off. If the receivers are all well covered when the ball arrives, suspect passer timing. Interceptions also result from poor timing. The secret of good timing is that the ball *must arrive* when the receiver is in the open. For correction of poor timing, refer to Chapter 2 where it is discussed in detail.

## Loss of Accuracy

Loss of accuracy is easily spotted and may be caused by many things. You may find it necessary to go back through all of the fundamentals of passing to discover the difficulty. But some troubles can be spotted merely by watching the pass.

*Underthrown Pass.* Underthrown passes result from poor follow-through. If a ball is released late from an overhand throw, it will be short of target. A pass will fall short if the step with the left foot is taken too soon, or if the step is too large. Also if the arm is not fully extended, if it is cramped down near the head, the ball will be underthrown. Should the passer take one step back just after the pass is thrown, it will also be short. All of these bad habits are easily spotted. Remember that an underthrown pass is much more dangerous than an overthrown one because the receiver has a chance to tackle an interceptor on an overthrown pass.

A good deal of practice throwing to moving targets should correct an underthrowing or overthrowing problem. Moreover, a passer should be very familiar with the speed of each receiver, for if a passer misjudges a receiver's speed, he will underthrow or overthrow. Refer to Chapter 3 for running-pass techniques if your passer is underthrowing while on the move. In high-school football we seldom see an overthrown pass compared to the number of times we see underthrown passes.

*Loss of Lateral Accuracy.* Should a passer throw very often to the left or right of his receiver, I first check to see if he is lining his body up properly with the point to which he is throwing. If he is doing this and still has the same problem, I immediately suspect that his passing motion is no longer overhand but sidearm. A sidearm passer is less accurate horizontally while an overhand passer will be apt to be more inaccurate vertically. A sidearm throw is easy to spot merely by watching where the boy's hand is at the end of his follow-through. In a good overhand throw, the boy's throwing hand follows a diagonal path across his body and winds up at the left hip. I also observe the boy's ability to lead a receiver properly.

Lateral inaccuracy may often be quickly corrected by observing the boy's body-lineup, his overhand throw and his leading ability. Should you be unable to correct his problem in this manner, you will have to go back to the fundamentals of the pass. This isn't very difficult because you will find yourself preaching many of these fundamentals indirectly during practice.

The best remedy for any accuracy problem is to have the passer throw as much as possible. Set up drills that concentrate on areas where his problem is the greatest. Many of the passing drills outlined elsewhere in this book will serve this particular purpose.

### Loss of Spiral

Many coaches don't care whether a pass has a good spiral as long as it gets to the right place at the right time and gets the job done. If a pass is completed it is well thrown. A completed pass is, after all, our objective. I think, however, that a properly thrown ball should spiral and that if it does not the passer's accuracy will not be as consistent as it should be.

It is very easy to locate the cause of loss of spiral. The problem is the wrist or hand. The boy's grip is not suitable for him, or his hand is not wiping itself across the ball properly at the moment of release, or finally his wrist may be twisting at the moment of release instead of being snapped forward. A twisting of the wrist is easy to spot because the ball flutters.

Refer to the discussions on the grip in this book for methods to bring back the boy's spiral. Your corrections will probably not bring immediate results. But if the grip, hand action, and wrist action are proper, you will notice an immediate improvement and the spiral will come with practice.

### Throwing a Hard Pass

If all your receivers have trouble catching a certain boy's passes, you should suspect that he is throwing a "heavy" ball. A ball that spirals through the air with its nose tipped slightly downward is hard to catch if it is thrown with a lot of power. By merely playing catch with the boy, you will quickly find out if his passes are hard to catch. I have seen several passers who, though they threw very accurately, had only mediocre success because of throwing a "heavy" ball.

The problem is how to correct such a difficulty. A "heavy" ball is hard to correct because, if the boy "softens" up his pass, he may lose his accuracy. We attempt to correct this problem by continually telling the boy that his passes must be "catchable." Not only must the ball arrive at the right place at the right time, but it must not be hard to catch. We try to get the passer continually to consider the point of view of the receiver who must catch his pass. We have had our best success in correcting this problem by taking this approach.

### The "Gun Shy" Passer

If you find that your passer is continually being chased out of the pocket or caught with the ball for a loss, you have quite a problem. You should work on your pass protection blocking naturally but it is just as important to look at your passer.

We may spend a considerable amount of time and effort training a passer, only to find that he is "gun shy" under actual fire. There are some boys who watch the rushers more than their receivers. Given the best protection possible, such a boy still thinks he is being rushed. He will roll out of a good protective pocket, throw early, throw the ball away and commit a multitude of other sins. Yet he may pass beautifully in dummy scrimmage. The passer who is "gun shy" is easy to spot. Don't kid yourself about such a boy no matter how well he passes. When the chips are down he won't do the job.

The best way to correct this problem is not to select a "gun shy" boy for passing training in the first place. However, if you do train him you may find that you can use him quite a bit in a game. You may have a boy in a halfback spot that has had passer training that you could rely upon when the pressure is on.

Do everything you can to build up the boy's confidence. Some boys can be taught to overcome this weakness by continual exposure to rushers in practice scrimmages. Remember that it takes a great deal of courage for a boy who is afraid of something like this to continually come out to practice faithfully, knowing full well that he will be exposed to the very situation that causes him his distress. Don't give up on this boy; he may very well turn out to do a fine job. But be prepared with another passer in case he should fail to overcome his weakness. A boy who is "gun shy" can never do the job right. A good passer is a cool customer who will stand right in there and throw his pass in the face of the most determined rush.

## Perfection Is Your Goal

The development of a good passer requires constant effort by both the boy and his coach. Perfection will never be attained but it must always be striven for. A boy must desire to practice continually and improve himself in the various skills of passing. The coach must make himself an expert passing teacher. He must constantly teach, correct, observe, and guide his pupil.

FIVE

# THE RECEIVER

One of the most difficult jobs we seem to have at Marblehead is finding good receivers. A boy must have many qualities to fill such a position but few boys have them all. Any boys who are so outstanding are usually in your backfield, so chances are that your backs will be fairly good receivers.

Two of the three men in a position to move quickly downfield for a pass are your ends. This creates a problem, because your best receivers are probably already in the backfield. Quite often, in a smaller school, you may have to compromise and select boys as ends that do not possess one or more of the necessary characteristics.

## Qualities of a Good Receiver

Before discussing the desirable physical qualities of a good receiver, it would be wise to emphasize the fact that a successful receiver must have a little more courage than is ordinarily expected. A receiver who is going up to catch a pass will often be hit viciously from the blind side. Not only must he absorb this punishment, but he must hold onto the ball as well. This takes courage. In practice he is required to do a tremendous amount of running and must discipline himself to attain a high degree of conditioning. In a ball game he does more running than anyone else.

Our right end was the only player that didn't require a period of rest at some time during a ball game last season. Although weighing only 150 pounds, he played both ways and was in excellent condition. His hustle and "esprit de corps" led to his being elected captain for this coming season. One thing that we can be sure of next season is that we will have leadership by example from this boy.

A good pass receiver should have good hands, good moves, speed, and size.

*Good Hands.* If a boy excels only in the ability to catch the ball, he may very well be your best receiver. It is amazing how many boys who upon entering high school can't catch a ball while running. The number of capable ball catchers seems to be getting smaller each year. If a boy catches the ball in his fingers, drawing back his hands at the moment of contact ("giving with the ball"), he should be considered as a receiver. If a boy can't catch the ball, all the size and speed in the world won't make him a good receiver.

*Good Moves.* There are some pass patterns in every team's offense that are designed to place a particular receiver in the clear without any unusual faking on his part. The pass pattern is an attempt to break down pass defense rules by running certain receivers along certain paths. But a receiver may also get into the clear by "breaking down" the defender who is assigned to cover him. We believe that faking ability is second only to pass-receiving ability. If the boy with the good hands can get free for an instant by using a good fake, and the pass is well timed by the passer, then there is little the defense can do to stop the reception. We seem to have more than our share of average speed receivers. A pass receiver with average speed must have good moves. A fast pass-receiver who also has good moves, should become a great receiver.

## Speed and size

You will sometimes have to choose between speed and size depending upon the job you want done. A receiver who is usually split wide needs speed more than size. A tight end who does a lot of blocking on the line of scrimmage needs size. While I consider speed to be more important than size, I certainly would want at least one receiver who was big even though he was fast.

### Improving a Poor Pass-Receiver

You may have boys who, though they don't catch very well, you want to develop into receivers because of other factors. If you are 50 per cent successful you should be quite satisfied. You have to face the fact that some boys will never be able to catch. However, many things may be tried to develop catching ability.

1. See that the boy has a football at home and see that it is thrown to him on a year-round basis. When the weather is good he should catch at least three times a week. During the summer, he should spend some time catching every day. By catching constantly he may develop the "feel" for catching that only repetition can bring.
2. Encourage your receivers to come out early to practice or to stay afterwards to do some extra catching. These suggestions, I might add, are not only for the poor receivers but for the good ones as well.
3. Develop a punishment system for passes dropped during the actual practice session. Don't make the punishment too severe for the poor receiver because this would discourage him. Have special rules for your starting receivers to make them concentrate even more on improvement. For example, have non-starters take one 50-yard sprint after practice for each pass over five dropped and starters take one 50-yard sprint for each pass over three dropped—the total not to exceed five 50-yard sprints. You may set your own limits depending on the boys and the circumstances of the practice.
4. Take charge or place a coach in charge of the receivers and work on catching techniques prior to and after practice.
5. Include in your practice plans some time each day for pass

receiving. This is easy to do because each day should include some passing work for your quarterbacks.

## Techniques for Catching a Football

The techniques in catching the ball are loose hands properly positioned, catching with the fingers, "giving" with the ball and developing an intense concentration.

### Loose hands

Because the ball should be caught in the fingers, a boy's hands must be loose and supple to receive the ball. I can remember a defensive end who was nicknamed "Clang" for his pass-catching inability. He couldn't catch well at all and the ball would bounce off his fingers as if it were hitting a stone wall. Through his entire college career, never once did he play on offense. In the days of two platooning, he played defense and was outstanding. He had all the assets of a good receiver but one—he couldn't catch.

You are indeed fortunate if you are able to teach a boy with stiff fingers to learn to catch. One gimmick is to tell him to clench his fists tightly before he moves down-field. The theory is that this clenching will loosen up the hands for a moment afterward and make him more ready to receive. This has helped some of our boys but not others.

### The hands and the arms of the receiver

We teach our receivers to catch short and medium passes with their thumbs behind the ball. Since the ball is thrown rather hard on these passes, the thumbs should stop the ball from slipping through the hands. If a boy is standing facing you and a pass is thrown at his face, his hands receive the ball in this manner. Translate this now into a moving position. If he were running from right to left, the ball would be caught with his left hand on top. This makes many a coach shudder because he is actually crossing his arms to catch the ball. Experience has shown us that this is by far the best method for catching a firm or hard pass. Only on the long over-the-shoulder pass do we teach a boy to catch with his hands parallel. Naturally, you can't catch a pass below the waist with your thumbs behind unless you are a contortionist. Our passers are trained to throw chin high, however, so that most of the time the thumbs are behind.

### "Giving" with the ball

When the ball strikes the hands, they must be partially relaxed and should "give" with the ball. That is, the hands should be drawn back to take the sting out of the ball when it strikes the fingers. There is an excellent drill for developing hand techniques. Stand the receiver about 15 yards from a passer, or a coach, facing him. This is a stationary drill. Begin by throwing at his face. Once he begins to catch the ball well, throw at different spots: over his head, high right, high left, low, waist high. The receiver must move his hands to a correct position for a ball thrown anywhere near his body. When he catches these well, throw far enough to the left or right so that he has to move from his stationary position. This will make him coordinate body, hand and arm movements.

We have one boy who has learned to catch fairly well by using this drill. Although he does not have "good hands," determination and continual practice have made him into an adequate receiver. If a receiver has a bad day, take him aside for 15 minutes after practice and go through this drill with him. Make a game of it: count each dropped pass as one point. You should not catch them all yourself, of course. You'll be amazed how quickly one of these 15-minute sessions will restore a boy's confidence and ability.

### Concentration

A boy who catches very well in dummy scrimmage may be a poor receiver in a game. I'm not talking about a timid boy. You're in trouble if a timid boy is the best you have. The problem may be that the boy now has other things on his mind. He may be thinking about being hit though he doesn't know when, or he may be glancing toward where he's going to run with the ball before he has even caught it.

Successful pass catching requires complete concentration on catching the ball. When the ball is in the air, a receiver must think of nothing but catching the ball. Any distraction at this critical moment will affect catching ability. Only when a receiver has firm possession of the ball may he turn his mind to other things. A receiver must have perfect concentration to be able to hold onto the ball when he is hit immediately after catching it, because he may receive severe punishment when hit in so vulnerable a position. Great receivers can hold onto the ball in such a situation because of their concentration as well as their courage. A boy can learn but you must constantly stress the necessity of concentrating. He must learn that after his eyes pick up the ball in flight, they must stay glued to it all the way.

## Some Boys May Never Develop

As I have said before, some boys will never be receivers no matter how much you work with them, while others have natural ability. An amusing incident involving natural ability occurred at a football banquet recently. It is our custom after winning a game to give the game ball to a deserving senior. At the end of the season, two seniors—an end and a fullback—hadn't received a ball. An interested townsman donated two footballs so that they could be appropriately marked and presented to the boys at the banquet.

It happened that both boys were sitting at the far end of the team table away from the front of the hall. After making a few comments about each boy, I asked them to stand and threw each his ball. The boys had nicknamed the end "Hands" because of his outstanding catching ability. I threw the ball high and he had to stretch for it and made a fine catch. The fullback had various nicknames, all of them referring to the fact that he was never able to catch a pass. The boy was a fine football player, so I kidded him a little about this by mentioning that we moved him around whenever we could so that he would never have to run downfield on a pass pattern. Before throwing him his ball, I said, "Kent, now is the time to disprove all these things they have been saying about you." I threw the ball, and sure enough, it bounced off his brittle hands. Kent and everyone else had a good chuckle over the incident. All through Kent's high-school career, we spent a great deal of time trying to teach him to catch. He never showed any improvement. The end had natural ability, and all we had to do was see that he had plenty of opportunity to practice.

## Individual Faking Moves

Most of our pass-receivers are not as fast as the defensive halfbacks, so we have to rely on pass patterns and deception to get a man into the clear. With a good fake, a slower man will still be able to get a couple of steps on a faster man before being covered again. I have pointed out already that the ball should arrive while the receiver has this advantage.

A man fakes to make the defensive man think he is going to do something he is not. The receiver has an advantage in that he knows where he is going. A sloppy fake or "rounding" the corner takes away this important advantage. The defensive man is usually as fast as or faster than the average high-school end. This is not usually true for a flanking back. A man who has a speed disadvantage can get a few steps on the defending back by making a good move. The faster defender will recover and move into a good defensive position on the receiver. There is a moment when any receiver should be free and it is up to the passer to hit him then. The passer's timing, as I have already said, requires much hard work.

If the receiver is as fast as or faster than the defender, a good fake will increase his advantage, but if he does not fake well, he gives the defensive man a chance to defend on even terms. One of the better fakes for a faster boy is the change of pace.

The fake is all important on the individual pass pattern and on an individual variation of a normal pass pattern. Receivers should fake on a normal pass if it is possible to keep the proper timing.

### The "wrinkle" fake

The first move we teach is the "wrinkle." A coach stands 10 or 15 yards in front of a line of receivers and they come down and use him to make their fake on. A single wrinkle is merely a fake in one direction before going in the other. If the boy is going to the left, he fakes right first. When he reaches the point for the fake and lands on his left foot, he steps off to the right (see Figure 14). As his right foot lands, he twists to the right, looks over his right shoulder in the direction of the passer, and places both hands up by the right shoulder as though he were about to receive a pass. He then pivots on his right and steps off to the left.

A wrinkle to the right is executed by reversing the wrinkle to the left. This move has to be taught to the beginner in slow motion, because he will have a tendency to round the corner instead of making a sharp angle move. Inexperienced boys usually make a feeble attempt at a body fake also. Even your

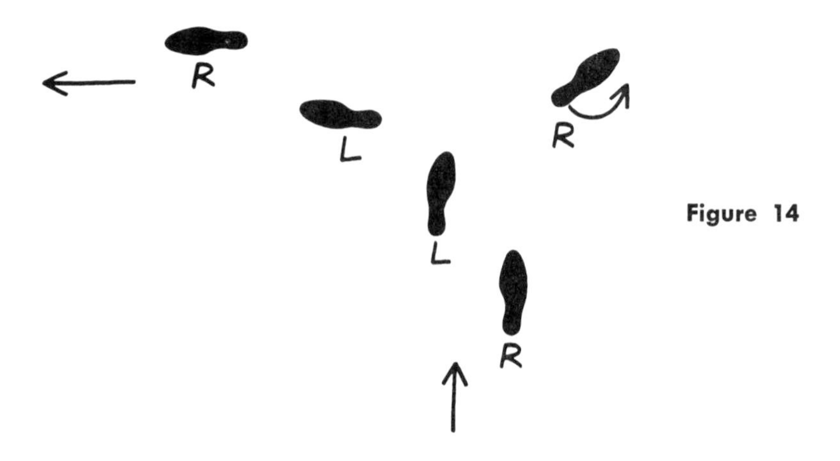


Figure 14

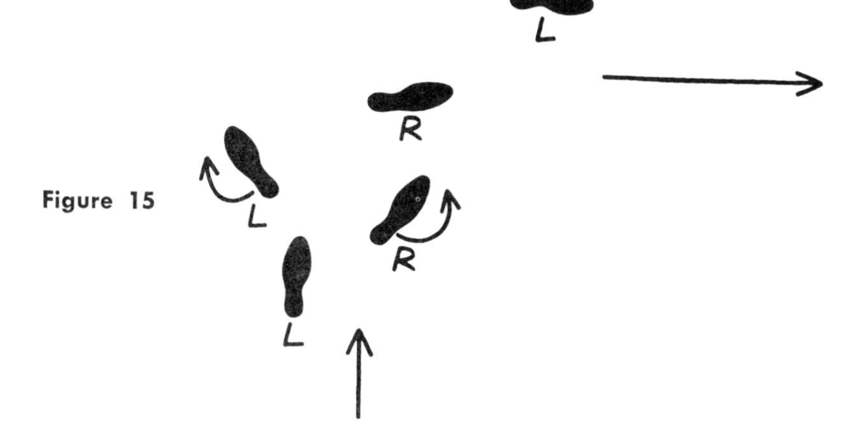

Figure 15

best receiver will have to slow down a little at the moment of the fake in order to make an effective move.

### The double wrinkle fake

Once a boy has this move down fairly well, we introduce the double wrinkle. If he is going to the right, he fakes right, then left, then moves to the right (see Figure 15). The boy is nearly standing still for a moment while making this fake. The move is merely one wrinkle following another without a pause.

If your receivers use both the single and double wrinkle, the defensive backs will hesitate even when the single wrinkle is performed, because they will not know which fake is coming. Thus one fake helps make the other more effective. The single wrinkle move can be used on sideline patterns, across-the-middle patterns and deep angle-out or angle-in patterns. Because the double wrinkle takes more time, it is advisable to make this fake on a sideline pass or a short pass into the middle.

### Z-in and Z-out

Z-in and Z-out are two of the more difficult moves. Actually, they are the same move. *Out* means the final direction is toward the sideline; *in* means that the final direction is toward the middle of the field. If your final direction is to the left, the fake is left, right, then move to the left. To the right, the fake is right, left, then right. Remember that for any move requiring a double fake, the first fake is in the final direction.

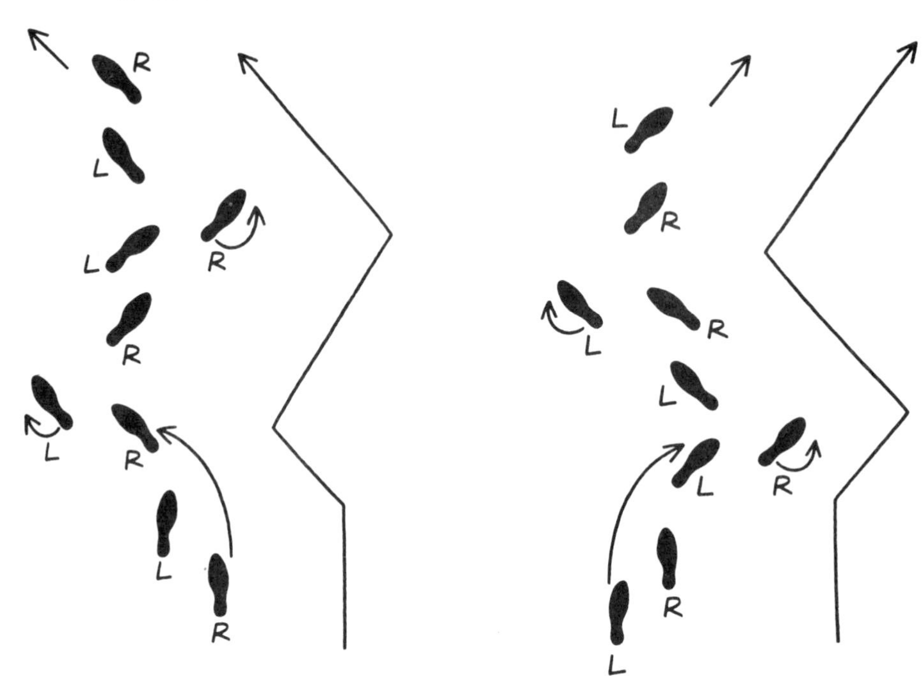


**Figure 16**

The first fake is two steps, then three steps, and then moving in the final direction (Figure 16). Notice that a cross-over step is needed to get into the first direction. Perform this move in slow motion and then increase the pace. It should eventually be performed at full speed. There is no need for a head or hand fake while executing the maneuver. This fake employs only sudden changes of direction.

This move is used for a deeper pass. We use it with a one-on-one individual pass pattern and we may use it with a variation of one of our team pass patterns. It is an excellent fake for several reasons. It can be executed at full speed. Because of the three steps in the second fake, the defender is lulled into believing that you are in your final direction.

When this fake is executed at nearly full speed, the body has a natural rolling motion that is very deceptive and hard to follow. If the receiver is slowed down on the line of scrimmage, he will not have time to make this fake. To give your passer more time to throw to a man making this move, you may find it essential to design your pattern with a roll-out motion.

### The hook

In making any move, a good receiver is trying to mislead his opponent. When running a hook pattern he must really move downfield fast to create the impression that he is trying to get behind the defender so that the defender will back up and be out of position when the hook is made. Because most teams are very concerned about the deep pass, they will try to cover the hook areas with their linebackers. This means that once a deep back has started to move back, he will not come up to protect against the hook until after the pass is thrown. The only halfback who will come back up to defend against the hook is the defensive back covering a wide flanker.

We instruct our receiver always to turn inside toward the ball when making a hook. In Figure 17 the position of the ball is on the right. Notice that the turn is made on the outside foot and that the leg receives a lot of force because it is also stopping the forward movement of the body. The body pivots on the outside foot. Then one step is made back toward the line of scrimmage. The feet are now parallel and the ball should arrive. Timing is very important and to insure perfect timing, the quarterback may not be able to fade all the way back because he may have to pass sooner.

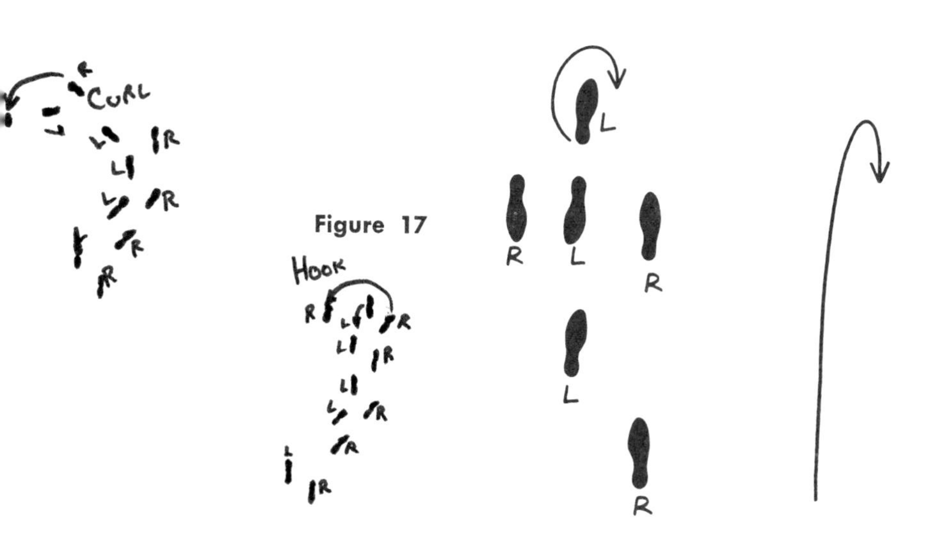

Figure 17

We must consider what should be done if the ball does not arrive on schedule. If the move is made in the middle area of the field, the receiver should drift left or right to slide into open spaces between the linebackers who are moving back. If a receiver is flanked wide and he does not receive the ball at the proper instant, he knows the defensive back will be on him in a moment and should break off to the left or right at full speed for a diagonal pass.

At Marblehead when a wide flanker hooks, the quarterback usually rolls to that side so that he doesn't have as far to throw. Most high-school quarterbacks don't have the strength to throw a ball hard on any short pattern near the sidelines. Also, the passer is in a better position in case of an interception. Our passer for this coming season has a very strong arm so we will throw sideline patterns from a normal pocket. The advantage of passing from a normal pocket is that you can threaten both sidelines when you don't roll out.

Many coaches think that a hook pass should be thrown to the stomach. We throw at the chest because we have had better luck. When the ball is thrown higher fewer defensive hands get in the way. The defender's hands are in a good position to receive the ball. The one disadvantage to this is the interception. If a ball is thrown higher on a hook pass and bounces off the receiver's hands, it goes up in the air and is easy to intercept.

### The hook-go fake

The hook-go fake should only be run by a man who is split wide. The wide defensive halfback may become more concerned about the hook and may come up. When making this move, the receiver should be more deliberate about making the hook. The passer fakes by stepping forward and slapping the ball into the left hand. Then the receiver rolls to the outside and runs deep along the sideline (Figure 18). He should avoid drifting toward the middle of the field because this is a one-on-one pattern and the safety man should not be brought into the play.

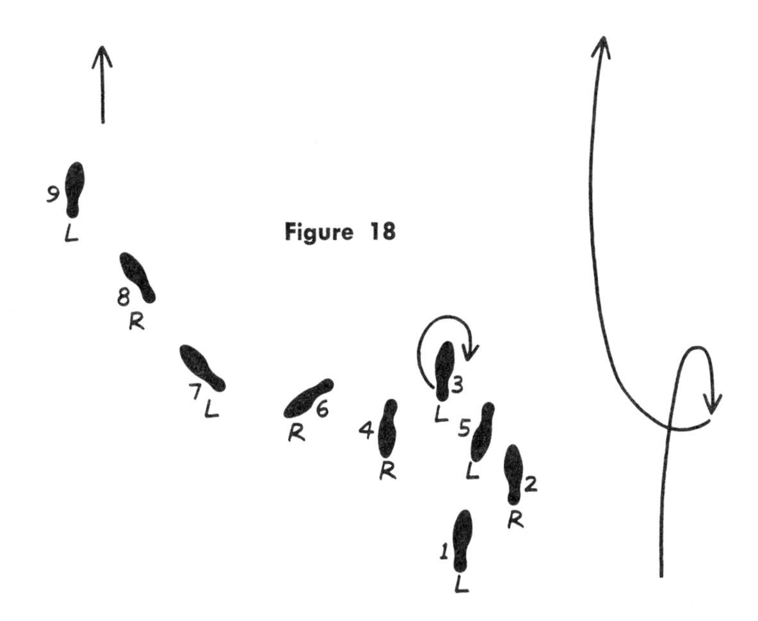

Figure 18

This pattern involves making the hook and then rolling to the outside and downfield. The boy should bring his hands up as though he were going to receive the ball before he rolls out of the hook to go deep.

**The fake block**

This is the best move there is if you wish to have a receiver downfield alone. To get a man into the clear downfield, this move must be used with an action pass. The defensive halfback must not know while the play is developing whether it is pass or run. The receiver can convince him it is a run with the proper fake.

One year we had a senior end who suddenly began to get far downfield without being covered. In one game, the situation was fourth down and two on the opponent's 20-yard line. I called for our 46–0 pass in which we belly the off-tackle left and then roll out left to pass or run. We planned to get the first down either by having the passer run or by throwing into the flat for short yardage. Suddenly, our left end was standing alone in the end zone. The passer floated the ball to him and we had six points instead of the first down.

This prompted me to ask the boy after the game how he had suddenly become so successful in getting clear. He told me he had developed a great new fake and had meant to tell me about it. He would run straight at the defensive halfback and bring up his arms as if he were going to run over him with a good shoulder block. Because he was a big boy, the halfback would jump out of his way to avoid the block, and he would keep going on his pass pattern. This end had only average speed, and yet he was often able to get a tremendous jump on the defender with this fake.

It was amusing to hear him tell of his discovery of this move. He felt that because he had discovered it, it was his personal fake and he took great pride in becoming expert with it. I let him think he was completely responsible for originating the move in our attack. But I had mentioned this fake several times during the season and apparently had made no impression on him at all. This incident has persuaded me to spend more time working on this fake in the future. The incident also illustrates a boy will do something better if he takes pride in his ability to do it.

We also use a fake block on the line of scrimmage to try to shake a man free. On our 27–0 pass we double team the tackle with our slot back. One of our variations is to have the slot man fake a block and then run a pattern straight down the middle of the field. We do this if they try to cover our halfback in the flat with the safety man. The slot back fakes a block on the tackle and keeps his eyes on the safety man. As soon as the safety man leaves his position, the slot back releases and goes right through the area the safety man left.

Once a tight receiver goes into a block at the line of scrimmage, high-school defenders will take their eyes off him. He must then find a way to move from his fake block so that he will not be picked up by a defender again. We used a 23 power pass in one ball game and scored an easy touchdown. Our scouting showed us our opponent lined up in the goal line defense shown in Figure 19.

The line blocks very aggressively and attempts to drive

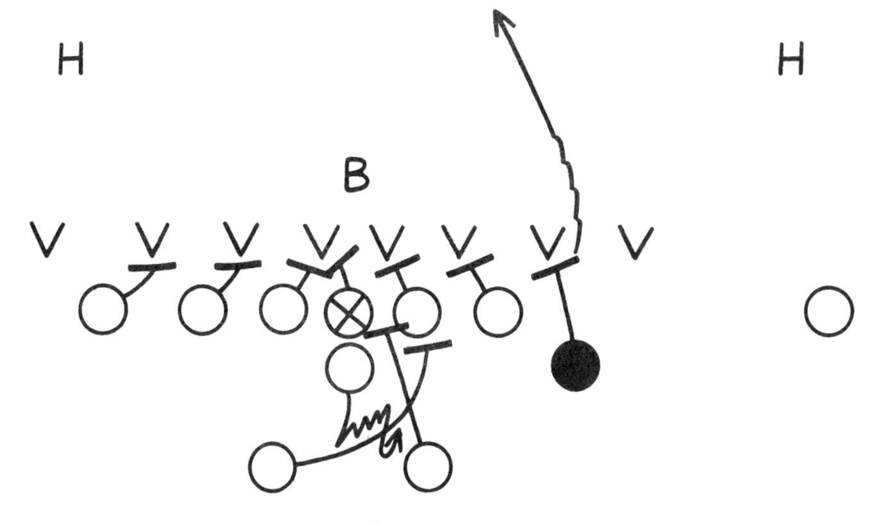


**Figure 19**

their men downfield. The slot man blocks for a moment, then releases and goes into the end zone. The quarterback rides the halfback into the hole and then draws out to make an easy pass. The beauty of this play is that if the receiver is not open the quarterback can run the three hole because the aggressive blocking is in operation. In this game the receiver was wide open and scored. The situation was first and ten on their 8-yard line. Notice that we passed in this situation, thus gaining the extra advantage of surprise. Because our opponent was much larger than we were, chances are that if we had run two plays, we would have had to pass on third down anyway. Chapter 13 will go into play calling in detail.

On all of our screen passes and fall-off passes the intended receivers actually block a defensive end for about two counts before releasing. On our off-tackle play we drive the defensive end out with our halfback. On the off-tackle pass he fakes this block by contacting the end for an instant before slipping into the flat. The fake block on a pass has been one of our most effective fakes and we try to use it whenever it is feasible.

## Change of pace

The change of pace can only be used by your fastest men. You are wasting your time if you work on this move with a receiver of only average speed. The idea is to get the defender to run the same speed as the receiver who runs at about seven-eighths full speed. Once the defender starts running with him, the receiver suddenly pours it on full speed. Since the defender doesn't know when this change is going to come, the receiver should be able to pick up a couple of steps before the defender can react to the different pace. Then he can use his speed to real advantage and get behind the defender. The only disadvantage is that the passer needs more time and your blocking may be unable to give it to him. By rolling out to the side of the fake, the passer may be able to gain his time.

You can use a change of pace with several other moves. If a man were running the hook pattern, he could start off slower, then pour on speed, then come back in a hook. The sudden change of pace should cause the defender to start to backpeddle, and he should be completely out of it on the hook. You can do the same thing on a sideline pass. What you want to do is make the defender rush backwards to cover the deep zone.

## Change of direction

A receiver should change direction at sharp angles. This is not an absolute rule, but any receiver who "rounds" his corners is easier to cover. A change of direction is part of nearly all of the moves presented. These changes are abrupt for the purpose of misleading the defender as to the final direction of the move.

We usually try to incorporate direction changes into our pass patterns. Most teams play a zone or a modified zone defense. If a receiver changes direction and heads towards another defensive zone, some sort of swapping usually takes place. A zone defense requires a certain number of rules. By having several receivers changing directions, you are putting these rules to their severest test—perhaps forcing the defense to break them. Several of our pass patterns are designed to make normal zone coverage difficult to attain.

## Breaking Down a Pass Defense

You can design a pass pattern to break down any pass defense if you know the defense rules. Once during my college days, the reserve quarterback was throwing pass patterns against the varsity during preparation for a coming ball game. Suddenly a receiver was all alone downfield. The coach asked the boy to run the pass pattern again and the same thing happened again. The reserve quarterback, knowing the pass defense rules, had designed a pattern that would put a receiver into the clear if the defenders followed the rules. Needless to say, this quarterback is now a very successful high-school coach.

We make every attempt to determine exactly what type of pass defense will be used against us, and we try to figure out its rules. Usually one, sometimes several, of the pass patterns we run will be effective against a specific defense. One of the duties of our scouts is to try to furnish all the information possible on pass defense. Often, by analyzing the films of the past few seasons, we discover a lot about the type of pass defense a certain coach uses. How to break down various types of pass defense is discussed in detail in Chapter 11.

## Working with Receivers and Passers Together

The most time-consuming part of developing a successful passing attack is coaching the passer. But once you have a good passer, he can only be successful if he has good receivers. You can save time by training your passers and receivers together. Whenever you are working with your passers, have them throw to your receivers. If possible, work with the passers yourself, and have an assistant coach work with the receivers.

Once you have a capable passer and good receivers, you can start enjoying yourself. You can begin developing an attack, knowing that you are pass capable. I am not implying that your offense is undecided until after you've trained your personnel, but I want to emphasize that your first job is to train them. At Marblehead our offense pattern is developed on the assumption that we will have the personnel. Once you know exactly what these boys can do, it is simple enough to modify your offense to suit their capabilities.

SIX

# A PASSING OFFENSE

Passes fall into two categories. The pass that is a pass from the very beginning. We'll call this the standard pass play. Pocket passes, screens, and short rollouts fall into this category. And the action pass which simulates a running play before becoming a pass.

## Advantages of Standard Pass Play

There are many advantages to the standard pass:

1. This type of pass affords the best protection to the passer.
2. It is nearly always used when everybody in the ball park knows it's going to be a pass.
3. Your quarterback will usually have time to set up before he throws.
4. By using combinations of any of the five potential receivers, you can attack any of the zones of the pass defense. You may also place your best receiver against the poorest defender and really go to work on him.

## Disadvantages of Standard Pass Play

Despite the advantages of a standard pass, it has obvious disadvantages.

1. The defense will recognize "pass" immediately.
2. The defensive zones may be extensively covered. Or your receivers may be held up. Or the defense may rush successfully. (Not all three together.)
3. You lose the element of surprise.
4. The pocket pass affords a poor set-up for the quarterback to run from. This may not be true if a defensive end is foolish and rushes from the inside.
5. The defense will rush better.

## Terminology

There are many ways to call pass plays. In college we called some set plays, but most of the patterns were called by the quarterback in the huddle. A receiver would have perhaps eight or ten moves he could make. If a receiver was not told where to go, he planned his route to fit in with the routes of the other receivers. A sample call might be "51 pass, 2 hook, 9 angle out" (see Figure 20). Number 51 calls the play and

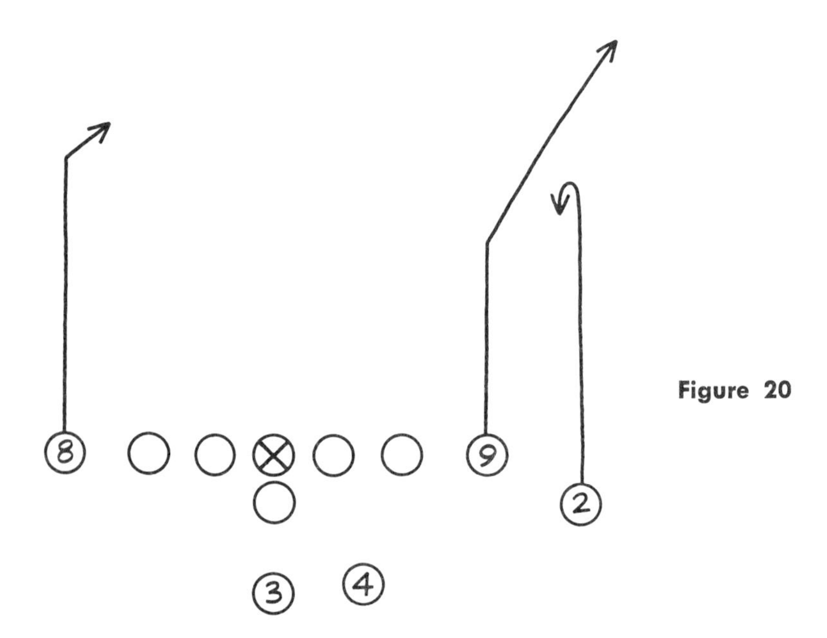


Figure 20

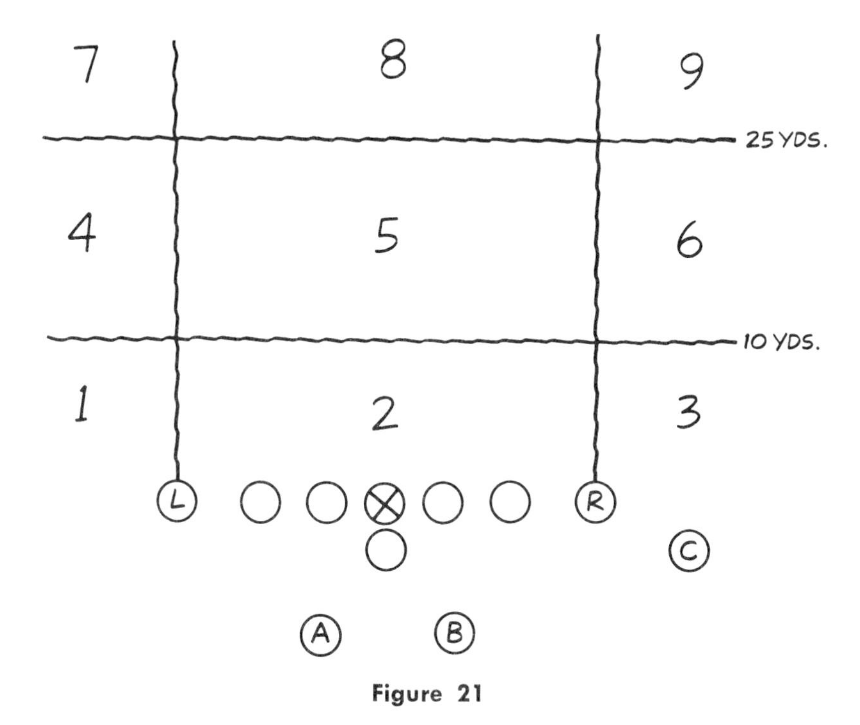


**Figure 21**

2 and 9 are the receivers who are being given their paths. The other receiver (8) then follows a complementary path.

Although this method was very successful at the college level, it would not work out well in high school. You need mature passers and receivers to achieve such a flexible type of passing attack. When I first tried using this in high school, several set patterns developed and these were the only ones used.

Many coaches number both the receivers and the defensive zone (see Figure 21). For example, the quarterback could tell the receiver R to run a pattern into zone 8. This set-up is only an illustration. And there are many excellent systems developed from this general scheme. Again, I feel that at the high-school level, this plan would develop certain pet pass plays and actually defeat the primary purpose of these set-ups, which are designed to produce a very flexible attack.

At Marblehead we have been successful with just a few basic pass patterns. Each pattern may have a variation or two to give the attack some flexibility. We give the pass pattern a descriptive name to help the receivers remember their patterns. Incidentally, the last word of the call for *every* pass play, standard or action, is "pass." If any linemen forget the play, at least the word "pass" will keep them from going downfield. Also, the wording of the play refers to the side on which the two receivers are.

## Our Offensive Set-up

Before proceeding further I will outline our offense set-up. We normally run from a slot right formation with varying splits on the right end (see Figure 22). Often our left end will also

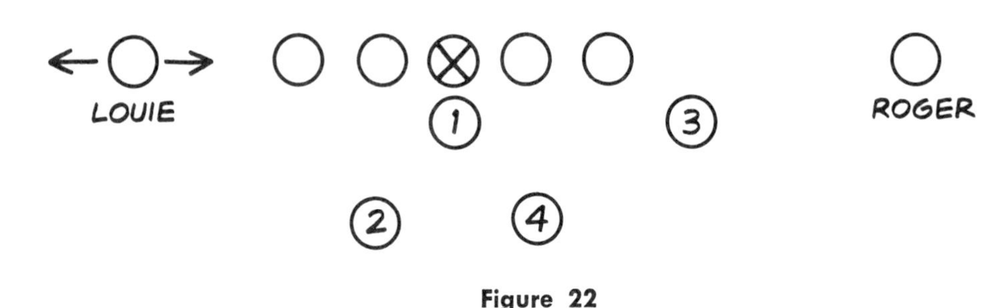


**Figure 22**

split at varying distances. If no formation is mentioned in the huddle, we come out in our normal slot right. If we wish to go to the left, "Slot Left" is called in the huddle. We call our right end "Roger," our left end "Louie." The slot is always the 3 back; the deep back on the left is the 2 back; the one on the right is 4.

When going from normal to slot left, it is perhaps best always to have the same man in the slot. However, we have rotated our backfield in the past because of personnel and our running attack. Our 2 back is usually our best and we have a very effective trap he can run from slot left.

## Standard Pass Patterns

### Trail-out pass

The maneuvers of our standard pass patterns are executed by the two primary receivers on the slot side. In the Trail-out Pass, the inside man, whether an end or a back, trails behind the other man to the outside. Note in Figure 23 that the outside man must run deep and toward the defensive halfback to prevent a "switch" between the safety man and the defensive halfback.

The outside receiver must drag the defensive halfback deep. The primary receiver runs a path straight downfield for 10 or 15 yards and then breaks directly toward the sideline. The off-side end is a release man and runs downfield toward his halfback for 10 or 15 yards and then breaks diagonally across the field, running at about three-quarter speed. This pass pattern is very good in that the passer has his two primary receivers in the same line of vision. It is also the pattern that seems most to complicate the problem of pass defense.

Many teams try to defend against this pattern by having an outside linebacker drop back to the flat area and pick up our trail-out man. We then run a variation of this pattern by calling for a rollout action toward this linebacker, thus placing him in a bind. If a team rotates too quickly, we would want to throw to our off-side end who should then be wide open.

There is another variation of this pattern that is very difficult to cover, but it requires a lot of time to execute. The deep receiver drags his halfback deep and then into the middle. The slot back then executes an out and down pattern making it almost impossible for a linebacker to cover him (see Figure 24).

The Trail-out Pass is one of our basic patterns because it is difficult to defend against it. Be careful of the interception, however, because your opponent will probably run any pass intercepted in a flat area back for a score.

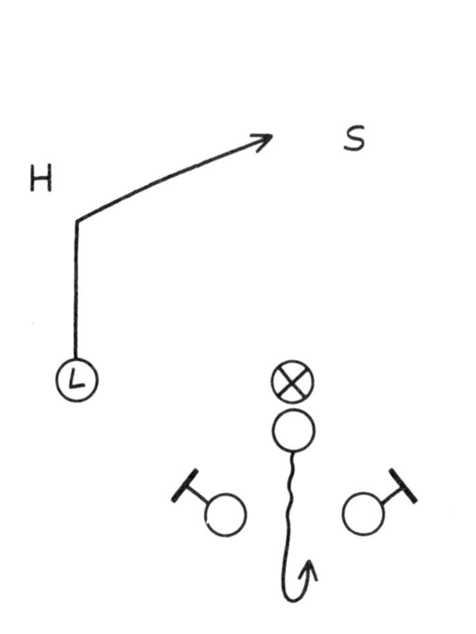

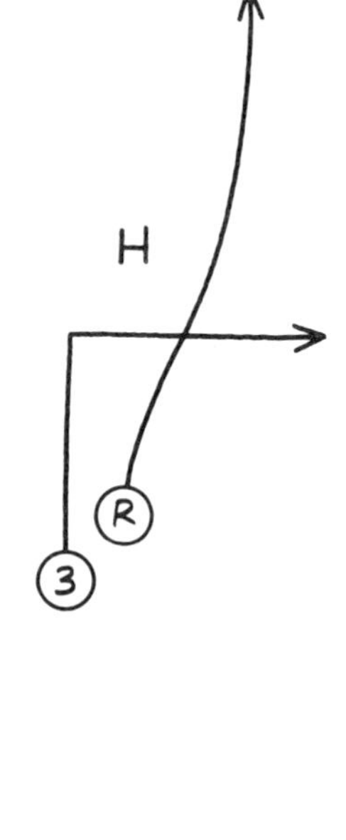


**Figure 23**

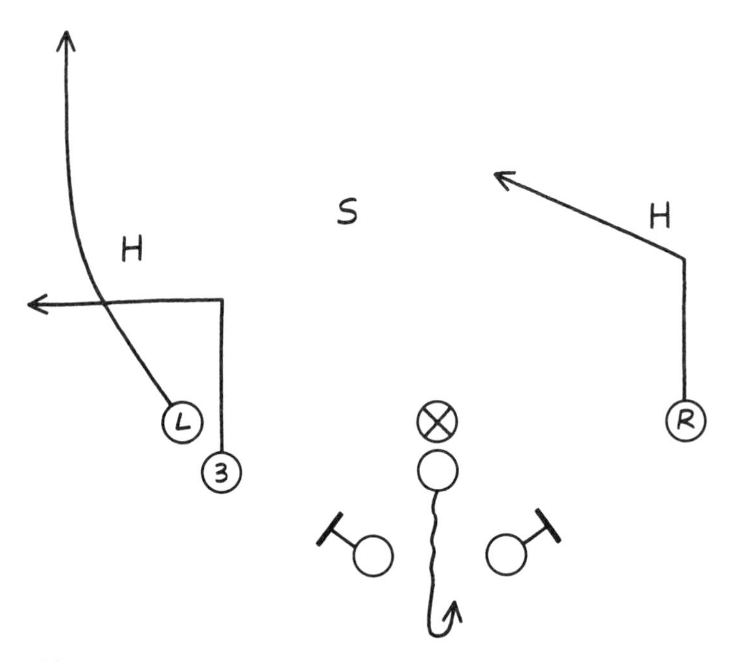

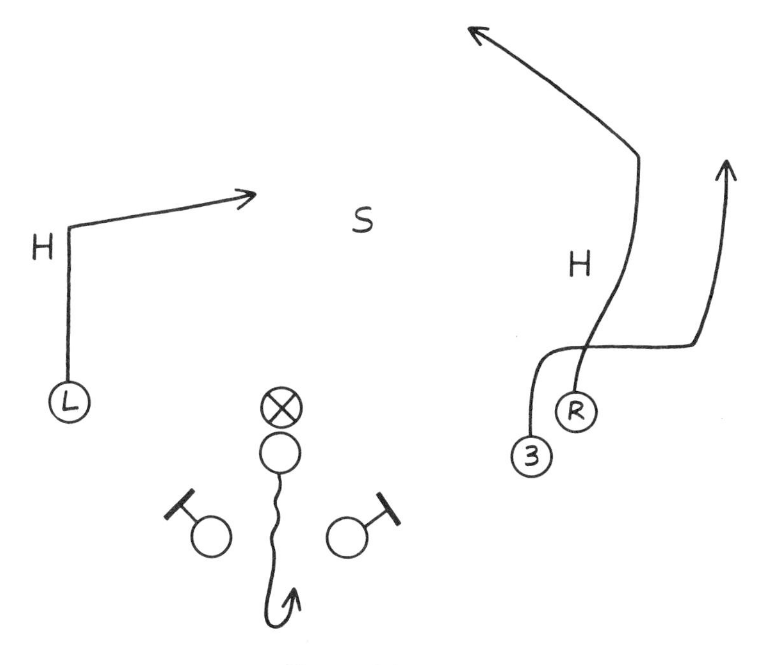


**Figure 24**

**Trail-in pass**

This pattern should be easy to remember because the outside man trails in behind the slot man who is going deep through the safety man's position (see Figure 25). Of our standard patterns, we rely on the Trail-in Pass the most and have the greatest success with it.

The slot man (inside man) must run into the deep middle zone to pull the safety man deep. We instruct him to run directly toward the goal posts and stay in the middle of the field. If this inside man is fast, this is a good opportunity to run a Z-in fake to get into the deep middle zone.

The trail man (outside man) moves straight downfield for 10 or 15 yards and, using a simple wrinkle fake, cuts flat across the middle. His final path should be nearly parallel to the line of scrimmage, and we usually hit him at just about 15–20 yards deep. The inside linebackers usually determine the depth of the trail-in man's path. If they are slow moving back, which is usually the case, he runs a deeper path behind them. If these inside linebackers are "flying back," he runs a shallow pattern.

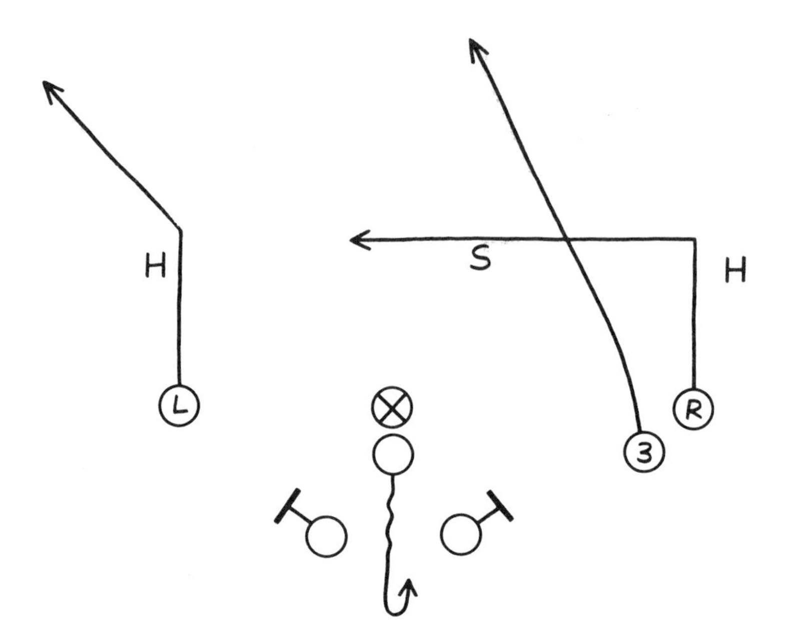


**Figure 25**

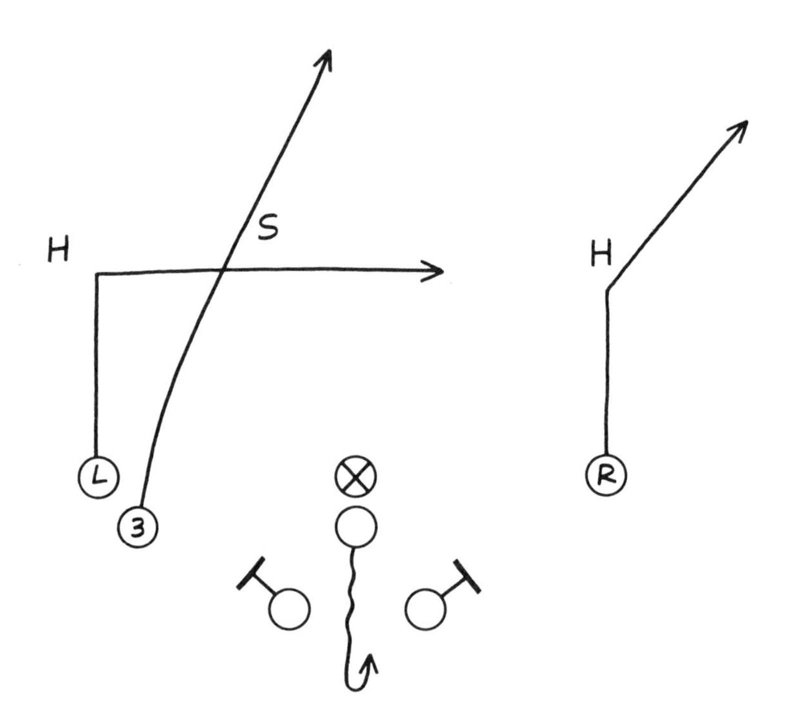

The passer again has the advantage of having his two primary receivers in the same line of vision, one shallow, one deep. The off-side end, who has the job of dragging his halfback out of the middle, is often a good alternate receiver. Release time is all important for your passer here. The receiver will be moving in and out of clear areas, and it is up to the passer to see that the ball arrives when the receiver is clear. Refer to Chapter 2 for a more detailed presentation of proper timing.

A very effective variation of this pattern is to roll out on the Trail-in Pass. The passer rolls out away from his strong side (see Figure 26). With two blockers in front of him, the passer can exert tremendous pressure on the weak-side halfback by using his run-pass-run technique.

**Figure 26**

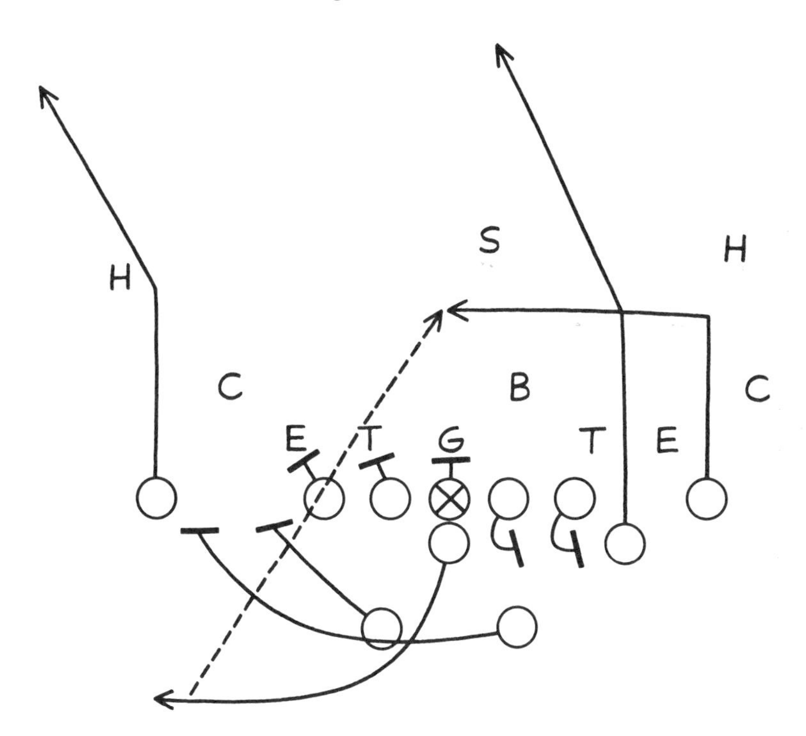

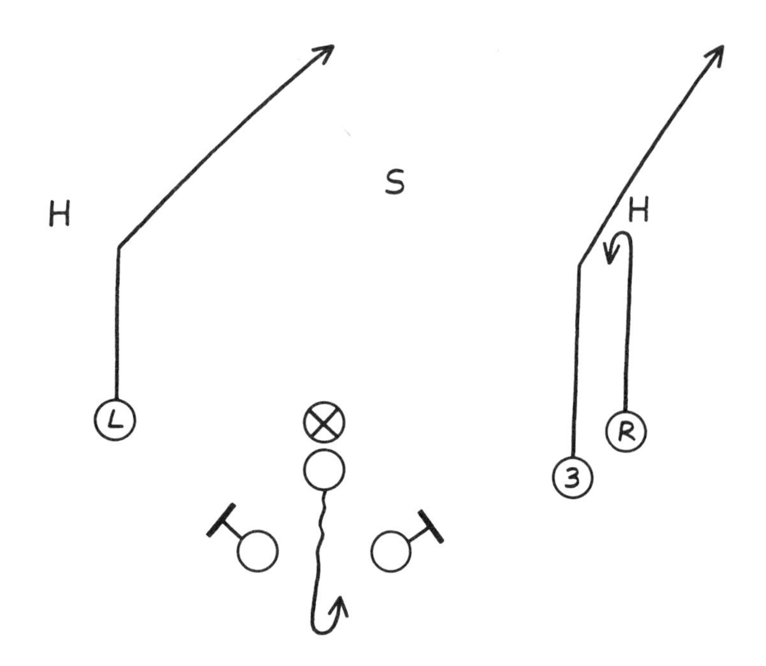


**Figure 27**

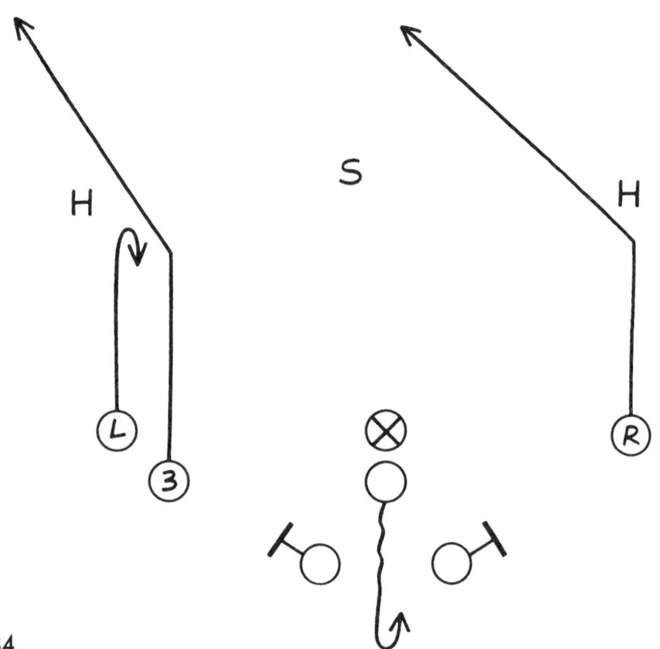

### Hook-go pass

The purpose of this pattern is to drag deep men downfield to hook a man quickly in front. The timing has to be exceptionally good because if the defensive linebackers are given time, they will move back to spoil the play. Again, the maneuver is run by the two men on the strong side, and the off-side end runs a complementary path (see Figure 27). The two men in the action should line up quite close together and stay no more than a yard or two apart while moving downfield together.

The outside man hooks at about 12 yards deep. As he hooks, the inside man breaks and runs a deep angle-out path. Timing is very important on any hook pass. The passer must have the ball on the way just as the receiver is completing his hook maneuver. The two primary receivers are again in the same line of vision. The deep receiver will sometimes be clear because of confusion in the defensive backfield. If the passer fakes the short man well, the deeper receiver should be able to break into the clear.

We have several variations of the hook-go pattern. On the "Hook-Go Pass with a Lateral," the off-side end breaks directly for a spot about 5 yards in front of where the hook man will catch the ball, and the hook man laterals back to him. He should have running room down the sidelines. Another variation we have used is rolling out to the right with the hook man running a hook and out path. We call this play "Hook-Go Pass, Roger Hook and Out, Roll Right."

### Deep cross pass

The purpose of this pattern is to defeat a zone defense that tries to cover their men closely while they are in their zone. In Figure 28, the pattern would be working on the defensive right halfback.

We do not use this pass very often because its purpose is mainly to defeat a tight zone pass defense. Louie runs a little shallower path than Roger because we want to slip Roger into

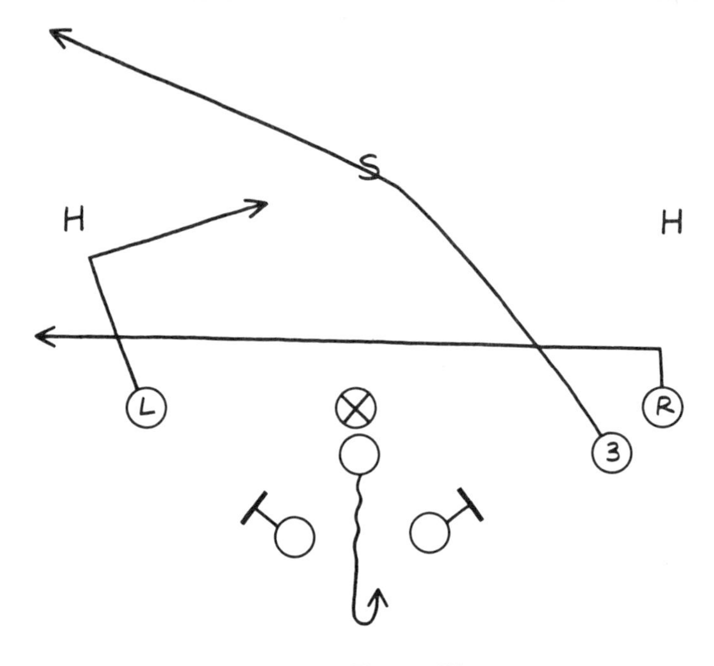


Figure 28

the deep outside zone behind the weak-side defensive halfback, and it is a good play for this. One problem is that the passer needs a lot of time. We only have enough time when we run this pattern as an action pass off our "Cross" running series. One reason I keep this pattern is that it has been used very successfully against us. However, if the defensive backs talk to each other, it is very easy for the safety man to pick up the intended receiver if the halfback has not dropped back quickly enough.

The trail-out, trail-in, and hook-go passes are our basic standard patterns. Because there are only three patterns, they are easily learned. But with left and right formations, and their variations, the problems of defense are multiplied while the offense remains simple.

## Miscellaneous Standard Passes

The following passes are standard passes because they do not fake a running play first. However, they are a mongrel type and often require a different blocking technique or a slightly unusual maneuver. For the sake of a clear presentation it would be best to collect all these patterns into one group.

### Fall-off pass

If a defensive end is giving us a particularly bad time on any of our standard passes, one of our two deep backs "falls off." A back "falling off" blocks the end for about two counts and then slips behind him. The quarterback just drops the ball over the defensive end to the halfback who is now standing off to the side waiting (see Figure 29). The receiver then has a lot of running to do on his own. This is not a screen pass although there is some similarity.

### Pro pass

Our pro pass can be considered a standard pass although it does differ in some respects. Our linemen block aggressively to prevent the defensive linemen from standing up (see Figure 30).

**Figure 29**

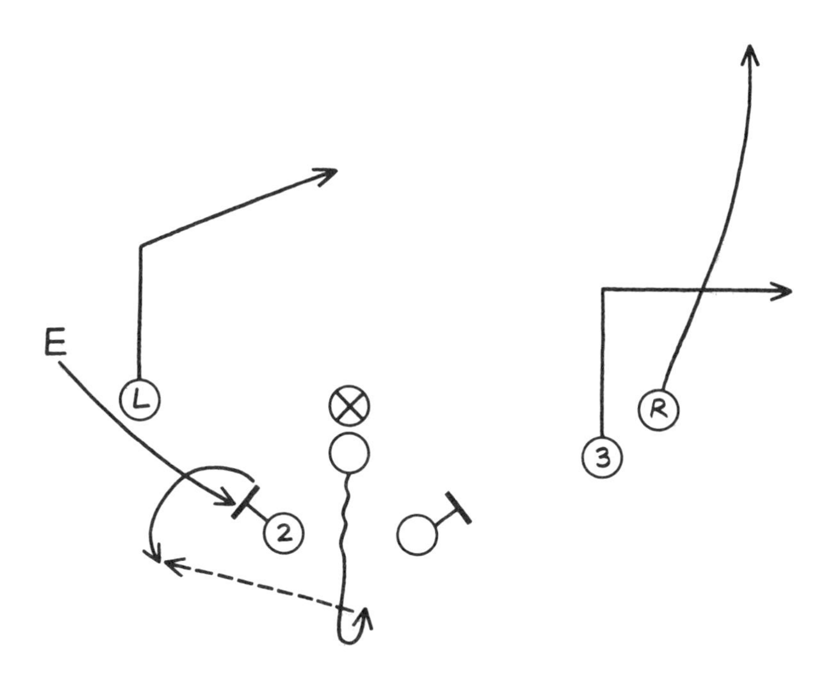

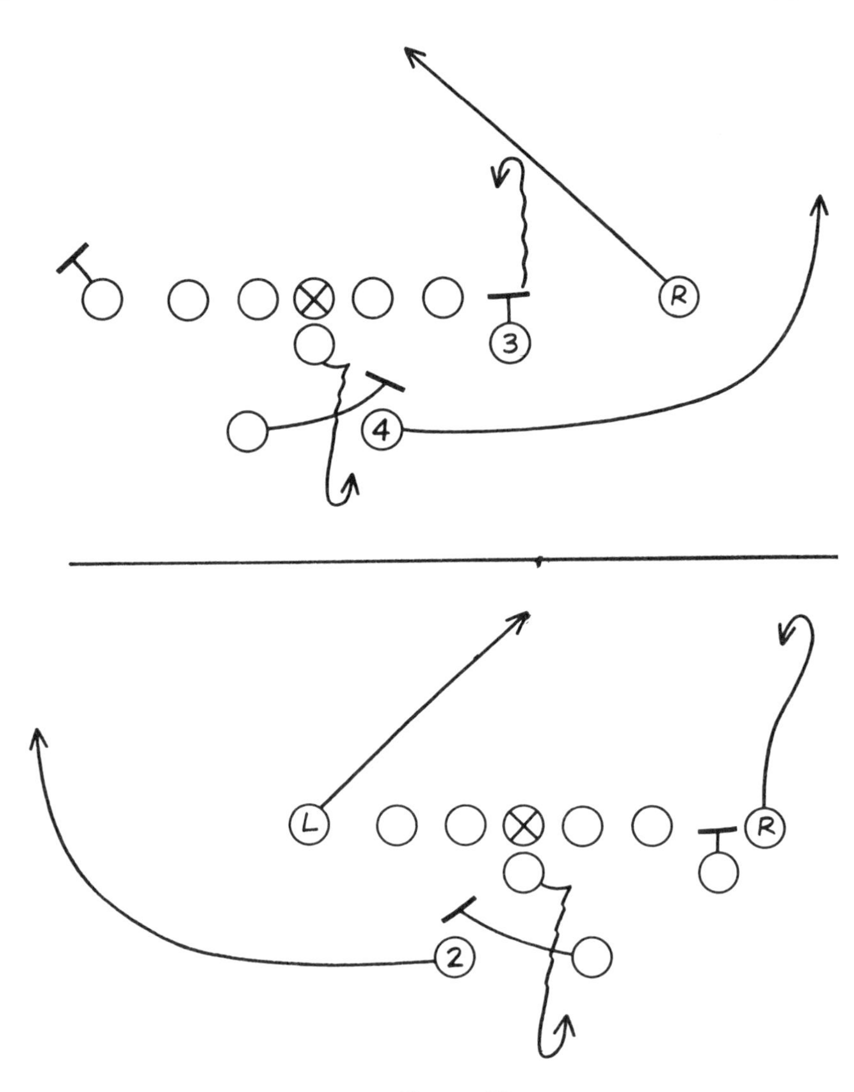


**Figure 30**

The slot back blocks and hides until all people have cleared the area in front of him and then hooks into a clear spot to become the release man. The end can be hit immediately or later. If the quarterback finds he cannot throw quickly, he must drop back to a deep set position very fast. The second receiver is the swinging halfback. A throw to the second receiver is very often a touchdown pass, either for you or for the defense. If it's intercepted the defensive man will, in all likelihood, go for the score. The risk is smaller if the flaring back has turned up-field before the ball is released. He is a good man to hit. But it is very dangerous to pass to him and your passer should be warned of the dangers. We also run the pro pass to either side from our slot left formation.

## Screen Passes

Our screen passes are run in about the same manner as our "fall-off" pass. The screen can be run with any of the standard pass patterns. The man responsible for blocking the end on the side of the screen receives the pass. The tackle and guard on that side and the center form the screen after making a normal pass block for two counts. Since the screen can be thrown on any standard pass, there are many variations of the screen. For example, if your "Trail-in Pass" is working, run a trail-in, screen right pass (see Figure 31). The defensive backs

**Figure 31**

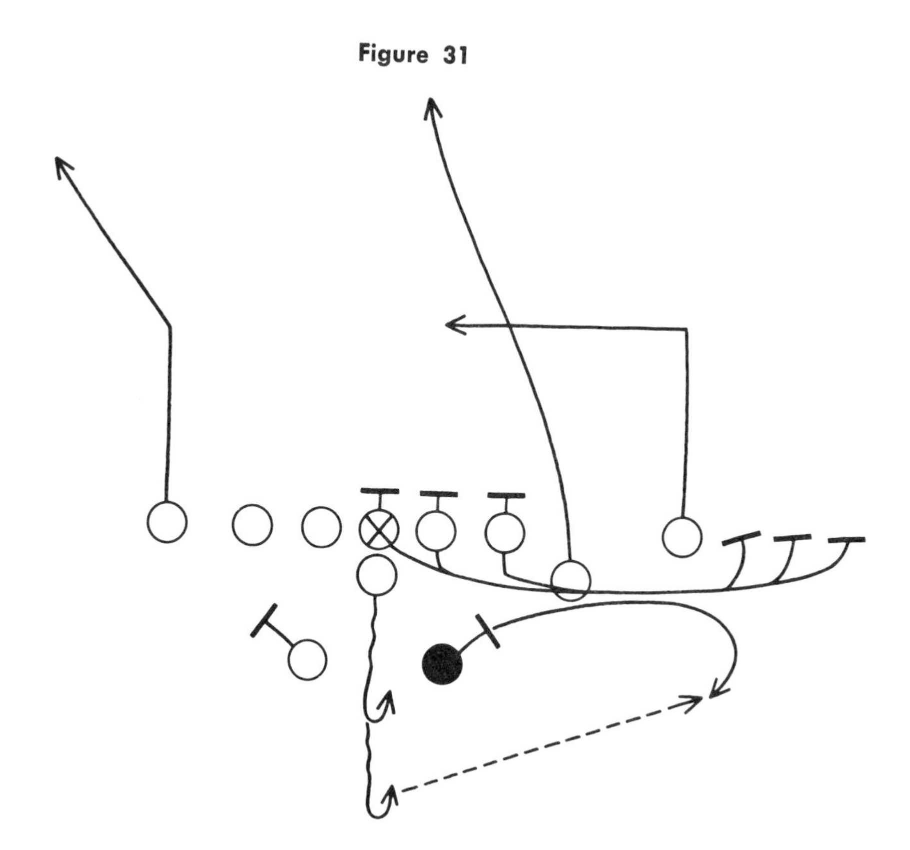

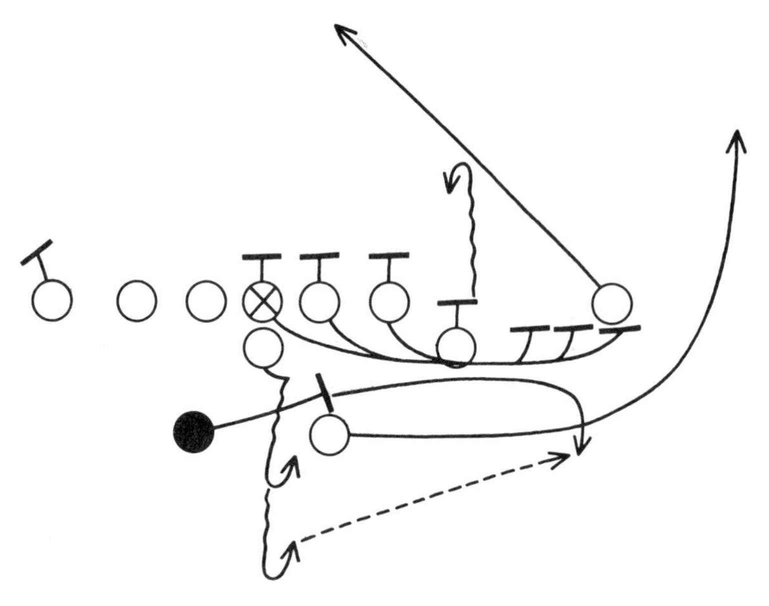

**Figure 32**

should react to the pattern that has been causing them trouble and thus give the receiver of the screen more running room after he has caught the pass.

Pro right, screen right pass (see Figure 32) has been particularly effective for us. Often the defensive corner will get into the screen and spoil it. On this play the swinging 4 back will keep this man honest. We have thrown several touchdown passes to the 4 back because the corner became anxious and came up into the screen, leaving the swing man wide open. In one game Tom Manning was unable to throw the screen so he ran to the right to pick the screen men up as blockers. When the defensive halfback came up to stop the run, Tom, still running, threw a touchdown pass to the swing man downfield. This is a good example of a running passer putting the pressure on the defensive halfback.

On Pro right, screen left pass (see Figure 33) you'll notice that the end, who is assigned to block the defensive end, is the receiver of the pass. This pass won a ball game for us during the past season. This was the only time we used it and I don't recall running it often in practice. The simple method we have for calling screens enabled everyone to remember his assignment. The opponent was a big team and we were having trouble moving on the ground. Late in the fourth quarter with the score tied 8–8, we were on their 30-yard line with fourth down, three yards to go. The play worked perfectly, giving us a first down on the 15-yard line, and we went on to score.

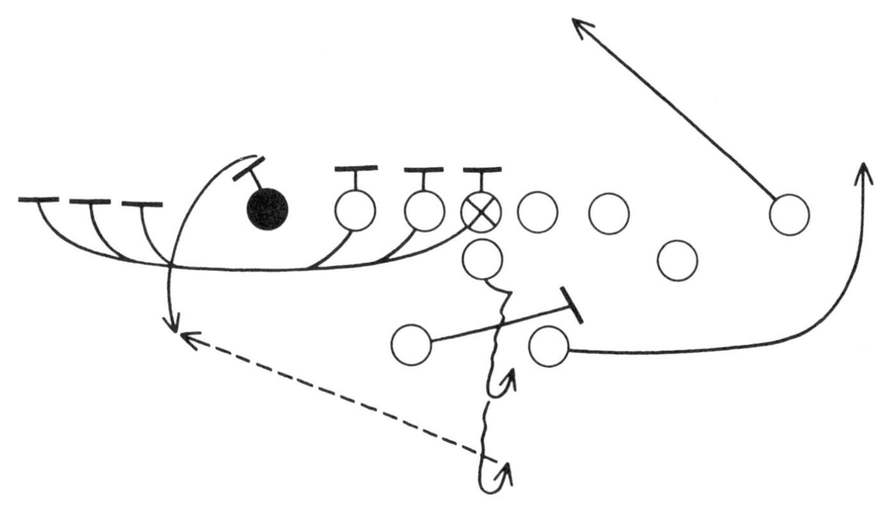

**Figure 33**

## Executing a screen pass

Our screen first develops as a standard pass play, everyone blocking normally, the three men in the screen releasing after two counts. Caution them that they must block for the two counts because the quarterback sets up in his pocket first before moving back again. The quarterback moves back as he would in a normal pass and sets. When he feels pressure he starts to drift back to throw the screen. The pass is released high because often it must be thrown over outstretched arms. The pass must be firm because the backward movement of the passer will make a firm pass softer for the receiver. Since the passer will be off-balance, he should have had plenty of practice with off-balance techniques.

If the screen is not open, the passer may be able to hit a receiver downfield, or he may have to eat the ball. If so he may be able to pick up some blocking by running to the side where the screen is forming. The screen, like the fall-off pass or swing motion, is very dangerous if intercepted because a pass intercepted off to the side is usually a score for the defense. A quarterback has to learn to "eat" the ball and take his loss.

**Halfback technique on the screen pass**

On the screen pass the men blocking the ends use a slightly different technique than they normally would. For example, in the "Trail-out Pass, Screen Left" (see Figure 34), the 4 back, who holds his block, cannot allow the end to rush deep from the outside as he normally does. He goes out to greet the end, but instead of hitting him with the left shoulder to steer him deep, he uses a body block. He must get a little more in front of the end than he normally does. His body still appears to be in position for a reverse shoulder block but he moves into a reverse body block. He will not be able to contain the end for very long, but he will prevent him from catching the passer deep and from the blind side.

The back receiving the screen pass goes into his initial block just a little different from normal. He strikes hard with his left shoulder. The block should stop the end in his tracks but when released he should be able to resume rushing from the outside. A half-hearted block attempt by the 2 back will not fool a good end.

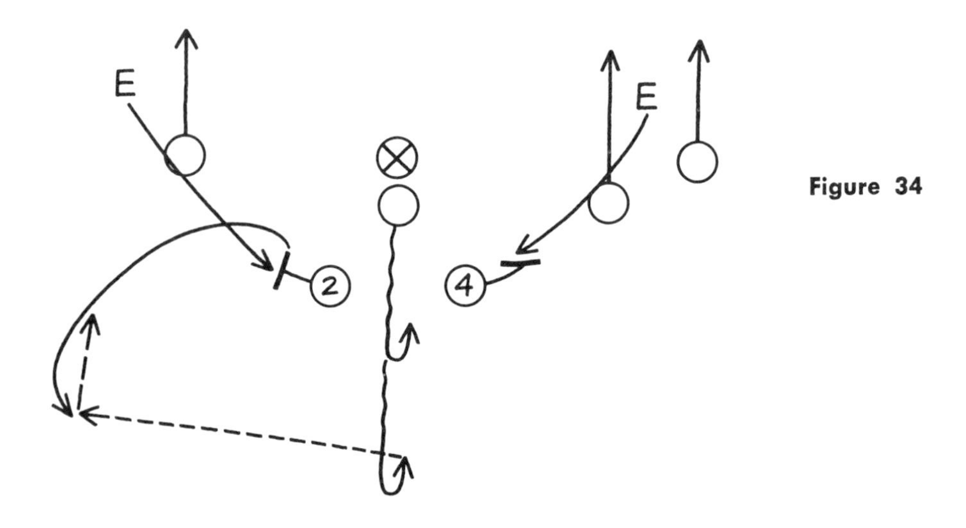


**Figure 34**

After hitting the end, the 2 back slips inside him and follows the course in the diagram, moving in an arc toward the line of scrimmage and then drifting back. When he catches the ball, he is about five yards deep and ten yards to the side in a standing position facing the passer. His first move should be with the left foot straight up-field so that he can move in any of three directions. Many screens are designed so that the runner is committed to a direction as he is receiving the ball. We do not do this.

## The Individual Pass Pattern

If you have a particularly fine receiver who has good hands, good faking moves and real speed, it is quite easy to develop individual pass patterns to suit his talents. This type of pass pattern is used when the defense attempts to cover a wide split end or flanker with only one man. In fact, the receiver doesn't have to be great, just better than the man attempting to cover him.

The pattern is run by the usual three men and the blocking is normal pocket protection. The intended receiver is the only man given an assignment, the other two men are on their own but must run a complementary path. That is, they should run a path that will pull a defensive man away from the intended pass area to prevent double teaming of the intended receiver by the defense (see Figure 35).

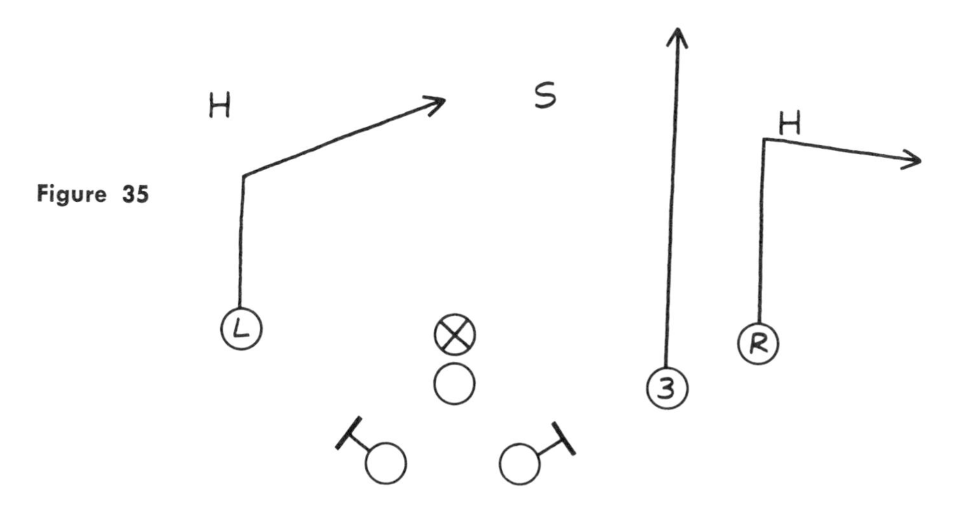


**Figure 35**

## Rolling out on an individual pass pattern

If your passer does not have the strength to throw to the sideline accurately, he could roll out to that side. The only trouble with rolling out on the individual pass is that the safety man will move as well, and you may end up with a double team on the intended receiver. On the Roger sideline pass the safety man could now help his halfback out if the pattern were the sideline and deep path.

## The stay pass

One year we had a left end that could run like a halfback and we would split him out a good distance to see if we could get one-on-one coverage. We scored several touchdowns on this one simple play (see Figure 36). If the defender plays him loosely, the quarterback throws out to him as quickly as possible, and there is only one man to pass for the touchdown. If the halfback covers him real tight, the end and passer fake the Stay Pass and then run a "go" pattern deep. We hope the fake of the short pass will pull the halfback up.

## Individual pass moves

We have quite a few individual paths that Roger or Louie can run. They are given names that indicate what the path is. Figure 37 shows the paths as Roger would run them.

Figure 36

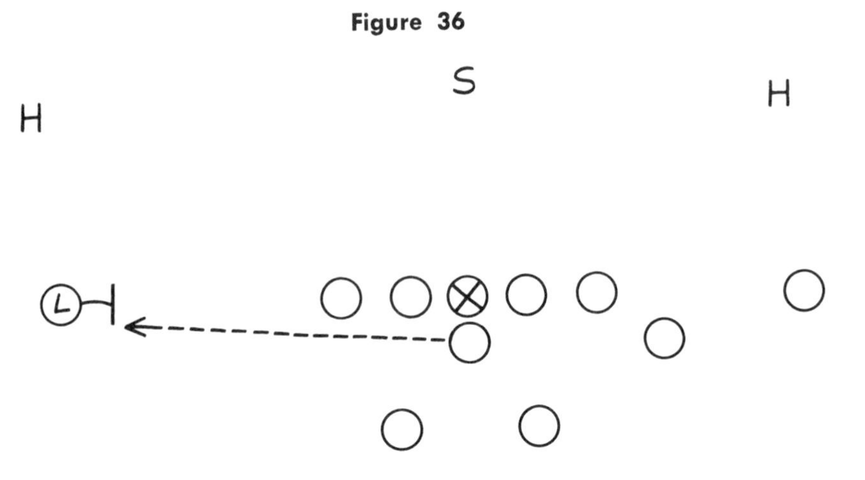

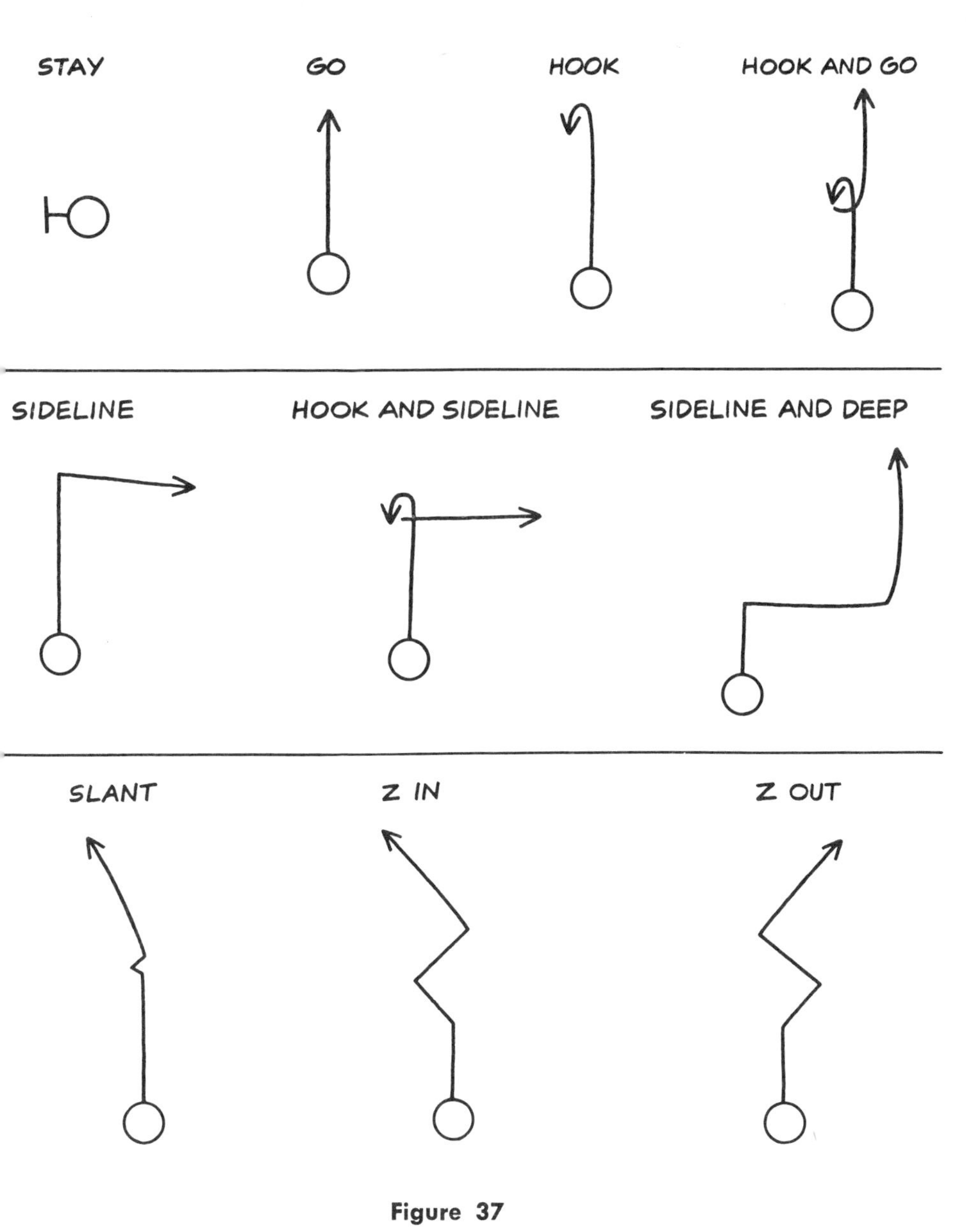


**Figure 37**

In addition to these standard passes, there are many others that you could almost originate during the course of a game. Just give them names that quickly tell the receivers what to do, for example "Everybody Hook Pass," or "Three Deep Pass."

## Our Offensive System

We now come to a discussion of the most potent part of our offense, the action pass. In order to discuss our play passes it is necessary to outline briefly our numbering and play calling system.

The holes are numbered odd to the right, even to the left (see Figure 38). The position of the hole is on the outside leg of the linemen, the exception being the end-sweep holes (8, 9).

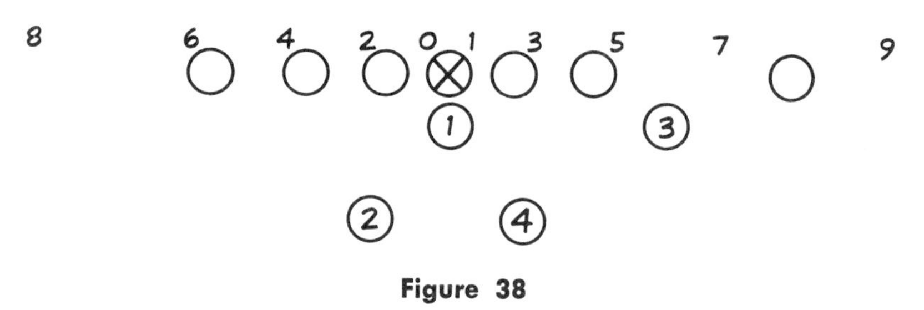


Figure 38

In addition, the "on-side" guard is number two or six. On either number he pulls; on two he blocks the end out; on six he leads the play. The off-side guard is the 0 guard; whenever he is called he leads. In Figure 39, the 29 tells the back and the hole, the 60 tells who will pull.

### Our cross series

In addition to these straightforward plays we also have several series. Each series has several running plays and at least one action pass. Figure 40 shows a play from our "cross" series.

The word *cross* tells our backfield to execute the same maneuvers no matter who is taking the ball. The running plays from this series are 23 cross, 42 cross (from either normal or slot left), 36–0 cross from normal, and 37–0 cross from slot left. We run a "cross" pass, 36–0 cross pass, and slot left 37–0 cross pass. These are discussed a little later in this chapter.

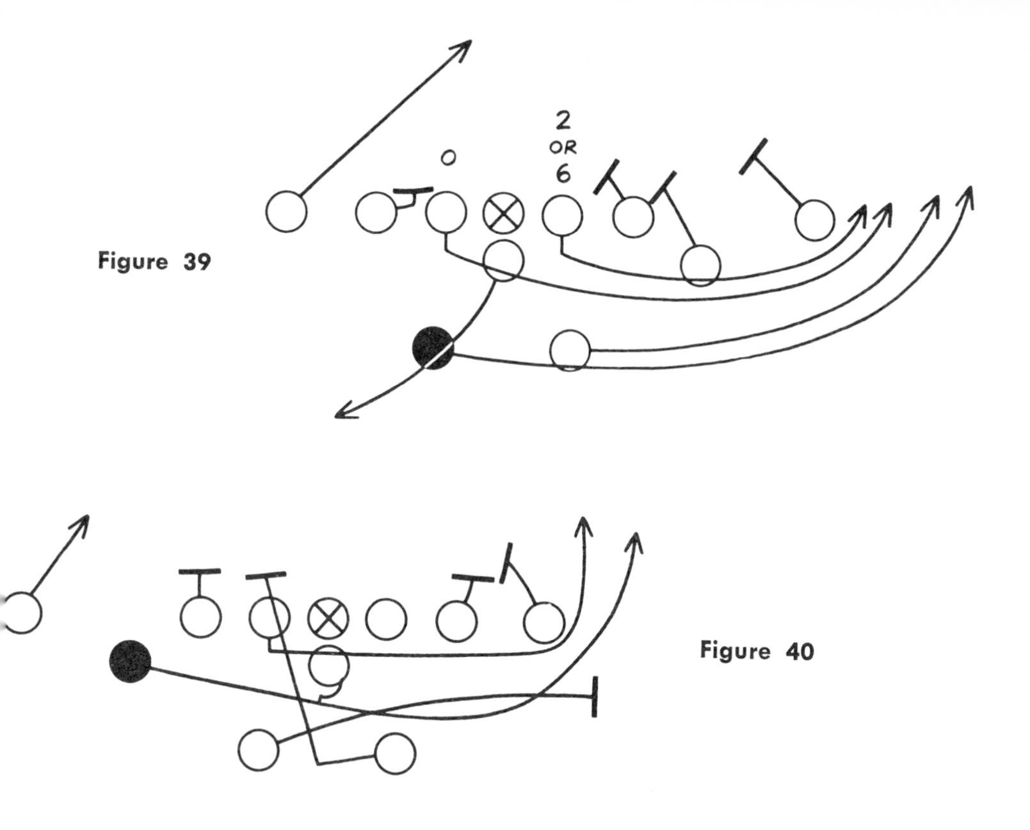


Figure 39

Figure 40

## Off-Tackle Run

Like almost every other offense in football, our offense is only as good as the off-tackle play, illustrated in Figure 41 against a 5–4 defense. The running play coupled with the action pass off it is our greatest threat. We split our right end way out so that he must be covered man to man in the deep outside zone as a pass threat. We have found that if he lines up in tight, he merely pulls the defense in with him. Any block that he then makes is offset by the defensive men that he has brought in with him. If he runs the pass pattern even on the running play, the right end takes a man out of the play and also sets him up for the pass.

The most important aspect of this play is the belly fake by the quarterback and the ball carrier. The quarterback must "ride" the ball carrier nearly into the hole before releasing for his bootleg fake to the outside. This action makes the pass and

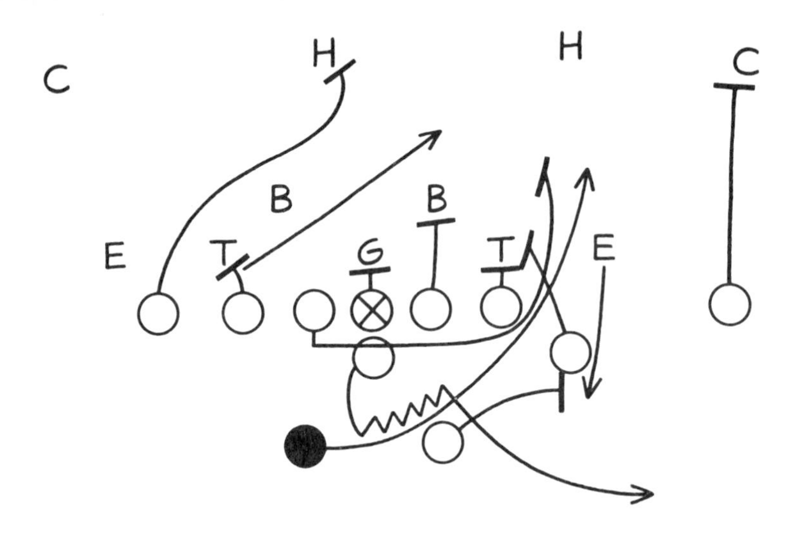


**Figure 41**

the run look exactly the same until the play is well under way. The defensive end must be made to remain inside and try to close the off-tackle hole. If he does stop the play by defeating our blocker, we then are able to confuse him with our pass. Also the on-side linebacker must be frozen for a moment in fear of the run. Then he will be unable to cover the flat on the pass.

## The Off-Tackle Pass

Our off-tackle pass must look just like our run in order to be effective (see Figure 42). Our linemen block aggressively on the "on-side" and we still include the double-team block on the defensive tackle. The quarterback rides with the 2 back, using a sliding lateral step. He makes a "belly" fake for two steps and on the third step he goes behind the 2 back and out to the side on his rollout action.

The right end, who is split very wide, runs a straight "go" path down the sidelines and forces the defensive halfback to play him man for man. The 4 back, who blocks the end on a running play, hits the end on the pass play, using a running shoulderblock. This contact is necessary to get the proper reaction from the end. This halfback then slips off the end and runs a pattern into the flat 5–10 yards deep.

The object of this pass play is to get outside the defensive end in order to put pressure on the outside linebacker. He should be the only man capable of making a good rush and the only man in the right position to cover the halfback in the flat. When the passer is outside, he can really put pressure on an outside linebacker if he is a good runner. Frequently the off-tackle pass will end up with the passer running for good yardage. A passer that can and will run makes this play the best one in our offense.

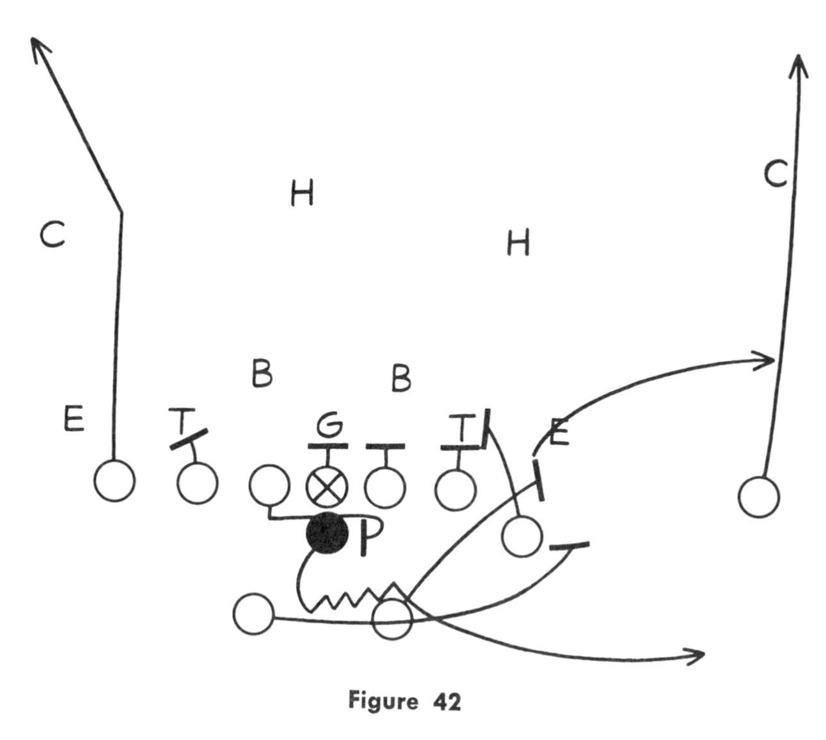


**Figure 42**

## 27–0 pass against an overshifted defense

The defense in Figure 42 is quite vulnerable to both the run and pass. Let us examine a different set-up. In Figure 43,

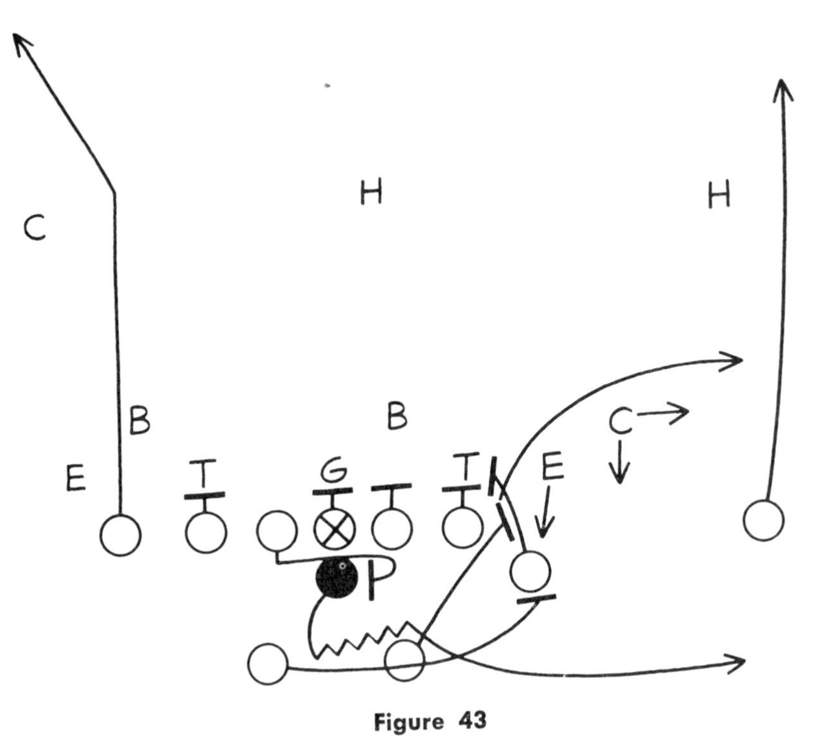


**Figure 43**

the defense, being somewhat overshifted, is now a little better able to cope with the run. The defensive end, who now has outside help from the corner, can seal off the hole with a good charge. This presents the back with a difficult block on the running play.

You can see how great the amount of pressure on the corner man is. If he comes up to stop the run, the flat is open. If he stays to cover the flat, the passer has running room. The off-tackle pass and running play to the slot side has been presented only from the slot right formation. We run the slot left off-tackle plays to the slot side in exactly the same manner.

## Weak Side Off-Tackle Run and Pass

### The run, 46–0

When we run off-tackle to the side away from the slot man we have a problem in that we have one less blocker. If our left end splits wide on the run, he must do the same on the pass.

We keep our weak side end lined up tight so that he can double team block on the run (see Figure 44). This means that our off-tackle pass loses the benefit of a wide-split end on the weak side. The running play to the weak side is therefore run in the same manner as it is to the strong side, although we lose the advantage of having a wide-split end always running the pass pattern.

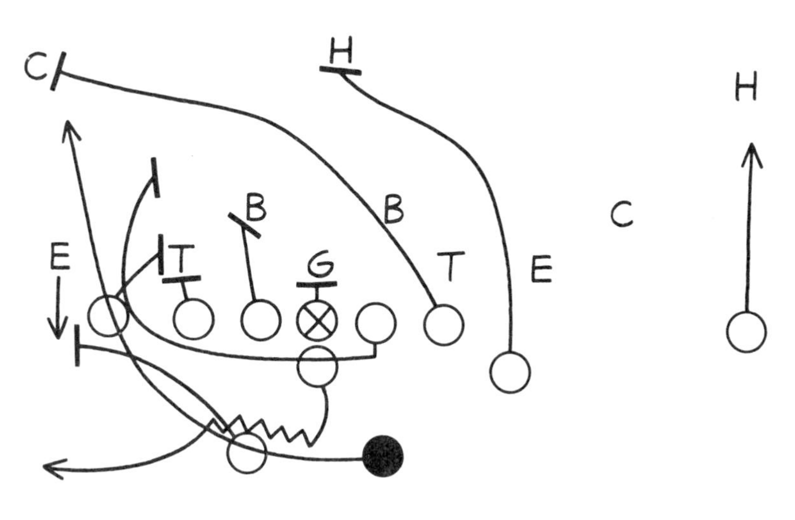


Figure 44

### The 46–0 pass

On the weak side off-tackle pass, our end moves directly downfield, running a deep angle-out pattern (see Figure 45). We lose the effect of having a double-team block on the pass. The on-side lineman blocks aggressively and the backfield execution is the same for all the off-tackle series plays.

There is the obvious advantage in the run of having Louie lined up tight for the double-team. However, we lose the advantage of the split end for the pass. You have to decide which formation you want and use it for both the pass and the run. You could mix it up by running 46–0 and later in the game

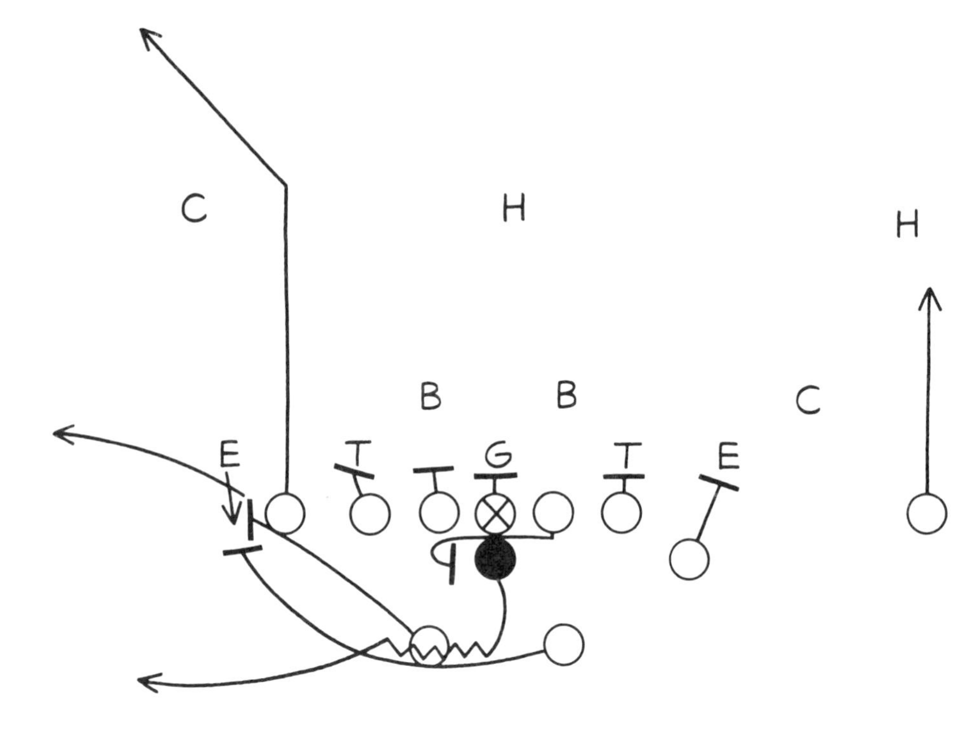


**Figure 45**

run Louie-split 46–0. There is a natural temptation to run with him tight and pass with him loose. This is, of course, a dead giveaway on your weak side off-tackle series.

## Defensive Adjustments and Variations

We expect our opponents will, in setting up their defenses, make a particular effort to stop our off-tackle combination. We try to anticipate the various defensive moves that will be made in an effort to contain our off-tackle series. By preparing for various defensive adjustments in practice, we are better able to cope with them when they appear in a game. Five different defensive adjustments have been used to contain this series.

### Loosening the end

Some defenses give their end the job of outside containment, and this end provides the outside rush on the rollout pass. This enables a corner linebacker to stay back and cover the flat. The defensive tackle and the inside linebacker are given the assignment of stopping the off-tackle run. The offensive solution to this type of defense is to run off-tackle continually. If your off-tackle run fails against this set-up, then your offense is in trouble for the day because you have more men at the hole.

### Covering the flat with an inside linebacker

On a rollout action many teams try to cover the halfback in the flat with an inside linebacker. This allows both the end and the corner linebacker to rush the rollout passer. Real good faking by the quarterback and the 2 back should confuse the inside linebacker. This linebacker must help stop the run, and if he is slow recognizing the pass, he will be too late to catch up with the halfback in the flat. If the linebacker is worried about the pass, he will find that in getting to the flat area faster, he will be overrunning the hole on the running play. Good backfield faking is a must for your off-tackle series and must be continually worked on.

### Safety man covering the flat

A very effective way to stop both the run and the pass is to assign the safety man the flat area on a rollout toward any wide-split end. In Figure 46, the inside linebacker, corner linebacker and end concentrate on the run and on rushing the passer. This type of pass coverage leaves the deep middle zone wide open because there is a man-to-man coverage.

We have a variation of our 27–0 pass that takes advantage of the deep middle zone when this type of pass defense is tried. In the 27–0 pass, slot middle, the slot back hides while faking the double-team block until he sees the defensive safety man leave to cover the flat. Then he slips right down the middle and may wind up all alone. This past season we scored one touchdown with this play. The passer cannot roll as far and consequently fades deeper. Since nobody is blocking the corner, he may very well spoil the play with a good rush.

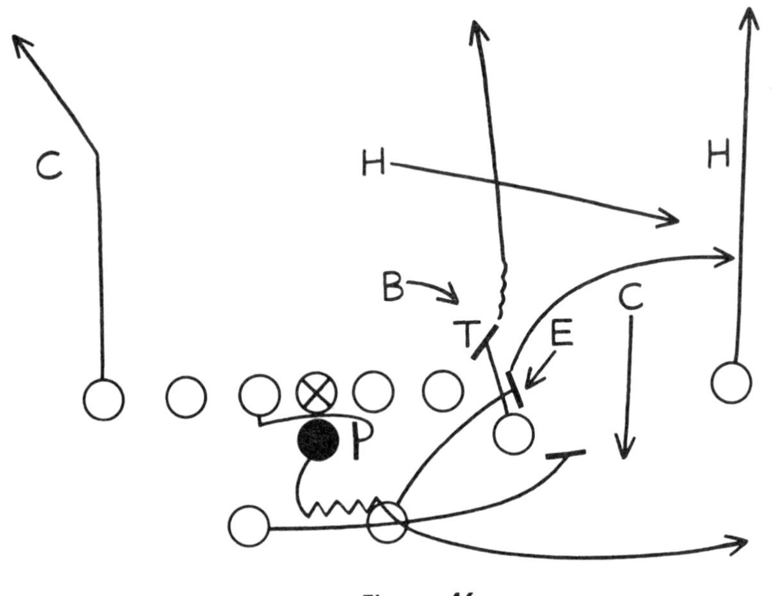


Figure 46

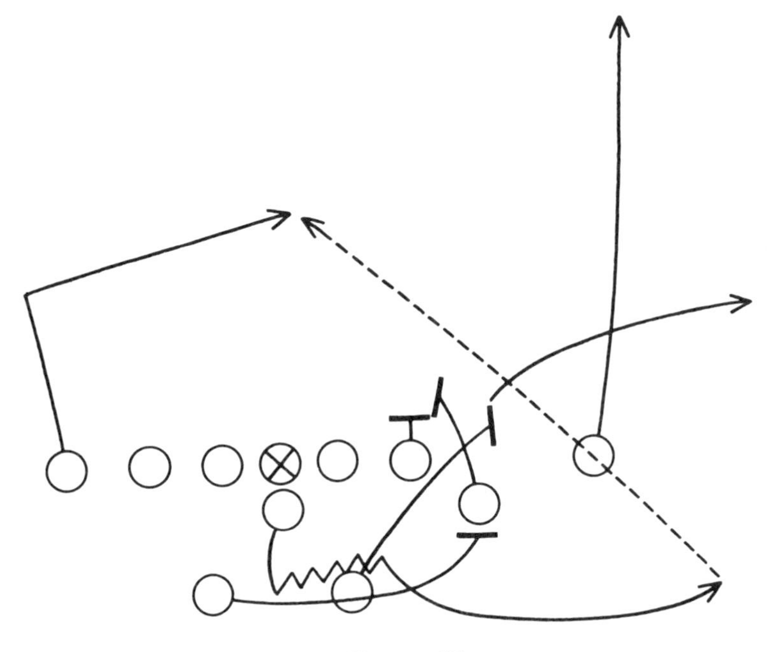

Figure 47

### The defense may run with you

Occasionally, as soon as the ball moves, the entire defense pursues it and the side you are working on becomes overcrowded. The natural solution is not to roll quite so far and have your quarterback throw cross-country to the left end. Most high-school passers don't have the strength to throw cross-country, so we vary the path of the left end in this situation. The 46–0 Pass, Louie Trail-in has the left end running a trail in a pattern about 15 yards deep. This variation (see Figure 47) is so timed that the left end is running well behind the passer and still requires the passer to throw back somewhat on the idea of a shorter cross field pass. If the defense is overpursuing, the left end slows down coming across the middle and is usually wide open.

### The defense may overshift

In the event that the defense overshifts in order to stop your strong side off-tackle series, your plays to the weak side will be your best plays.

It should be emphasized that weak side plays are run on their own merit. They do not exist just to complement the strong side attack even though the strong side attack is run most often. You must have an effective attack to the weak side and use it, or the defense will overshift and really place you at a serious disadvantage. When your opponents are planning their defense, you have got to make them afraid to overshift by the threat of your weak side attack. If they overshift, you must attack them to the weak side first.

## Series Action Passes

### The cross series

Our cross series is designed to make it more difficult for the defense to key our backs. The action of the backs is always

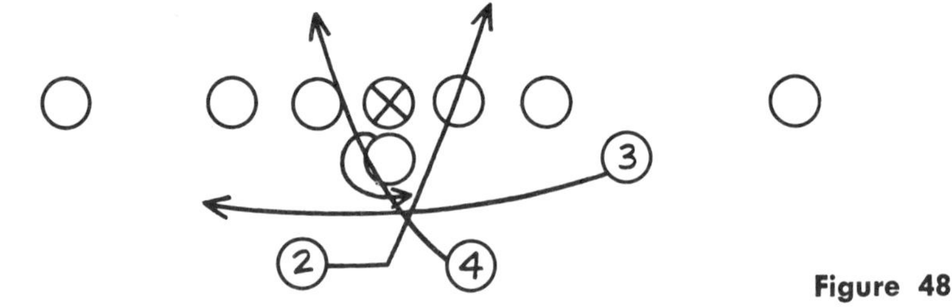


Figure 48

the same. The 4 back always goes first (see Figure 48). The 2 back takes a jab step to the right in order to clear the 4 back and then cuts for the guard hole on his side. The 3 back is the third man by the quarterback to complete the backfield movement. The running plays are 42 cross, 23 cross or 36–0 cross. On the 36–0 cross the 4 back blocks the end after making his fake, and the 2 back "picks" the hole left by the pulling guard. The quarterback reverse pivots to the 4 back and does all of his faking standing in a spot one foot behind his center.

**Cross series passes**

The cross series pass is run with the same backfield movement. The 4 back has to be able to sneak through the line in order to get in his downfield pattern. As the 2 back is picking, the right guard pulls to the right to block the end. Notice in Figure 49 that the downfield pass pattern is our standard cross pass pattern.

We also have an action pass developing from our 36–0

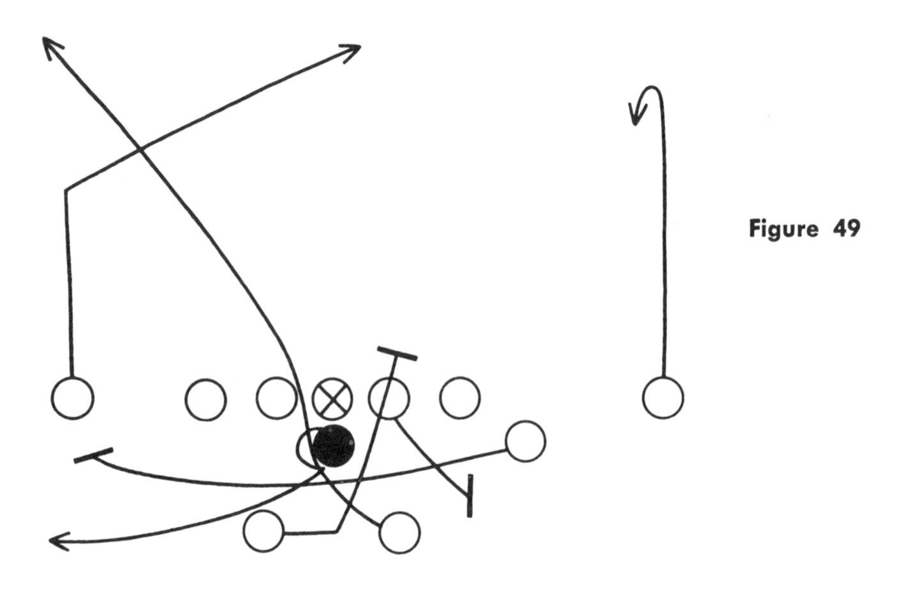

Figure 49

cross running play (see Figure 50). This is the only play we have in which a player other than the quarterback throws a pass. We have had good success in going for the two points after a touchdown using this play with a pass-or-run option.

## The fan series

The other series we use is the fan series (see Figure 51). In this we have the running plays, 19–60 fan, 36–20 fan, 30 fan trap, and 41 fan wedge. The 3 back goes behind the quarterback on everything except the trap where he receives a forward handoff.

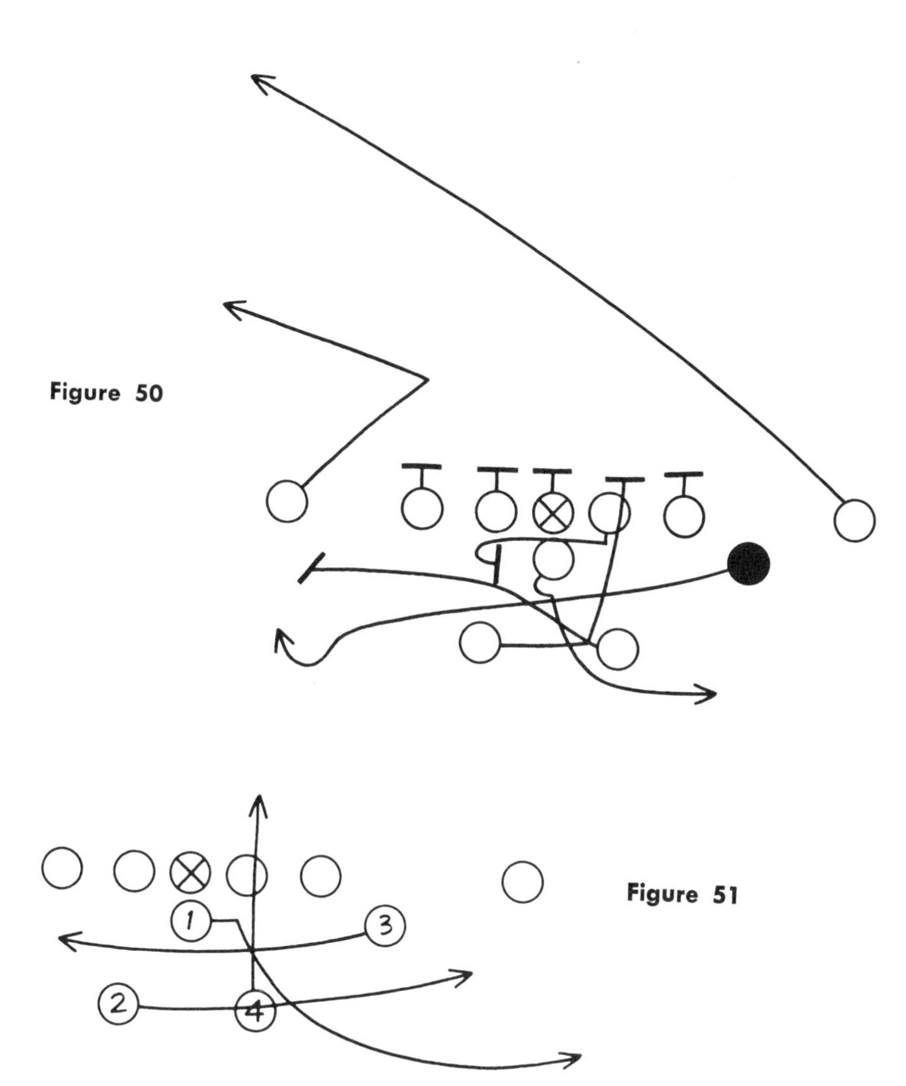


Figure 50

Figure 51

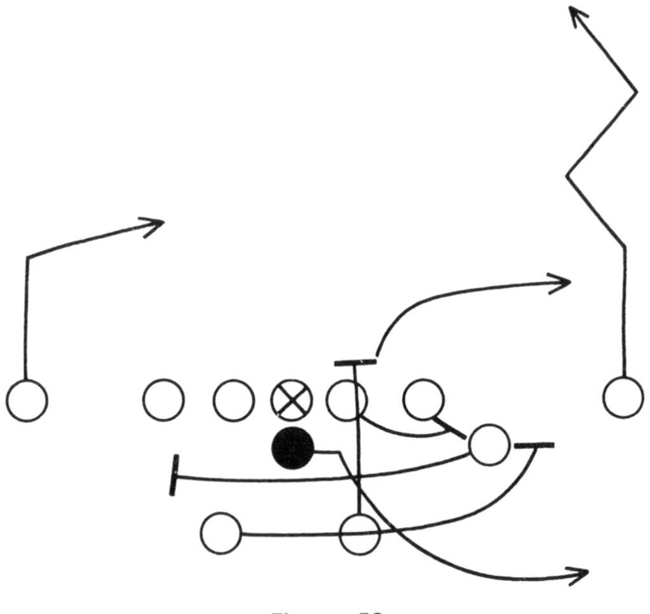

**Figure 52**

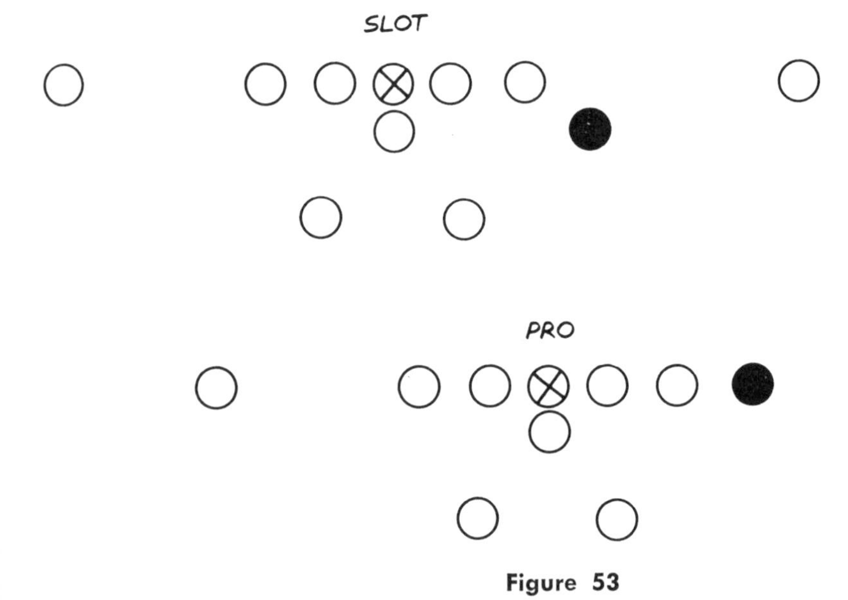


**Figure 53**

### The 19–60 fan pass

The 19–60 Fan Pass is diagramed in Figure 9, Chapter 3. The success of the pass depends upon good backfield faking, good passer timing and proper path selection by the right end. One variation of this pass that has worked very well for us is to have Roger run a Z-in path instead of his normal deep or shallow angle-out path (see Figure 52).

The complete cross and fan series can be run from slot left formation as well. Only slot right plays have been illustrated, but if you reverse the diagrams you will have the companion plays from slot left.

## Slot "T" Line-up Compared to Pro "T" Line-up

To see how a team running a pro style attack can make use of any of the standard or action passes, let's take a quick look at the slot formation to compare it with the pro style line-up.

The only difference between the two is that in going to the pro line-up the slot moves forward and becomes the tight end and the right end drops back as a flanking halfback. You can see that it would be very easy for us to change to a pro line-up and still have basically the same offense.

Consider the man in the shaded position in Figure 53. There are several advantages to having him up on the line of scrimmage. The biggest advantage is that he is favorably positioned to block on the line of scrimmage. He is in a much better position to double-team on the off-tackle play. Another, lesser, advantage is that he can get down-field just a bit quicker for a down-field block or to run a pass pattern. With him positioned here, however, we lose the threat of him as a ball carrier.

By having him back in the slot, we are handicapped most on our off-tackle play. He must double-team and his job becomes tougher as he is further away. He can still do the job

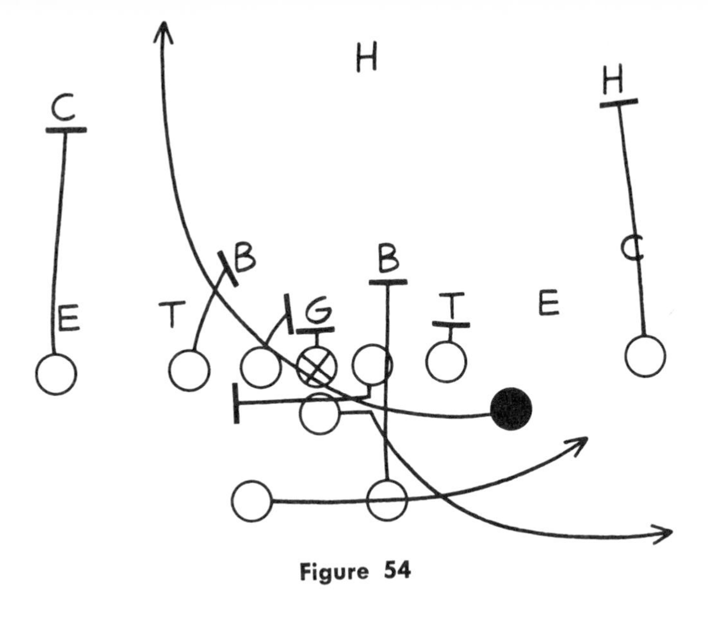


Figure 54

and he gets a great deal of work in practice at double-teaming in this set-up. We have decided to position him in the slot because of the running threat. Our two deep backs are fairly good keys and by having a strong play coming back with the wing back we keep the defense fairly honest. Figure 54 shows our most effective play of this type.

## The Short Pass versus the Long Pass

Throw short and the long pass will take care of itself. You will find that it is very difficult to get a high-school passer to appreciate the value of the short pass. Your passers will practice their long passing game most if you don't control them. In a ball game they will tend to throw the long "bomb" rather than shorter passes. The short pass is the foundation of our passing game and our passers are continually impressed with this fact and made to work a great deal on short passes.

We may open the game with a long pass in an attempt to surprise the defense. The chances are, however, that the first time we pass it will be for the short distance. As a player and as a coach, I have called the sideline pattern many times with success. Then when the defense has become annoyed with our continual gains on these completions, I call the sideline and down pattern. Just this past season, we made two large gains by throwing this pattern long after being successful on the sideline pattern. The long pass is therefore set up by the success of your short passing game, which is, of course, dependent upon the timing and accuracy of your passer.

The short passing game includes all passes that are not thrown real long. On our trail-in pattern, we have been able to hit our end fifteen yards down-field consistently. Our pro passes, to the end or halfback, have also been consistent gainers. Our Roger and Louie individual patterns have been successful on the shorter patterns, particularly the sideline pattern.

The remarkable thing about our short passes is that quite often our gains are considerably more than we expect. If the end catches a trail-in pass fifteen yards down-field, he will often run the ball even farther once he's caught it. If your receivers move well, chances are that they are capable ball carriers and their running abilities will add yardage to your short passing game. Our Roger, or Louie "stay" pass has actually scored some touchdowns for us. We hit the split end with a quick pass right at the spot he is lined up on. Only the defensive halfback is out there to tackle him, and our ends have avoided him and gone all the way for the score.

The long pass has won a number of games for us although we do not employ it often. By exploiting the short passing game, we make our long pass very effective when we use it. The threat of the long pass also keeps the defense more honest and helps our shorter passes go. Coaches instruct defensive backs never to let anyone get behind them. If a defensive back has to give away a completion, it will be to the shorter pass. This is correct defensive training and is reason enough to dictate the use of the short pass.

## Summary

After reading this chapter, you may think that it would be impossible for any high-school team to run all these pass plays and still have time to work on other phases of the game. Since this book is written for the coach, it goes into great detail regarding coaching techniques and strateg However, I keep things as simple as possible for the boys.

The less they have to remember in the way of assignments, the more they will be able to concentrate on carrying out their assignments successfully. As far as our players are concerned, we have seven standard passes and three action passes.

I. Standard Passes
   A. Normal
      1. Trail-in
      2. Trail-out
      3. Hook-Go
   B. Miscellaneous
      1. Fall off
      2. Pro Pass
      3. Screen
      4. Roger or Louie individual pass
II. Action Passes
   A. Off-Tackle Pass
   B. Cross Series Pass
   C. Fan Series Pass

There are only ten pass plays. Variations of them along with the ability to run them from several formations compound the actual number of situations you can present to the defense. In planning any offensive maneuver, make it as simple as possible for your boys; at the same time, make it as difficult as possible for the defense to counter the maneuver.

SEVEN

# PROTECTING THE PASSER

If you wish to have a successful passing attack, you must devote much time and effort to developing good pass protection. Your passer and your receivers must be given sufficient time to do their jobs. This means that a successful passing attack requires a complete team effort.

Most coaches feel that the best way to stop a high-school passing attack is with a very determined rush of the passer. You can expect that your pass protection blocking will be severely tested in every game. Since we are primarily a passing team, we try very hard to provide our passer with the best possible protection. If you are indifferent about this phase of the passing game, you will never realize its full potential.

## Rushing the Passer

Some coaches feel that the best pass defense is to rush the passer hard and to punish him physically as well. I don't think that a beating will have much effect on most passers. The boy you select as a passer will certainly have courage. But if the defense denies him sufficient time to pass, then he is in trouble.

During my own experience as a passer, the thing that bothered me most was a determined rush by the defense. Given sufficient time, a quarterback finds it much easier to complete a pass. It doesn't matter how many men drop back to cover as long as there is time to throw. Since the field is much too large to cover completely, there will be moments when a receiver is free somewhere. I really enjoyed passing against a waiting defense that rushed with only the minimum of men. My coaching experience has shown me that extensive coverage down-field in high-school football is not a very good pass defense and that rushing the high-school passer is. So you must be prepared to combat a concentrated rush by your opponent.

One other thing to keep in mind is the investment in time and coaching that you have in your quarterback. There is no better way to have a quarterback injured than to give him poor protection.

## The Time Element

To have sufficient time to throw a pocket pass a normal distance, the passer must have at least four and one-half seconds in which to throw. If the pass pattern involves an intricate fake by the receiver, or if it is to be thrown real long, even more time is needed. Four and one-half seconds do not seem very long to keep anybody out. A boy of average speed, however, can run 30 yards in four seconds. The passer is only 5 yards deep in a pocket pass, so the defensive man must be contained for most of the four and one-half seconds.

On a rollout pass, the passer has more time. We expect our blockers to provide the passer with at least five and one-half seconds. Often, when our pocket pass protection is not providing us with the needed time, we throw the same type of passes with a rollout action to either side. In these cases, the rollout protection has provided us with just enough extra time to get our passing attack rolling again.

The time I give for passer protection is only a minimum. A boy doesn't block four and one-half seconds and then stop because he has done his job. We insist that a blocker must keep his man out as long as he is able to do so. His objective must be to see that there will be no penetration even if the passer should take two minutes to throw. We continually tell our blockers to block "forever" and hope that we can achieve at least our minimum time requirements. We have a stop watch on the field, and whenever we do any live work on passer protection, we have a coach timing the protection. You must continually emphasize time. And remember that your objective in pass protection is to give your passer "all day" to pass.

## Normal Blocking for Linemen

Pass protection blocking can be aggressive, normal, or waiting. Our normal block is used on most all of the pocket passes, and sometimes on an action or a rollout pass. A lineman who is executing a normal pass block must:

1. Break the defensive man's initial charge
2. Stay on his feet
3. Keep between the man and the passer
4. Give up as little ground as possible
5. Contain his man as long as he possibly can.

### Lineman with the defensive man head on

The offensive lineman who has a man in his immediate area strikes out and hits this defensive man in order to break his charge. He strikes him with the "near" shoulder while stepping with the "near" foot. He does not continue his forward movement as he would if it were a running play. After the initial contact, he brings his other foot up under his body and assumes the position of a boxer who is in a balanced position waiting for his opponent's next move. His feet are set at approximately shoulder width, one foot a little in front of the other. This stance will enable him to move forward, backward, or laterally. The blocker must be able to move in any direction quickly and keep his body under control. His weight is on the balls of his feet, his knees are bent, and his body leans forward. His arms are at shoulder level, his forearms rotated up and his hands "locked" to his chest.

During the pause that usually occurs after the first contact, the blocker gathers himself into this position to wait for the defensive man to resume contact. From this crouch he must be prepared to bend quickly at the knees and to strike upward and into his man as the rush is resumed. If at any time contact is broken, he must go back into his crouch to wait for the next thrust.

Once the charge of the defensive lineman is stopped, the task is to screen him out. The blocker's footwork is much the same as a boxer's. He must slide laterally, keeping pressure on the man and keeping himself between the man and the passer. He will have to begin to give ground to maintain good body position. When he feels he is losing his man, he will go into a cross-body block. A man of less weight can effectively hold off a bigger man for four and one-half seconds by proper lateral movement and by giving some ground.

### Withdrawing pressure

The biggest difficulty a lineman has in pass protection is keeping on his feet. If there is any weight on his heels, he will be tipped over backwards. If his weight is too far forward, he will fall on his face. Our linemen learn quickly how to deliver the initial shock to break the man's charge. They then have difficulty in screening him out.

When you have pressure on the man you are blocking, it is very hard to refrain from lunging forward after him if the pressure is released. For example, if the offensive man is effectively screening his man, the defensive man may try to spin out. As soon as he starts to spin, the offensive man feels less pressure and will automatically drive forward and lose his man. When the offensive man feels a release of pressure, he must break off contact, wait for his opponent to come out of whatever maneuver he is in, and then resume contact when his man tries again to penetrate.

### An uncovered blocker

If a lineman has no one on him, he takes a jab step forward and then withdraws to the protective crouch. He must be prepared to move laterally to either side to help a teammate or to pick up a linebacker who may be attempting to "red dog."

On our pocket protection our linemen "show" pass immediately. It doesn't matter if the defense quickly recognizes the pass because most of our pocket passes are thrown in definite pass situations. The offensive lineman can protect better by going quickly into his protective stance. To offset this somewhat we do run our draw play with the lineman first showing this pass blocking.

## Aggressive Blocking for Linemen

Our pro passes, action passes, and rollout passes require aggressive blocking. On the pro pass we don't want the defensive linemen to stand up and raise their hands because the passer throws quickly and is still on the line of scrimmage. On the action and rollout passes we use aggressive blocking in certain areas in order to prevent penetration by the defensive men in those areas. The advantages of an aggressive pass block are that it forces the defensive men to remain low and it prevents any immediate penetration of the offensive line. The disadvantage is that it will not contain the man as long as the normal block.

### Aggressive techniques

When blocking aggressively we teach our lineman to strike at his opponent's knees using a "near shoulder–near foot" block. This action should cause his opponent to bring his hands down. The blocker then follows through by bringing his other foot up under him and continues to drive through his man as in a running play. When he feels he is losing his man, he must whip into a body block and try to contain his man longer by "crab" blocking. If a blocker is to block aggressively an opponent who is not shoulder or head on, he must drive through this man by using a reverse shoulder block. In this case, he first takes a jab step with his near foot and then a cross-over step with the other foot, which will bring him into proper position to execute a block by driving for his opponent's far knee.

**The uncovered blocker**

If no one faces him head on, the blocker should aggressively move out after the linebacker lined up with him. We assume that the linebacker usually keys the lineman he is lined up with and that he will move forward to make contact. If the linebacker fades, the blocker cannot go after him. If there is no linebacker for the uncovered man to go after, we instruct him aggressively to block either side, thus effecting what amounts to a double-team on one of the defensive linemen. In some of our action passes an aggressive double-team block is part of the design of the play.

## The Waiting Block

A lineman is seldom called upon to execute a waiting block. We use it for the off-side blocking on our rollout and action pass. Coming up from his stance, the blocker takes two quick steps backwards while gathering himself into his protective crouch. The defensive man now has a longer distance to come in order to make contact. Just before the moment of contact the blocker "uncoils," striking forward into his opponent. He then must recover his balance. He hits and recovers until he feels he is finally losing his man and then he must whip into a cross-body block.

The advantage of this block is that it can contain a man much longer than the normal block. But a great deal of ground must be given up in the process. This is the reason why it is such a good method for containing the off-side defensive linemen on a rollout action. You may use modified waiting blocking on your pocket passes if stunting linemen are bothering you. The brief wait permits a blocker to pick up his man after his final direction is established.

## A One on One Drill for Pass Protection

Our linemen get quite a bit of practice in protecting the passer in actual scrimmage, either one on one, line against line, or entire team scrimmages. Any such drill is more effective if the defensive man doesn't know whether it is to be a run or a pass. There is one very effective drill, one on one, in which we are able to work on defensive play, offensive blocking and some pass protection.

Have two men hold two dummies about one and one-half yards apart to simulate a dive hole and to restrict the movements of the players. Pair off your linemen according to ability and allow each pair in turn to have one play; switch positions and run one more play. We work a center, a quarterback and a dive halfback in this drill as well (see Figure 55).

The coach gives a number with his fingers and each lineman must try to defeat the other. The dive halfback must hit very hard and must step to the same side that his blocker's head is on. The defensive man must not only shed the blocker

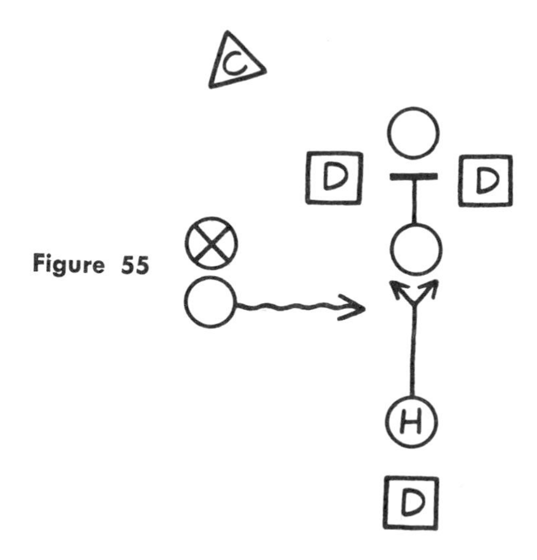

Figure 55

but make a tackle as well. If the coach, after giving the number, raises one hand high, it means pass protection. The quarterback then fades back and the offensive man makes a pass block. We place a tall dummy behind the dive halfback and if it is a pass, the defensive man must rush, hands high, and tackle the dummy high. A coach has a stop watch to time the blocker and we carefully check the time the blocker contains his man. We can learn a great deal about an individual lineman in this drill and therefore use it often. We are cautious about using too many live drills. But in this drill, there is not much chance of injury because no one gets a chance to build up any great momentum.

### Normal Backfield Blocking—Pocket Protection

The problem for the blocking backs is somewhat different than for the linemen in that the rushing defensive end will have plenty of momentum by the time he reaches the blocking halfback. The problem is aggravated by the fact that the ends often outweigh the back who is assigned to block him. For these reasons it is necessary for us to use different techniques for backfield pass protection. The linemen attempt to screen out their men while our backs try to channel the ends' momentum along paths from which they will not be able to get at the passer.

The position in which the back waits for the end is about three yards behind his own tackle. A halfback who is lined up behind his tackle has merely to pivot on his outside foot and place his inside foot so that his body is facing outward at about a 45 degree angle. A back lined up in the middle must move so that he is in position by the time the end arrives.

The position of the back invites the end to rush from the outside. The back is facing slightly outside as he waits for the end. His body position is very similar to that of a boxer. His feet form a wide base for the purpose of body balance, and he must be able to move laterally without losing his balance. His knees are bent, weight on the balls of his feet. He is in the protective crouch for pass protection, and he must be able to dip at the knees and "fire out" violently if the end tries to run over him.

## Situations Faced by Protecting Back

Four different situations will be faced by the blocking backfield man and each should be discussed separately. However, for all of these situations only one general method of pass blocking is needed.

### Blocking the end who rushes from the outside

The defensive end can and should rush the passer from the outside: he should take the outside path that is open to him.

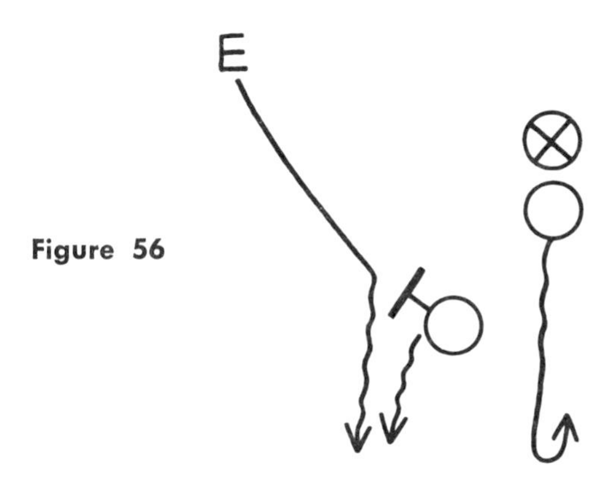


Figure 56

As the end reaches the back's position, the halfback steps with his outside foot and hits the end with a reverse shoulder block (see Figure 56). His head is always in front of the end's momentum. Making use of the end's momentum, he drives the end out along a path that will take him behind the passer. Since the passer usually steps up as he throws a long pass, there should be more room behind him into which to channel the rushing end. Perfect balance and agility are needed by the halfback. He must maintain solid contact and yet maintain a wide, balanced position for the lateral sliding he must do. A good end will rush from the outside because he's responsible for keeping the passer from rolling out of his pocket. The biggest problem is that the back will often over-extend his weight and fall forward. Should this happen he can recover somewhat by swinging into a cross-body block.

### Halfback block of end on inside path

The defensive end may try to fake outside and slip by on the inside in his anxiety to get to the passer. This of course is something an end should never do unless there is someone else stunting outside to contain the passer. If the end takes this path, we are delighted because our quarterbacks are taught to rollout to that side to place an immediate burden on the defense.

If the defensive end chooses an inside path, it is easy for the back to turn and use a reverse shoulder block, for example, to make contact with his left shoulder and drive him inside (see Figure 57). In this situation, the halfback has a good opportunity to do a really fine job on the end. The end will be a little off balance and should easily be moved. The back should really fire into him and drive him right into the pile in the middle of the line.

Since we would like the end to rush inside as often as he wishes, it is unfortunate that when he does it once, we have such an effective blocking angle that he will probably not do it again. However, the punishment he receives may very well soften up his charge for the remainder of the game. In our league we seldom encounter an end who will rush from the inside.

### Halfback blocking the tough end

If the defensive end is a good football player, he will attempt to defeat your halfback by driving through his outside

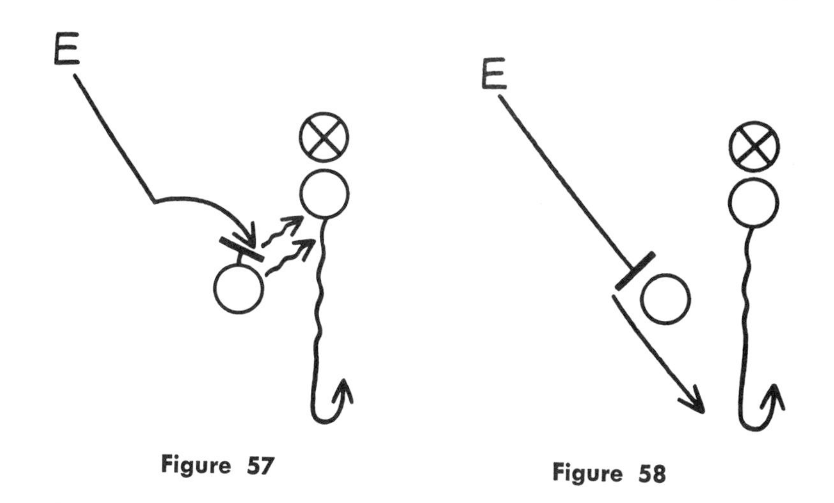


Figure 57

Figure 58

shoulder and on into the passer (see Figure 58). This is the type of end play we encounter most of the time and it takes a very determined halfback to get the job done.

We teach our own defensive ends to rush from the outside. They are to greet the protecting back with the inside forearm, keeping the outside arm and the body free so that they can keep outside position. They must defeat the back's block, push him away to the inside and squeeze the passer hard from the outside. This situation develops into a one on one contest between two men who must defeat each other's move. The better man will win.

The back will know immediately that the end is going to try to run over him. His first job is to arrest the end's momentum. Just before contact is made, the back dips at the knees and fires forward and up from the ground. Contact is made on the reverse shoulder because the end is still on a slightly outside course. The defensive back must really strike out hard because the end has quite a head start. The force of the contact will keep the back from falling forward. He should then recover a good protective crouch and drive the end in the direction that the end's second effort will now take him.

It takes a very determined effort by your back to do an adequate job of pass protection. The primary cause of protection breaking down is the back's failure to do his job. There is no place in this game for "prima donnas." If a boy feels his specialty is running and he won't put out 100 per cent on a block, there isn't any room for him in your backfield. A runner, even your best runner, should also take pride in his blocking and be determined to do a good job.

### The non-rushing end

The defensive end may have a stunt on and instead of rushing may drop back to cover the flat. When the back sees the end drop off in this manner, he merely turns back and faces forward to pick up any loose man rushing from his side. Chances are that there will be a free lineman rushing from the inside, whom the back must block. In this situation the back hits his man, recovers, and then drives him the way he wants to go. Do not allow your backs to leave their feet. They must have a wide base along with balance and good lateral movement.

## Blocking an Outstanding Defensive End

We have several ways to handle a particularly good end who is causing us a great deal of trouble. Sometimes the back will move directly at him and drive his shoulder into his knees. This is done to try and knock him completely down before he gets too much momentum. This should not be done often because if the end knows this block is coming, he merely dodges it and goes on to demolish the passer. We also use our fall-off pass (discussed in Chapter 6). If the back hits the end and then slides off for a little pass to the side, the end won't be so quick to shed the block of the halfback the next time. This, we have found, is a very effective way to make the end more cautious, as is a successful screen pass to his side.

## Aggressive Backfield Blocking

There are times when a back is required to pass block a man up on the line of scrimmage. Our sprint pass and rollout passes require the on-side back to execute such a block on the defensive end. The objective of an aggressive block is to prevent immediate penetration by the defensive man, containment being of secondary importance.

When blocking aggressively, the back moves at full speed directly toward the man he is to block. He must get to him as quickly as possible. He uses a low, running shoulder block, placing his head between the man and the passer. By hitting his man just above the knee, he should knock him down. As soon as the back feels he is losing contact, he must slide into a cross-body block and then roll into the man. The fullback blocking the end on our sprint right pass moves directly at him and drives his left shoulder toward the end's far leg. If the end should achieve deep penetration, he will spoil the pass by forcing the passer deep.

By blocking aggressively, the back will be unable to stay on his feet as long. Moreover, an aggressive block will not contain the opponent for a very long time even if it knocks him down. On our rollout pass we wish to strike the end as close to the line of scrimmage as possible and be well outside him by the time he recovers; therefore, we usually assign another man to get into an outside position to pick up the end when he gets away from the back's block.

## Backfield Pass Blocking Drill

We use only one drill besides a full team scrimmage to teach the backs to make their pass protection block. We run this drill dummy, semi-live, and live.

This drill is no different from most others in that you can accomplish more than one thing with it. We work on the proper charge of the defensive end as well as the pass protection block of the back. Actually this set-up is the same as if complete teams were involved (see Figure 59). The dummies laid on their sides merely spread the defensive end out to the proper width. At the snap of the ball, the ends rush the passer and the halfbacks must handle them. When we are going

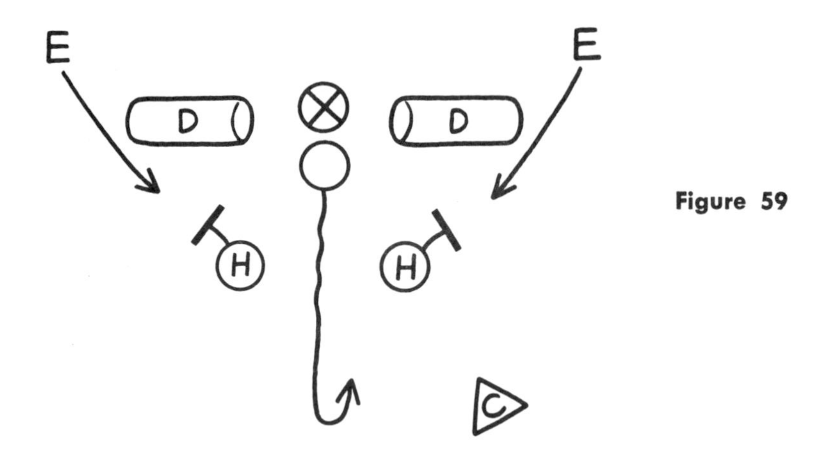


Figure 59

live, they grab the passer if they can get to him but they don't hit him. He's much too valuable to take such an unnecessary chance in a drill of this type.

### Dummy drill

In the dummy drill, the boys run at about half speed and though the offensive man is pressed, he is allowed to steer the defensive man along a proper path. This is done to give both backs and ends the "feel" of the various situations. The ends rush the passer who just stands back at the place from which he is to pass. The ends then go through the outside, inside and head on rushes so that the back can be instructed how to handle each of these situations. The passer also has a chance to observe these various situations and will benefit accordingly. We usually go through dummy drill for a few moments before we get more active.

### Semi-live drill

We most often run this drill semi-live. We give the rushing end an air dummy to charge with. Actually the drill is live; it differs only in that the dummies cushion the shocking blows. The boys work hard, hit hard, and get a great deal from the semi-live work. Yet, we do not expose ourselves needlessly to possible injury. No one has been injured doing the drill in this manner and this is most important.

### Live drill

Unfortunately some pass protection work for the halfbacks must be done live. When running this drill at full speed, we instruct the defensive end to get to the passer as quickly as possible by any means or any routes. Because we are doing defensive work with the ends at the same time, we don't allow them to rush on an inside path very often. Rushing on the inside path is a bad habit for an end to pick up.

This drill should be done live as seldom as possible and the coach must spare his best men. If your best back does a good job of blocking, let the other backs take more turns. The end has a decided advantage when this drill is run live. He knows it is to be a pass from the very start and can really get rolling by the time contact is made. If a back can block an end who rushes from the very start, he should do well in a game against an end who also has to think about stopping the running game. We find that our halfbacks have done a good job in pass protection over the years. This is something we've worked very hard on and it has certainly paid off for us.

### Aggressive drill

From this same set we also practice aggressive pass blocking on the end. On our off-tackle play we drive the end out, and on our rollout passes we try to knock the end's legs out from under him. By mixing rollout plays and off-tackle running plays with the normal pocket pass plays, we can also give the back necessary drill on blocking the end (see Figure 60).

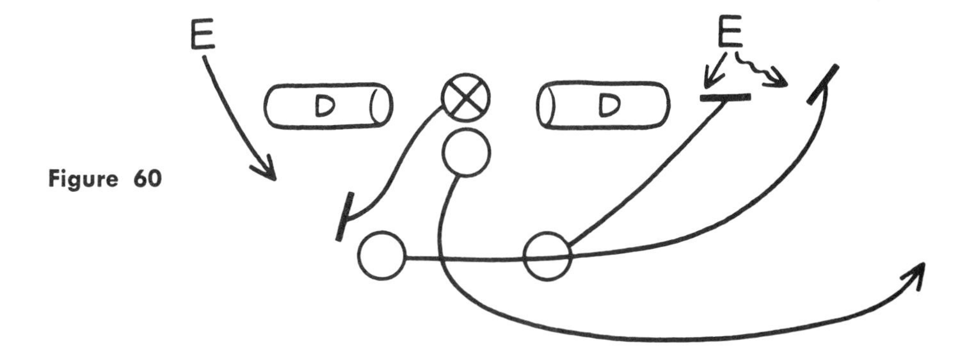


Figure 60

## Pocket Protection

We have tried to area block our pocket passes and have had little success. This is done very effectively by many teams but we have found that man on man blocking works much more successfully for us. Therefore, we spend considerable time with one on one pass blocking, the purpose being to contain, or screen out the defensive man. Pocket protection is a lot of individual, one on one, contests. There are usually some blockers available to help out a boy who loses his man.

### Pocket protection blocking rules

Since we block individual men instead of protecting areas, it is necessary to have a simple set of rules to tell our linemen whom to block. We merely number the defensive men on the line of scrimmage from our center out, not counting the man facing the center. Figure 61 shows the way we number some defensive alignments.

The guards are told to block the first man and the tackles are to block the number two men. The backs block the ends.

Figure 61

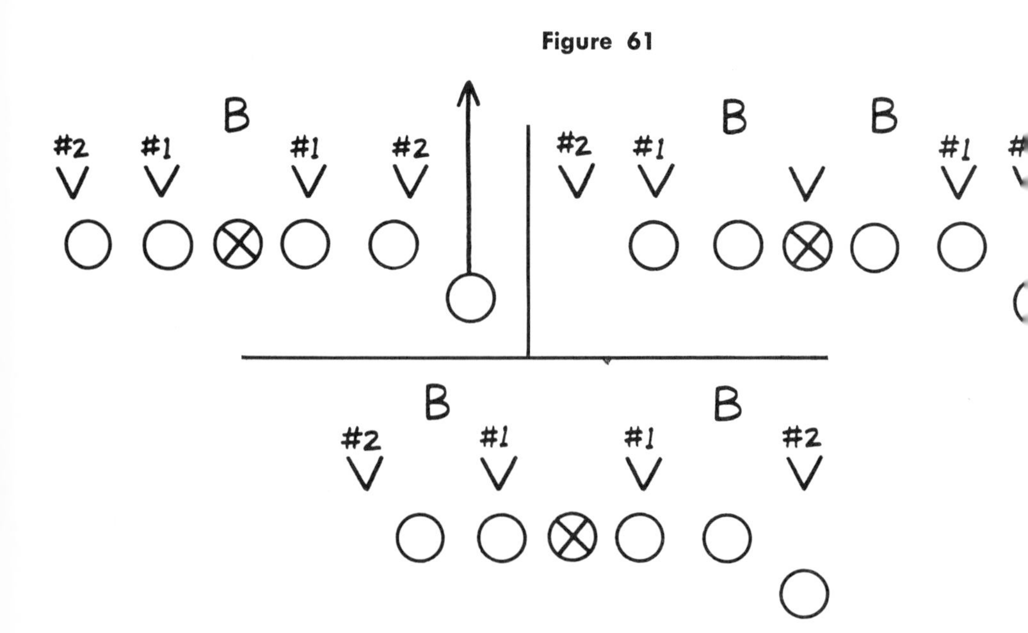

You will notice that on some of our alignments, an end is blocked by the tackle. If the back does not have to block the end, he should look inside as well as outside to block where he is most needed.

### The tight linebacker

If a linebacker is up close to the line of scrimmage, the tackle and guard will count him and block accordingly. We do

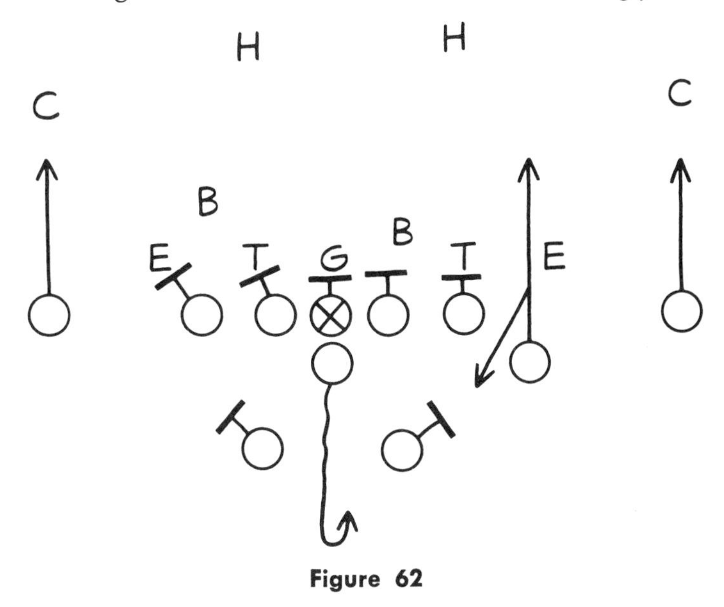


**Figure 62**

not count a linebacker if he is loose or drifts back on a pass. If a loose linebacker decides to rush, he will be late and our free back will pick him up in the backfield when he arrives.

When we split both our ends against a 5–4, we would apply our rules as shown in the defensive adjustment in Figure 62. The left halfback in this instance does not have a man to block and can help out by picking up the first defensive man breaking through into the pocket. This blocking rule enables us to run four man pass patterns without any great problem in blocking assignments arising.

## Handling Stunting and Red Dogging Defenses

Our opponents continually test our pass blocking rules with stunting defenses and with shooting linebackers. Because we have a reputation for successful passing in the shorter passing zones, the stunting defenses do not usually rush with many men. If a linebacker shoots, an end may drop back to cover a flat area. The objective of these defenses is to outnumber our blockers in one area or to cause us to use a double-team block and leave one man free.

### The stunting defense

When our linemen use their normal pass blocking technique against a stunting defense, we sometimes run into difficulty. When two men on defense execute a cross stunt (the first normal move of our blocker is aggressively forward), we end up with two blockers on one defensive man. In Figure 63 two such stunts involving linebackers are illustrated. In both of these situations a defensive lineman slants into an uncovered blocker. The blocker who fronts this slanting lineman first strikes out on the normal pass block to break the defensive man's charge. The defensive man thus draws two blockers while the linebacker is in free.

As soon as stunting defenses begin to confuse our pass blocking rules, we execute the waiting pass block. By using this block, the blockers are able to pick up each man as he comes out of his stunt. Though the blocker gives some ground initially, this is compensated for by the fact that the defensive men have less forward momentum because of their slanting.

**Figure 63**

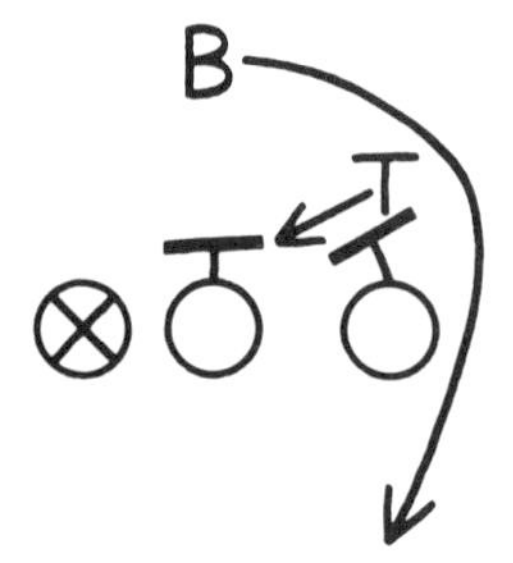


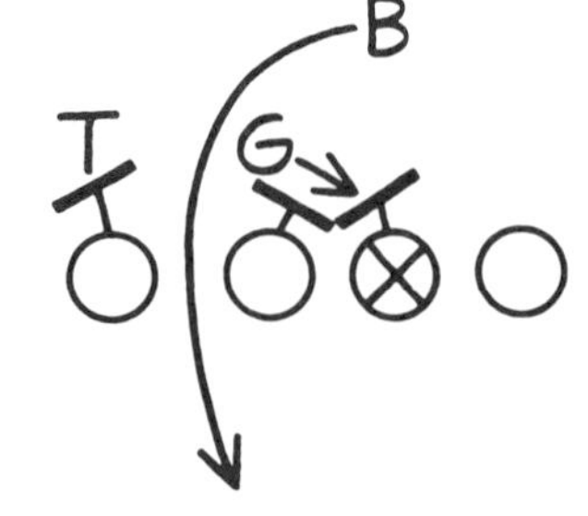

## The shooting linebacker

In some situations a defensive team will outnumber your blockers in an area because they shoot a linebacker up between two defensive linemen. It has been our experience that when a team does this, some rushers from another area usually drop back to cover a shallow zone (see Figure 64).

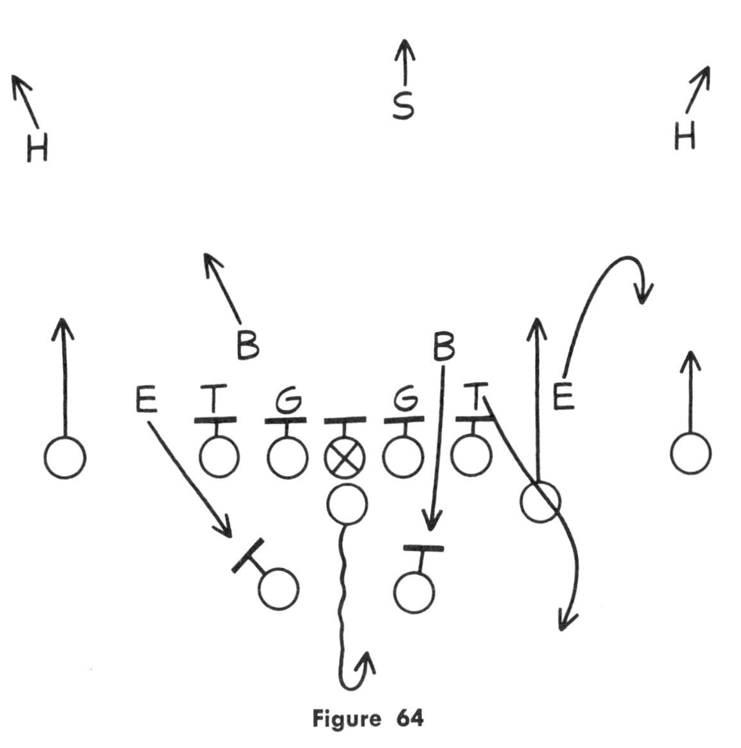


**Figure 64**

Our pass blocking rules handle this situation automatically because the back whose end is not rushing would then look inside. The shooting linebackers will always be picked up as long as another rusher drops back to cover a shorter passing zone. Should linebackers shoot while all original rushers keep rushing, special consideration and handling is in order.

## The Concentrated Rush

Quite often teams are willing to gamble by rushing with more men than there are blockers. Such an action puts a great deal of pressure on both the defense and the passer. The defense must reach the passer before he is set to throw because some downfield passing zones will be uncovered. Thus the passer will find himself hurried and must be cool enough to stand in his pocket and throw quickly to an uncovered receiver in a shorter passing zone. By rushing with too many men, the defense is gambling on catching the passer for a big loss of yardage or forcing him to throw poorly. But they take the chance that the pass will most likely be completed if they don't reach the passer quickly enough. We have successfully handled the problem several different ways, so this type of rushing doesn't bother us. Our pro pass is very effective in this situation.

### Holding in one receiver to block

Very often we receive the overload of rushers on our slot side, but it doesn't really matter where the excess is. We run our individual Louie and Roger passes with the slot back staying in to block the end. This leaves our fullback without a specific blocking assignment, so he is free to pick up the first man to penetrate the pocket no matter where he is.

In Figure 65, the safety man on an umbrella defense is shooting an inside gap and would not normally be blocked. One season we ran all our individual pass patterns with our slot back blocking because we were getting a great deal of overloading on our pass protection blocking.

### Throwing a short quick pass

When an outside linebacker is shooting in to rush the passer, the quick pro pass to the end on the side the linebacker has just left wide open is very effective. We run our pro pass with both ends split and slanting in. In Figure 66 the passer

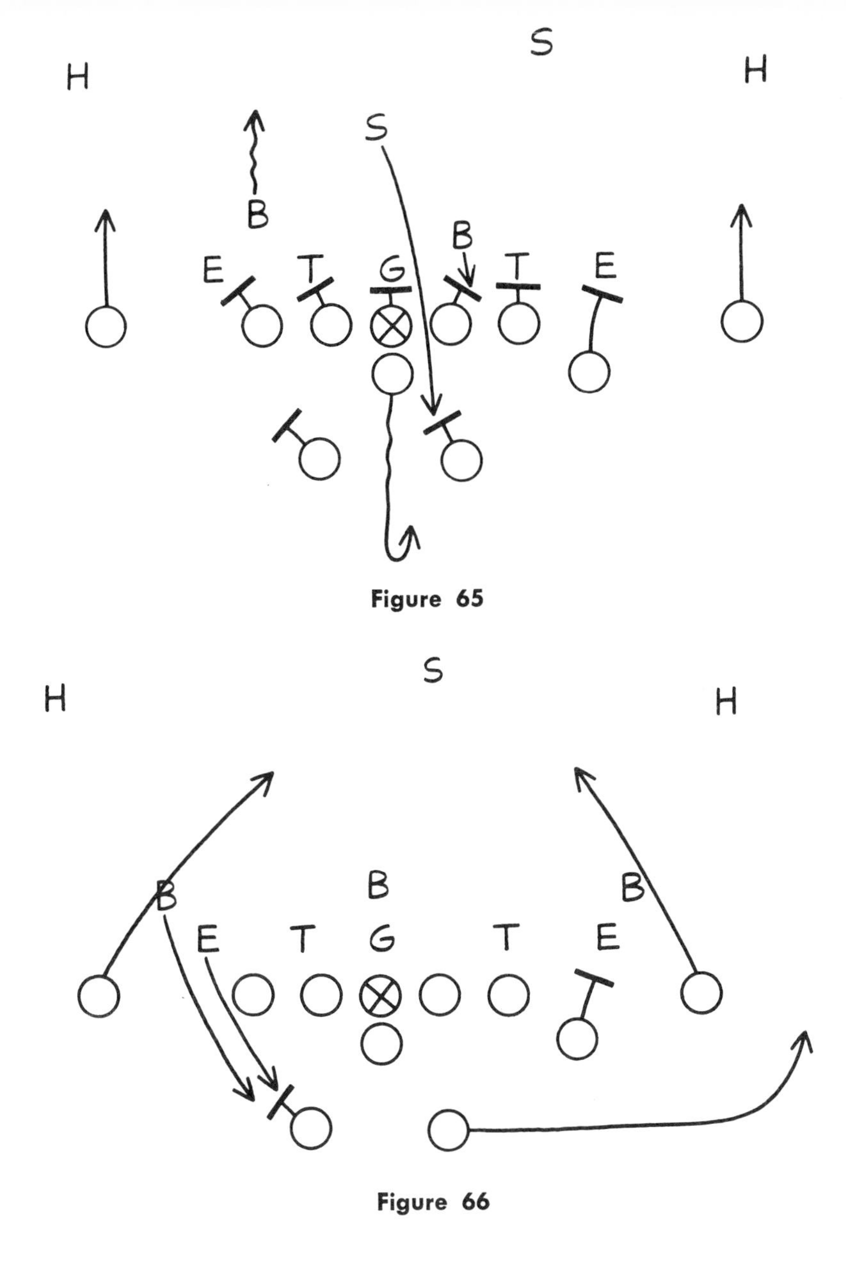


**Figure 65**

**Figure 66**

must quickly spot the linebacker who is shooting and throw to that side, in this case the left end. Fall-off passes, screen passes, and fan passes to a halfback are also very effective in this situation if thrown quickly into the area vacated by the shooting linebacker.

### Rolling out

A team that rushes with an excess of men often tries to compensate by having their deep defenders tighten up toward the line of scrimmage. By covering a split end very closely a halfback can effectively stop any quick passes to him. To get free the end must fake and then run a deep pattern. It is easy for a receiver to get behind a man who is covering him close. However, the passer needs considerable time to throw deeper and the plan of the defense is not to allow him this time.

If we wish to throw deep in this situation, we use rollout protection toward the split receiver we want to throw to. Our rollout protection places an excess of blockers on the "on" side. Moreover, normal rolling out gives the passer extra time, so our passer will have the time needed to throw deep. We love to see tight man-to-man coverage on a split receiver because if we complete a pass to this receiver deep, it results in a long gain and usually in a touchdown. By rolling out we cut in half the number of effective rushers. Unfortunately we also decrease the downfield area into which we can effectively pass.

## Protecting for the Rollout

The primary objective of a rollout pass is to complicate the defensive problem by presenting a pass-or-run situation. Our rollout passes fall into three categories. We can rollout on our pocket passes by merely adding the words roll right (or left) to the play when called in the huddle. Our individual patterns to a wide flanker are often run by rolling out to the flanker side. And we have our most effective rollout in our action passes.

Because any one of these roll-out passes is actually a pass-or-run option no matter how it starts, the blocking method is the same for all rollouts. The blocking is aggressive on the "on" side and is passive on the "off" side. The blockers on the side of the rollout go after their man while those on the other side wait for their man.

### Blocking the on side

The blocking must be aggressive on the on-side because the roll of the passer must be moving along a flat path. If these blockers wait at all or give any ground, the passers will drift back deeper. This must not be allowed to happen because the defensive pursuit will then have a chance to catch up and spoil the play. The aggressive blocking on the on-side will not hold out the defensive man as long. However, he will be blocked on the line of scrimmage and will not make quick penetration. By the time the defensive man recovers, the passer's speed should place him outside, leaving the defensive man to chase him.

One of the more difficult aggressive blocks must usually be executed by the on-side tackle because the defensive tackle is often outside him. In Figure 67, the defensive tackle may very well recover and be in position 1 when the passer is in 2. It is easy to see what will happen if the play is strung out, if the passer drifts deep, or if he slows down. At its poorest the aggressive block must allow the passer to run a flat path and get ahead of his pursuers. At its best, it should knock the man down and put him completely out of the play.

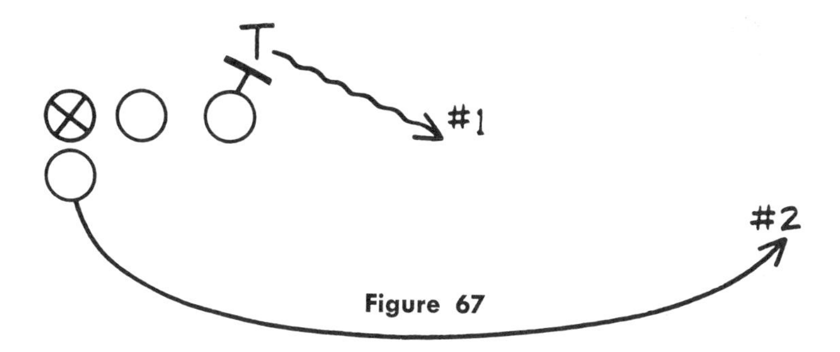

Figure 67

The secret of the rollout is that the passer must really move once he starts. The passer must be reasonably fast to rollout effectively. If your passer is slow, stick to the pocket pass or use a very short roll with pocket protection. A slow boy must be an excellent passer to play quarterback for us. Our rollout passes are too important a part of our attack to be put away for anyone but an exceptional passer.

**Blocking the off side**

The boys blocking the off side on a rollout pass execute waiting blocks. Their job is to stop any off-side defensive pursuit from catching the passer from behind. Instead of predetermining whom to block, they pick up the first man to reach their waiting position.

### Rollout Right Pass

Figure 68 shows a rollout pass to the right against an Oklahoma defense. The movement of the receivers is irrelevant to the blocking, in this case they are running the trail-out pattern.

**Figure 68**

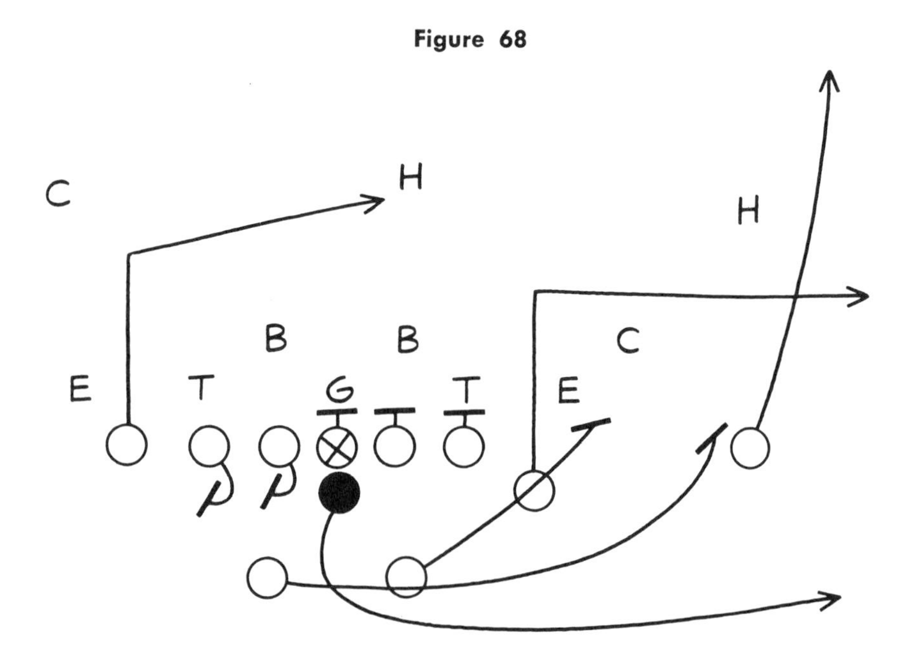

### Left tackle

Being the tackle on the off side, the left tackle would execute a waiting block probably on the defensive tackle. His job will be done better if he steers his man along an outside path and screens him off from pursuing the passer, because his job is to prevent his man from catching the passer on the blind side.

### Left guard

Being an off-side lineman, the left guard also performs a waiting block. If a man tries to penetrate his position, he will block in the same manner as the left tackle. In this set-up, the linebacker may very well drift with the flow of the backs. If there is no one to block, the guard will then drift back and cut off any chaser (usually the defensive end) from his side with a shoulder block aimed at the knees.

If the guard is called to pull, as on the 27–0 pass, his assignment is a little different. If he is certain a linebacker or a lineman is going to shoot as soon as he pulls, he doesn't pull. If he does pull he takes three steps and turns around to the inside to pick up chasers from the weak side.

### Center

The center blocks aggressively as he does on a running play. In this case, he goes after the man on his head. If no one is there, he waits and then drifts back to block any chasers from the weak side.

### Right guard

The on-side guard and the center have the same rule. Block aggressive if someone is there, drop back for weak-side chasers if no one is coming through you.

### Right tackle

The big block needed on this rollout pass is made by the

right tackle. He must strike for the defensive tackle no matter where he finds him. Usually he will be on the offensive tackle's outside shoulder. The blocker will drive his shoulder into the opponent's knee to knock his legs out from under him. If the defensive tackle is worth his salt, he will fight first to the inside because he will feel himself being driven out. If he turns to chase the passer, he is still in the clip zone and we teach our blocker to throw the clip block which is perfectly legal here.

## Backfield Blocking

### Fullback

The fullback or our 4 back in this play goes right after the defensive end. Because our backs drive the end out on our off-tackle play, the end will have a tendency to fight inside whenever a back comes straight at him. When the fullback reaches the end, he "dips" at the knees and drives right through him with a shoulder block, in this case with the left shoulder. His job is to shock the end and stop him in his tracks. Once he begins to lose contact, he should slide into a cross-body block. Although he will not contain the end for very long, it should be long enough for the passer to get outside.

### Halfback

Whenever a back is the second man to hit an end, he does not go directly after him on the rollout. He assumes a lead blocking position for the passer. Once he is outside the end, he turns upfield and looks inside if he has no one to drive out. He'll usually find the end chasing when he looks back inside. If there is no one to block, he should stop on the line of scrimmage to protect the passer.

Do not let your lead blockers drift along a deeper path because this only forces the passer deep. They must operate near or on the line of scrimmage. Many rollouts have been spoiled for us by our own blockers forcing our passer too deep.

This back will become a personal blocker should the passer run. Your passer should "holler" if he decides to run but the back can see if he's running merely by observing the reaction of the defense. As long as the defense hesitates, it still could be a pass.

## Expect a Determined Rush

When we have sacrificed putting pressure on the passer to drop more men back, we have been hurt. When our opponents don't rush our passer, we have been more successful. In professional football the trend is reversed. They rush with a minimum and defend with a maximum. Why the difference? It is obviously the quarterback. A professional passer has the experience to find the uncovered receiver downfield and pass to him even when rushed hard.

The high-school passer does not have this experience and his reaction to pressure will often be the wrong one. When rushed hard, the high-school passer will more often than not throw the ball at the wrong time to the wrong place. Because it is hurried, his pass will usually be poor and underthrown. He will often throw to his intended receiver even though he is well covered. In this situation we want our passer to eat the ball or, if he can, to drift to one side or the other to try to develop the play into a pass-or-run situation.

The action passes that are incorporated into your offense will also help in protecting the passer because the defense will delay a concentrated rush until it is definitely established as a pass play.

If your passing attack becomes successful, you can expect your opponents to try to rush your passer very hard. A good deal of time and hard work must be spent on protecting the passer. Your team must take pride in doing a good job and must not be allowed to consider a pass play a chance to rest. Pass blocking is not easy and requires just as much determination as any other part of the game.

You can expect your opponent to shoot linebackers, to overload one area, or to initiate stunts with their linebackers and defensive linemen. Your team must be aware of the different possibilities to be encountered, and your blocking rules must be flexible to compensate for any defensive maneuvering.

If you cannot adequately protect your passer, don't bother passing. Most intercepted passes come from the hand of a hurried passer. A coach must be willing to do a thorough job on passer protection because adequate pass protection is essential to any passing attack.

# EIGHT

# COMPILING AND KEEPING RECORDS

If there was no need to learn from previous experience, there would be little need to learn to read and write. A man should not only benefit by reading of the experience of others, but he should maintain some record of his own experience to receive the most from it. While a coach learns much from other coaches, there is little question that he learns most from his own experience. The greatest part of what we learn from our experience is carried with us. Each of us has developed his own way of working with young men, and there is little need for us to write this down. This material is actually a part of us and of the way we do things.

There is, however, much to be gained from the keeping of vital statistics and records of past performances. Any material that you prepare and organize for a game should be kept for future reference. Film studies of your team and of your opponents should be well organized and kept in a permanent file. It would be foolish to spend many long hours preparing a set of defenses for a forthcoming game only to misplace and perhaps lose this information after the game is played. A good coach should never find himself turning to an assistant to ask this kind of question: "Joe, do you remember the defense we used against Latin High School when we played them last year?" Much time was spent preparing for this game last year and for previous games. The coach should be able to go to his file on Latin High School and pull out not only last season's defenses against Latin High, but the defenses employed in the seasons before that. There should also be material on Latin High's offensive plays, pass patterns, scouting reports, etc. In setting up a system of permanent records, you must first determine just what information you wish to compile; then you must find the time and the means to do it.

## Be Realistic in Your Record Keeping

The information we compile may differ from what you would wish to gather. You may also think that our records do not hold enough information. Be realistic when you set up a system for keeping vital information. Don't attempt to keep a very detailed, all-inclusive record if you will be hard pressed to find the time to keep your file up to date. It would be far better to have only a single page summary of each game in a file than to have an assortment of incomplete forms scattered here and there about your office. If we chose to compile a more complex and inclusive record than the one we keep, we would no doubt have no permanent file at all. You know what your own time commitments are and should keep them in mind while you are deciding just what information you wish to compile and how you wish to organize it.

This past spring I dropped in to visit with coach Vic Fusia at the University of Massachusetts. At the time, he and his entire staff were involved in analyzing the films of their past season. One coach was busy screening the films for information on all the third and long yardage situations that had occurred. Another coach was working on all third and short yardage situations. All of the other coaches were involved in similar research. With so many men working full time all year round on football, a wealth of information can be compiled. No doubt the thoroughness of these coaches in compiling information is a contributing factor to their outstanding record.

The majority of high-school coaches unfortunately find

themselves in situations that are far from ideal. Most of us are full-time teachers and must fit any football activities around this full-time involvement. Any coach who has taught a full load during the football season knows how little extra time he actually has available. Your assistant coaches are full-time teachers too and during the off-season are often involved with other sports, as you may be yourself. Once the season is over chances are that you, as head coach, will be working alone when it comes to compiling information and keeping records. You know your own time requirements and how much help you can expect. Keep a record of only the information you know you will have time to keep.

## Our Record Keeping Organization

The information we compile and keep is not as inclusive as we would like it to be. Given more time, I'm sure we would still complain because there are so many ways of analyzing a past season. We keep only what we feel to be most important for us. Our system has evolved through a long process of evaluation and elimination. If you have more time, you will be able to incorporate more items in your review. I present my method to show that even if you are a full-time teacher, there is a great deal of research that you can actually do. Before discussing the various areas of research, I will present a brief outline of our organization.

I. Game-by-game record
  A. Scouting reports
    1. Scouting report and summaries
    2. Our game plans and defenses
    3. Play cards of all opponents' plays and defenses
  B. Game film analysis
    1. Offense
      a. Running
      b. Passing
      c. Summary

2. Opponent
    a. Offense
    b. Defense
    c. Our defense
3. Miscellaneous information

C. Game statistics

II. Seasonal summary
  A. Offense
    1. Running game
    2. Passing game
    3. Important statistics
  B. Defense
    1. Against running game
    2. Pass defense
    3. Important statistics
  C. Written review

## Game-by-Game Record

The primary purpose of this chapter is to present a method of compiling records so that you may continually evaluate and improve your passing game. Therefore, the areas of the outline that do not deal directly with the passing game will be touched upon only lightly. A complete discussion of the manner in which we handle our scouting report would of necessity be an involved and lengthy presentation.

### The scouting report

Our scouting report is routinely compiled. A play-by-play record is kept along with the vital statistics of each play situation. The important part of the scouting report is the summary. Each play is diagramed and also sketched with a magic marker on a piece of cardboard for use on the field. Each formation is diagramed and analyzed to uncover the most common plays from each basic formation. When they line up in a certain formation, many ball clubs do only a few particular things, which of course makes defensive problems fewer. Each defense is also analyzed and cards are made up on them for field use. These cards are also available to the squad in the locker during the week and are filed away after the game.

Before a scout goes out, he refers to our file for the game film analysis of the previous season. He then looks at the previous year's film to familiarize himself with the opponent he will be watching. When he goes to scout the game, he will carry the play cards from the file to quickly check the present season against the past season.

Our scouting experience has shown us that most coaches rely on certain favorite plays year after year, though they add a few wrinkles to keep the defense honest. Our chief rival is a very successful coach who has run the same plays from the same formations since I have been in Marblehead. His attack is very well balanced and very well executed and has given him a life-time record to be envied. The team with a new coach will give you the most scouting trouble until after you have had the actual experience of playing them.

## Game Film Analysis

### Offensive game film review

Our method of game review naturally includes our running game as well as the passing game, so the sample included contains both parts as well as the summary. The next chapter discusses the use of these records in evaluating your passing attack, so you need to use only the passing section for this purpose.

Our films are returned to us the day after the game and the film analysis is done immediately. It must be done quickly because there is little time to be spent on yesterday's game when there is so much preparation necessary for the coming game. During the season we use a game film only for the purpose of making us a better team for the next game. The forms used for game film analysis aid us in this and are very useful for our off-season review. In addition, this information helps us the following season when we again prepare for the same opponent.

Figures 69–71 show how we conduct our film review and what we keep a record of. Running plays and pass plays are numbered in the order that they appear in the film. The information is so arranged that the game summary is easy to fill in. The information in the game summary is so arranged as to help us compile the seasonal summary. With several coaches working together, it takes no more than two hours to complete our offensive game analysis form. Additional time is then spent on the defensive side of the game.

We find that keeping the summary sheet in our files is not sufficient. It can be somewhat misleading. In one game the sheet indicated that we had achieved our best results of the entire season on the ground. Our reserves ran nine plays in a

**Figure 69**

OFFENSE - RUNNING GAME SUMMARY

Offense - Running

Marblehead vs. OPPONENT #8 Page 1

Score 34-6 Date 11/18

| # | Down/Dist. | Position | Play | Carrier | Result | Defense | Comment |
|---|---|---|---|---|---|---|---|
| 1 | 1/10 | ↓ | 29-60 | THEW. | +6 | 5 EAGLE | |
| 2 | 1/10 | ↓ | DIVE RT. | THEW. | +2 | 5 | |
| 3 | 2/8 | ↓ | 23 POWER | JERM. | +1 | 5 | LG MISSED BLOCK |
| 4 | 1/5 | ↓ | 27-0 | THEW. | +5 TD | 7-1 | |
| 5 | 1/5 | ↓ | 27-0 | THEW. | +9 | 5 PINCH | |
| 6 | 1/10 | ↑ | 42 POWER | GOTT. | +1 | 5 EAGLE | LT MISSED BLOCK |
| 7 | 2/2 | ↑ | 23 POWER | THEW. | +7 | 5 | |
| 8 | 1/10 | ↑ | 46-0 | GOTT. | +1 | 5 EAGLE | |
| 9 | 3/3 | ↑ | DIVE RT. | GOTT. | +10 | 5 PINCH | |
| 10 | 1/10 2ND HALF | ↑ | DIVE RT. | GOTT. | +8 | 5 | |

OFFENSE - PASSING GAME SUMMARY

Offense - Passing    Marblehead vs. OPPONENT #8    Page 3

Score 34-6    Date 11/18

| # | Down/Dist. | Position | Play | Passer | Receiver | Result | Comment |
|---|---|---|---|---|---|---|---|
| 1 | 2/8 | ↓ | PRO LEFT | PRIN. | HASK. | +8 | |
| 2 | 1/10 | ↓ | PRO LEFT | PRIN. | THEW. | +13 | |
| 3 | 3/10 | ↓ | R SDL. | PRIN. | HASK. | INC. | |
| 4 | 4/10 | ↓ | L-DW IN | PRIN. | HASK. | +17 | DOWN TO 5 YD. LINE |
| 5 | 3/30 | ↓ | DELAY 3 MIDDLE | PRIN. | MAC. | +7 | |
| 6 | 1/15 | ↑ | TRAIL IN | PRIN. | STRAY | +14 | |
| 7 | 1/10 | ↑ | PRO LEFT | PRIN. | HASK. | INC. | |
| 8 | 2/10 | ↑ | R STAY | PRIN. | RAND | +8 | |
| 9 | 3/3 | ↑ | PRO LEFT | PRIN. | JERM. | +23 | |
| 10 | 1/6 | ↑ | 27-O PASS | PRIN. | RAND | +6 | TD |
| 11 | 1/10 | ↑ | #2 BACK DEEP | PRIN. | JERM. | +24 | |
| 12 | 1/10 | ↑ | L SLANT | PRIN. | HASK. | INC. | (NEAR TD) |
| 13 | 2/10 2ND | HALF ↑ | T ELIGIBLE | PRIN. | FACEY | INT. | TD FOR OPPONENT |
| 14 | 1/5 | ↑ | SPRINT LT. | PRIN. | STRAY | INC. | |
| 15 | 3/8 | ↑ | R ACROSS | PRIN. | HASK. | +8 | TD |
| 16 | 3/3 | ↑ | 2 MIDDLE | PRIN. | JERM. | +3 | TD |
| 17 | | | | | | | |

**Figure 70**

row at the end of this game without throwing a pass. However, our first team passed 38 per cent of the time and our success in passing was the direct reason for our winning. Our opponent was extremely cautious in this game and set up his defense to try to double-cover some of our receivers. By spreading out in this manner, he gave our running game an opportunity to succeed. This defense created too large a burden on their left tackle, and we ran eighteen plays to one or the other side of him. In addition our passer had excellent protection.

The summary shows that our passing success was achieved by the short pass. We seldom throw the "long bomb," using it only when such a pass has been properly set up by success on

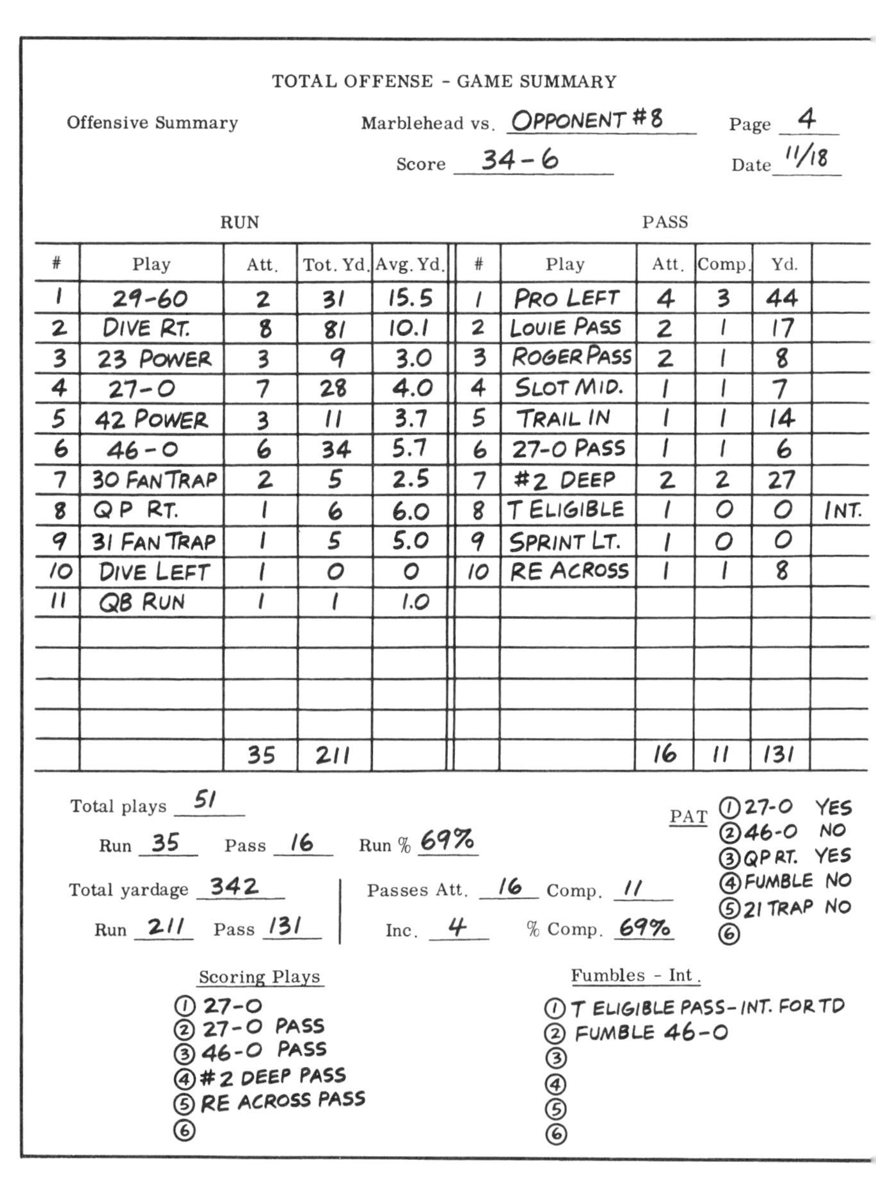

TOTAL OFFENSE - GAME SUMMARY

Offensive Summary — Marblehead vs. OPPONENT #8 — Page 4

Score 34-6 — Date 11/18

| RUN | | | | | PASS | | | | | |
|---|---|---|---|---|---|---|---|---|---|---|
| # | Play | Att. | Tot. Yd. | Avg. Yd. | # | Play | Att. | Comp. | Yd. | |
| 1 | 29-60 | 2 | 31 | 15.5 | 1 | PRO LEFT | 4 | 3 | 44 | |
| 2 | DIVE RT. | 8 | 81 | 10.1 | 2 | LOUIE PASS | 2 | 1 | 17 | |
| 3 | 23 POWER | 3 | 9 | 3.0 | 3 | ROGER PASS | 2 | 1 | 8 | |
| 4 | 27-0 | 7 | 28 | 4.0 | 4 | SLOT MID. | 1 | 1 | 7 | |
| 5 | 42 POWER | 3 | 11 | 3.7 | 5 | TRAIL IN | 1 | 1 | 14 | |
| 6 | 46-0 | 6 | 34 | 5.7 | 6 | 27-0 PASS | 1 | 1 | 6 | |
| 7 | 30 FAN TRAP | 2 | 5 | 2.5 | 7 | #2 DEEP | 2 | 2 | 27 | |
| 8 | Q P RT. | 1 | 6 | 6.0 | 8 | T ELIGIBLE | 1 | 0 | 0 | INT. |
| 9 | 31 FAN TRAP | 1 | 5 | 5.0 | 9 | SPRINT LT. | 1 | 0 | 0 | |
| 10 | DIVE LEFT | 1 | 0 | 0 | 10 | RE ACROSS | 1 | 1 | 8 | |
| 11 | QB RUN | 1 | 1 | 1.0 | | | | | | |
| | | | | | | | | | | |
| | | | | | | | | | | |
| | | | | | | | | | | |
| | | | | | | | | | | |
| | | 35 | 211 | | | | 16 | 11 | 131 | |

Total plays 51

Run 35 Pass 16 Run % 69%

Total yardage 342

Run 211 Pass 131

Passes Att. 16 Comp. 11

Inc. 4 % Comp. 69%

PAT
① 27-0 YES
② 46-0 NO
③ QP RT. YES
④ FUMBLE NO
⑤ 21 TRAP NO
⑥

Scoring Plays
① 27-0
② 27-0 PASS
③ 46-0 PASS
④ #2 DEEP PASS
⑤ RE ACROSS PASS
⑥

Fumbles - Int.
① T ELIGIBLE PASS-INT. FOR TD
② FUMBLE 46-0
③
④
⑤
⑥

**Figure 71**

the short patterns. Our idea is to throw short with consistency and to let the long pass evolve naturally from this success.

Notice also that our running game exploited the plays that were going for us. Our 11 pass completions were shared by six different receivers, and we attacked nearly every area of the pass defense zone. With respect to down and distance, our strategy was unpredictable. Our running attack was very right-handed, and we could expect that our next opponent would set up strongly on that side. Thus you are able to analyze your own offense from the point of view of your next opponent. You can see how much helpful information can be gained from the charts. This information will be an immediate aid in planning your practices for the next week. Your records will also help you evaluate at the season's end and will be available for reference when you meet the same opponent next year.

**Analysis of opponent**

We also do a film analysis of our opponent—usually immediately when the game is still fresh in our minds. Sometimes we are too busy to do this and it is left for the off-season. If you find you are pressed for time during the season, this area of research can be done later.

Our film review of our opponent is very similar to our scouting report and is summed up in the same manner. It is unnecessary actually to compile this information during the season but since we look at the films several times anyway, it is no problem to record this information about our opponent. The summary is done by an assistant or by myself during the off-season.

If you are not prepared to devote the time on Sunday afternoon and evenings during the season to football, don't even try to start keeping records. All the successful coaches I know spend a great deal of time working at the game. Also once the season starts, I see as many games as I can possibly fit into my schedule. If I were to attend a Friday night high-school game in the area, I would be surprised if I did not see certain high-school coaches there as spectators. These coaches often have neither participating team as an opponent but are there because football is there. A football coach who desires to be successful must be devoted: willing to give himself and his time completely to the game.

### Keeping of statistics

If you are fortunate as we are in having every game filmed, all the statistics you want to compile can be taken from the film. The statistics we compile are presented in our game film summary form. These statistics are formed into a yearly set. If you are unable to have game films taken, the job of compiling statistics becomes a good deal more involved. Fair results can only be achieved if the method is extremely well organized because each play is only run once.

Your problems are further complicated if you lack personnel to do the job. On game day you and your assistants are all very busy and you are the only people competent to do the job. The only satisfactory method is to assign an assistant to the task and have a reserve quarterback sit on one side of him and a team manager on the other.

If we were unable to have game films, I would attempt to take game statistics on the same forms as I now use for the film analysis because these forms are made to hold the information on the offensive game that I want. If the results of such statistic-taking should prove too complex and unreliable, I would have to cut out some areas that we now include.

Compiling information on our defense is just as complex. We want to know the type of plays being run against our defense, the performance of the defense, and the performances of individual players. Our defense usually involves stunts and we have to run the film several times just to determine what defense was being used on a particular play. Without films, we would be forced to omit much defensive information in the interest of efficiency. If you have no films, you should be sure to record the following information:

1. Position of ball on field
2. Down and distance
3. The opponent's formation and play
4. Your defense
5. Name of tackler.

If all of this can be accurately compiled on your defense during the course of the game, you have the most important information.

If this discussion convinces you of nothing else, I hope that you will understand how important it is to take films. If your school does not take game films, fight until you can somehow get them. If your opponent takes game films and you do not, you are at a distinct disadvantage before you even step onto the field.

## Seasonal Summary

A seasonal summary is compiled primarily for the purpose of evaluation. Most of us start planning for the next season the day after the last game. The game summaries, when tabulated into a seasonal summary, afford us important factual information for planning for the future. We can see where our passing game was successful and where it failed. The development of our passing game for the coming season should exploit our successes of the past. The areas where our passing attack failed should be studied and ways to overcome our weaknesses should be formulated. You must also consider the known abilities of your returning personnel. What has been successful for one team in one season may very well not be successful for another team.

### General seasonal passing summary

The first seasonal summary (see Figure 72) concerns the general offensive game and is the summary of the season Tom Manning established a State record of 25 touchdown passes in one season. This team had an outstanding right end and extremely capable receivers in all positions. The running game was excellent and the only real weakness of this team was its lack of depth. We played our key games with only thirteen boys and when one of them was injured, we began to have our troubles.

SEASONAL SUMMARY — Season of ________

| Game | Plays | Run | Pass | Comp. | TD Passes | Int. | Score |
|---|---|---|---|---|---|---|---|
| #1 | 37 | 25 | 12 | 8 | 2 | 0 | 40-0 |
| 2 | 49 | 27 | 22 | 11 | 2 | 0 | 18-14 |
| 3 | 57 | 32 | 25 | 13 | 5 | 1 | 50-14 |
| 4 | 43 | 24 | 19 | 10 | 3 | 0 | 36-14 |
| 5 | 48 | 30 | 18 | 6 | 2 | 2 | 20-21 |
| 6 | 39 | 26 | 13 | 5 | 1 | 0 | 20-14 |
| 7 | 43 | 14 | 29 | 19 | 6 | 1 | 46-22 |
| 8 | 47 | 27 | 20 | 14 | 2 | 0 | 30-8 |
| 9 | 43 | 29 | 14 | 8 | 2 | 1 | 12-6 |
| | | | | | | | |
| Total | 406 | 234 | 172 | 94 | 25 | 5 | 272-113 |

Pass Comp. 55%   Won 8   Lost 1   Tied 0

Pass Int. 3%   Running Plays 58%

**Figure 72**

SEASONAL SUMMARY — Season of ________

| Game | Plays | Run | Pass | Comp. | TD Passes | Int. | Score |
|---|---|---|---|---|---|---|---|
| #1 | 45 | 35 | 10 | 6 | 0 | 0 | 6-6 |
| 2 | 34 | 24 | 10 | 3 | 0 | 1 | 3-18 |
| 3 | 47 | 34 | 13 | 11 | 0 | 0 | 14-6 |
| 4 | 40 | 30 | 10 | 6 | 0 | 0 | 13-0 |
| 5 | 40 | 32 | 8 | 1 | 0 | 2 | 7-12 |
| 6 | 34 | 26 | 8 | 6 | 0 | 0 | 13-8 |
| 7 | 45 | 32 | 13 | 10 | 4 | 0 | 27-6 |
| 8 | 33 | 23 | 10 | 7 | 3 | 0 | 29-20 |
| 9 | 32 | 29 | 3 | 3 | 0 | 0 | 7-0 |
| | | | | | | | |
| Total | 350 | 265 | 85 | 53 | 7 | 3 | 119-76 |

Pass Comp. 62%   Won 6   Lost 2   Tied 1

Pass Int. 3.5%   Running Plays 76%

**Figure 73**

Figure 73 is the second seasonal summary of a team that passed less than normal for us but completed more passes than normal. This team was also a conference champion due to its defensive ability and the ability to come up with the big offensive play when it was needed. These two summaries furnish general information concerning these particular seasons—information useful for publicity purposes and for presenting a general offensive picture of a season.

### Summary of individual pass plays

Of direct interest to us in this presentation is the seasonal tabulation of our individual pass plays. This table is directly obtained from each of the nine game summaries. Figure 74 shows the pass play summary of a conference runner-up that finished with a 7–2 record—relying almost entirely on the passing game.

You can see that only four passes were able to achieve what I consider excellent results. Louie pass is the individual pass pattern for the left end, and there are many different moves that he can make. These individual patterns along with the Pro Left and Trail-in patterns can be found by referring to Chapter 5.

Some immediate conclusions can be drawn from this table and not all of them are very good. The first question I ask is, if the Pro Left and Trail-in passes were so successful, why weren't they thrown more often? Our screen passes, which have had their successful seasons, were not practiced enough to insure their success. The Sprint Pass series, which is discussed in Chapter 10, needs evaluation and revamping if it is going to prove a valuable addition to our offense. In the future I am going to keep this Pass Play Summary up to date, game by game, instead of totalling at the end of the season. Obviously this team had certain passing capabilities that we did not exploit as fully as we should have. Pro Left pass had a completion result of 12 for 13. We should have thrown this pass 30 times instead of just 13.

| # | Pass | Att. | Comp. | Int. | TDs | Results |
|---|---|---|---|---|---|---|
| SEASONAL SUMMARY - PASS PLAYS | | | | | | |
| 1 | LOUIE PASS | 33 | 21 | 1 | 3 | EXCELLENT |
| 2 | ROGER PASS | 24 | 11 | | 3 | GOOD |
| 3 | PRO LEFT | 13 | 12 | | 3 | EXCELLENT |
| 4 | PRO RIGHT | 10 | 3 | | | POOR |
| 5 | 46-O PASS | 5 | 3 | | | GOOD |
| 6 | 27-O PASS | 3 | 1 | 1 | 1 | FAIR |
| 7 | SPRINT RT. | 20 | 11 | | | GOOD |
| 8 | SPRINT LT. | 8 | 2 | | | POOR |
| 9 | TRAIL IN | 9 | 7 | | | EXCELLENT |
| 10 | SL TRAIL IN | 4 | 4 | | | EXCELLENT |
| 11 | RE ACROSS | 4 | 3 | | 1 | GOOD |
| 12 | LE ACROSS | 7 | 2 | | 1 | POOR |
| 13 | SCREEN RT. + LT. | 3 | 3 | | | POOR (SMALL YARDAGE) |
| 14 | SCREEN MIDDLE | 1 | 1 | | | GOOD |
| 15 | #2 BACK PASS | 3 | 2 | | 1 | GOOD |
| 16 | #4 BACK PASS | 1 | 0 | | | — |
| 17 | TRAIL OUT | 5 | 2 | | | POOR |
| 18 | TACKLE ELIGIBLE | 8 | 4 | 1 | 3 | EXCELLENT |
| 19 | MISC. + UNKNOWN | 12 | 9 | | | — |
| 20 | | | | | | |
| 21 | | | | | | |
| 22 | | | | | | |
| Total | | 173 | 101 | 3 | 16 | COMP. 58% |
| | | | | | | INT. 1.7 % |

**Figure 74**

At least the passes that achieved poor results were not thrown very often. The ability of the left end was exploited to the fullest, and although toward the end of the season they double-teamed him, we were still able to hit him consistently.

As a result, the rest of our offensive play benefited by being able to pit 10 men against 9 men. Our completion rate was very good as was the number of touchdown passes. It is quite satisfying to note that there were only three interceptions. I think the reason for this success is that we spend so much time on the fundamentals of the passing game. Our passers have been able to develop their accuracy and good timing to a high degree of proficiency. Considering that we made 11 interceptions on defense during the season, interception was a big factor in our favor during this season.

The pass summary chart is a fine source of material for planning our passing attack the next season. Along with the pass summaries of seasons previous to the just concluded one, it holds a wealth of information about the relative success of each of your pass plays. The summary in Figure 74 is the record of a team which was strictly a passing team. According to other seasons, our most consistent pass has been our off-tackle pass. Whenever we have had a team with a fairly capable ground game, the records show that our action passes, particularly the off-tackle pass, have had outstanding success. Our one consistent pocket pass has always been the Trail-in pass.

## Balance Your Attack

The ideal type of offense for successful passing should have a capable running attack. With a good running game we pass less often but with greater success. A team that ran 75 per cent of the time had a completion rate of 63 per cent. Another team that ran 58 per cent of the time had a completion rate of 53 per cent. If your opponents respect your passing and running attacks equally, your action passes, if well executed, will be consistently successful over a period of several years. Because of our usual lack of size, our game is quite slanted toward the pass. In the future, should we have a good sized team, our running game would be used considerably more.

NINE

# INTEGRATING A PASSING ATTACK INTO ANY OFFENSE

In order to get the most out of your passing attack, it should be well integrated into your basic over-all offensive pattern. Marblehead is primarily a passing team but 68 per cent of our plays are running plays. Your passing attack should complement your running attack, and you should not have a haphazard collection of passes just for the sake of having some. Even though you may not throw very often, the few passes you use should be a smooth outflow of your offensive pattern.

## Evaluate Your Present Passing Game

Before making any changes in your passing attack, it would be wise to conduct a systematic review of what you have been doing until now. During the winter months you could probably find the time to make such an evaluation. If you are well organized at the outset, you will find that this process is not as time consuming as you might think. You will evaluate well, I believe, if you go back over your past three seasons.

It is my intention to show you a systematic way to make such a review. Once you have completed your review, it should be relatively easy to continue keeping records from game to game and year to year.

## Diagram present pass plays

The first step in evaluating your passing attack is to diagram all of the pass patterns you have used during the past three seasons. By following this simple procedure you may find that you have plenty of patterns, many of which are actually duplications. You may also have many patterns that you have never used or never used successfully.

An excellent way to diagram your passes is on individual cards; 6 x 8 index cards should serve the purpose. On the front of each card diagram the pass pattern. On the back list the pertinent information regarding the pattern (see Figure 75). In addition to the diagram and name include the category of the pass on the front. On the back list the purpose of the pass, primary receiver variations, weaknesses, and any significant comments.

By using two notebook rings, you can make these cards into a small notebook. Notice that the information on the back side of the card is written upside down. This makes it possible for the card to be most easily read when put in notebook form. We keep several of these notebooks in the team locker room and in the training room so that the players will have easy access to them. With this system, it is possible to keep your material up to date merely by adding or withdrawing cards. We make up similar notebooks of cards for our running attack, defense, and special situations such as punts, kick-offs, etc.

## Place your passes in categories

Before making these cards into a notebook, you have to decide which passes you intend to keep, which passes you will reject, and whether you will add any new passes. Determine categories to organize your passes into and then sort them ac-

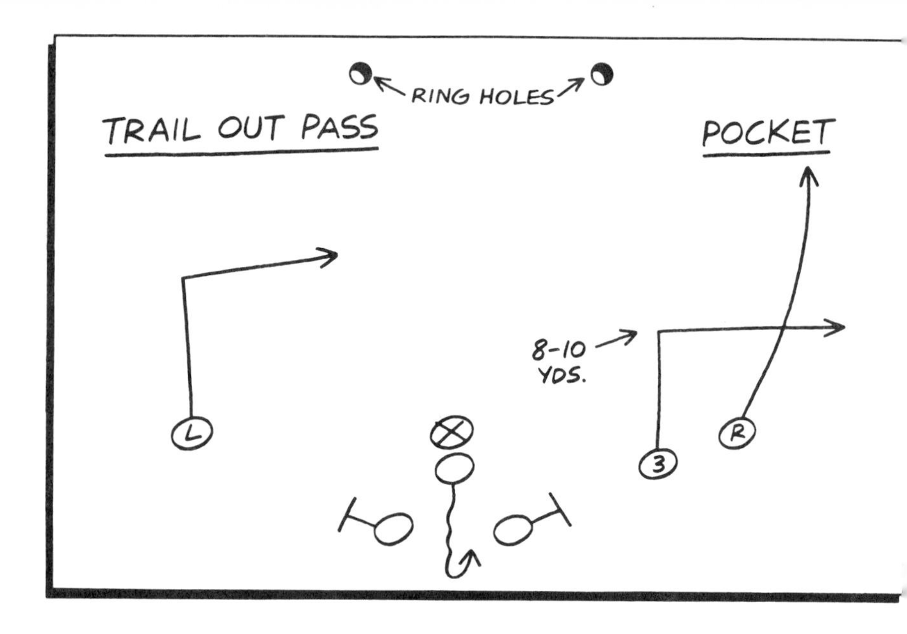


1. PURPOSE — FLOOD THE HALFBACK ZONE
2. PRIMARY RECEIVER — #3 OR R, DEPENDING ON DEFENSIVE H
3. VARIATIONS — ROLL OUT RIGHT, OR R HOOK AND LATERAL
4. WEAKNESS — R MUST NOT RUN TOWARD MIDDLE— POOR INSIDE 15-YARD LINE
5. COMMENTS — 1. CAN BE COVERED BY CLB DROPPING OFF; ROLLING OUT SOLVES THIS 2. BEWARE THE INTERCEPTION

**Figure 75**

cordingly. The easiest way to do this is to lay all the cards on the floor where you can see them all at a glance. Then it will be very easy to begin to group them.

Our grouping consists of two categories: the standard pass

and the action pass. The standard pass is a pass from the very beginning. Our action passes begin by faking a running play and then develop into a pass. These major categories are broken down into different areas. You may wish to organize your passes differently because of your patterns, philosophy of passing, type of offensive attack, or for some other reason. We could have, I suppose, categorized our passes as pocket passes, roll-out passes, action passes and miscellaneous passes.

For the purpose of analysis, write this organization into a simple outline form and list the passes that you have in each category. A very brief outline of our passes can be found at the close of Chapter 5. For evaluation purposes, I would also classify each pass in this outline according to its variations and the different formations it is thrown from. For example our Trail-out pass would be classified in the following manner:

ITEM A–2 Trail-out Pass

a. Normal formation
b. Slot left formation
c. Roger hook and lateral
d. Roll right.

**Test your memory**

Now that you have your cards sorted into the various groups, lay them out on the floor again. For the purpose of checking just how good your memory is, list these passes in the following areas:

1. Pass plays you have never used in a ball game
2. Pass plays you have seldom used
3. Pass plays which have been prone to interception
4. Pass plays you use often but with little success
5. Pass plays you use often with modest success
6. Pass plays you use often with great success
7. Special pass plays used successfully.

Categories 4, 5 and 6 will be rather small because all of us tend to rely on certain favorite patterns.

1. Patterns you have never used should not be taught.
2. Pass plays seldom used should be taught only if they

serve a particular purpose. For example, our 23 power play has a pass we have used only once but it resulted in a score. The purpose of this pass is to fake a power play up the middle first, and it works very effectively inside the opponent's 10-yard line.

3. Passes which have a history of interception should be discarded.
4. Patterns you use often with little success are obviously poor regardless of your prejudice toward them. Either discard them or alter them to make them effective.
5. Pass plays you use with modest success are worthwhile and should, of course, be kept.
6. Patterns that have been the best for you probably number no more than five or six. Our most successful passes have generally been our action passes, particularly the off-tackle pattern.

Do not discard any patterns until after you have completed your study. The listing I have suggested is for the purpose of testing your memory. Your memory may be the only guide you have used in setting up your passing game from year to year. Once you have completed your film survey, you will find it interesting to check the actual facts against your memory. You may find that a pattern you felt had been quite successful for you doesn't actually measure up to your opinion of it. Another pass that perhaps you thought little of may very well have a good history.

Our patterns have evolved to the point where their success ranges from modest to outstanding. The number of patterns we have discarded is huge. New patterns are continually considered and evaluated. Some of these are added; the rest have cards made up on them and are filed.

### Use of your game films

The greatest sources of information for evaluating your passing game are your films. Many of you, I'm sure, keep a file of game-by-game film analyses and could easily organize this information as I have suggested. If you do not have such material on file, it will not be as difficult as you might think to compile it.

I have suggested that your review go back over a three-year period. For us this would be a matter of going over a total of 27 game films. To review your passing attack only, each film should not take you more than one hour. Should you find you wish to include a review of your running game as well, each film will take a good deal longer. Once this task is completed, it should be relatively easy for you to keep your file up to date.

In Chapter 8 you will find the forms we use for making our film study. These forms are filled out when we review each game film the following week. The information is then collected on the game summary sheet. The game summaries are then compiled into a season summary, which is very helpful to us in evaluating our offense of the past season.

In this discussion, we are concerned only with a review of your passing game during the past three seasons. Should it be necessary for you to go over all the game films of these seasons, it might be well to take the time and record information regarding your running game, defense, and other aspects of the game. If you do not find the forms suggested in Chapter 8 adaptable to your situation, be certain to make up some sort of form that will suit your purpose. If you attempt to inaugurate a review without having this review completely planned and prepared for at the beginning, you will waste a lot of time and will probably leave things out that you intended to consider.

You now have duplicated game forms and summary sheets. Individual cards have been made on each pass play you have had in your offense over the past three seasons. You have sorted these passes into various categories. You have tested your memory as to the use of these passes and their relative success or failure. Now, let's go to our films and see if our passing game is what we think it is.

**The film study**

In doing our film study we include all passes that were

called in the game. Any passes that were called back because of penalties are nevertheless included in our records. For example, the fact that our left guard is off-side on a Trail-in pass has no influence on whether or not it is a good pattern. Information regarding the number of times and the reasons the passer is forced to run is also included in a separate part of the review of our running game. This information is very useful in evaluating pass protection blocking.

The forms we use for our review are presented in Chapter 8. You may use these or choose your own. Since you will probably undertake your film study during the off-season months, it may take you a long time to complete your individual game analysis. As long as these forms are not complicated, the job of summarizing should be comparatively short.

After you have compiled the pass summary, you will find it very interesting to check these facts against the facts as you remembered them before you began looking at films. I would be quite surprised to find any coach who had more than six pass plays that were used consistently and with success over this three-year period. Our 19–60 fan pass had great success one season but we never used it again after that. Passes like this that were successful only because they particularly suited certain players should also be noted. If this type of player comes along again, the information regarding this particular play should be readily available.

Amend the information you compiled in the seven areas of the memory check suggested earlier in this chapter. For the moment, disregard all pass plays except those in categories 5, 6 and 7, i.e., passes you use often with modest success, passes you use often with great success, and special pass plays that have worked successfully. I should imagine that these pass plays are few in number.

## Determine Your Passing Needs

You now know the pass patterns that are the backbone of your passing offense. In all probability they do not encompass all of the passing areas that should be a part of your offense. The next task is to determine what you want your passing game to do for you. You should list the needs your passing game should fulfill. Because we are a passing club, we want many more things from our passing game than you may want from yours. Many of the objectives that a coach might desire of his passing game are listed below:

1. Passes to aid running game
2. Passes to surprise opponent
3. Passes for use in a strictly passing situation
4. Passes to be used against a determined defensive rush of the passer
5. Passes that enable you to place your best receiver against the poorest defender
6. Patterns that confuse the various types of pass defense
7. Passes that have a history of high completion and low interception.

**The element of surprise**

One of the major tasks of any offense is to keep the defense off-balance. Keep your opponent guessing right up to the last possible minute. Because of this I feel that it is an absolute necessity that an action pass is coupled with your most effective running play. Our best running play is off-tackle (discussed in Chapter 6). One of our most important passes, and one we practice most, is coupled with our off-tackle play. We attempt to make the pass look like the run as long as possible. This is done by aggressive blocking on the on-side with a double-team on the tackle still taking place. In addition, the quarterback "rides" with the halfback before rolling out. There is no question that the run and the pass mutually aid each other. Once the pass has been used effectively, the defense will react less quickly to the run. The success of the run will cause the defense to be less concerned about the pass.

I think it is generally agreed that we all will be more effective if our best running play is coupled with an action pass. You may wish to use more action (or play) passes than this.

We use several other action passes, although with less frequency than the off-tackle pass. Our running game is successful, I believe, only because our opponents have so much respect for our action passes. They will not commit themselves as early to a run for a fear of a pass.

Surprise is an important element of play passes. There are, of course, other ways to surprise an opponent. Some coaches have some pet pass plays for certain situations. We have used out 23 power pass on first down inside an opponent's 10-yard line and caught them off balance. The only purpose of such a pass is to surprise an opponent, and thus it is used very seldom. We wish to have some surprise passes in our repertoire.

The element of surprise can also be effectively employed in your game strategy. When and where to call a pass play is discussed in detail in Chapter 13. The effectiveness of surprise is evidenced by the fact that the odds for completion are about the best on a first and ten situation.

To harness the element of surprise, a receiver should practice faithfully and learn to make good fakes while moving down-field. A good receiver masks his intentions by deliberately trying to mislead the defender. If he can get the defender to try to begin guessing his intention, he has the defender at his mercy. I recall one game in college in which we kept hitting our left end on a down-and-out pattern. When we finally ran the down, out-and-down pattern, the defender was so used to coming up to cover the sideline pattern that when the receiver turned downfield again there was absolutely no one near him. Surprise certainly must be a major consideration in the development of a passing attack.

## Collect Your Findings

Your evaluation of your passing game has now reached the point where you can look at your past and plan your future. You know from your film study the areas where your passing attack has been successful. The same source will clearly point out the weaknesses of your over-all passing game. You have listed the objectives of your passing game and have an outline form for sorting your pass plays into their various categories.

When you put the passes with a successful history into your outline and match the outline against your objectives list, you will find quite a few holes in this over-all picture. You now must be able to come up with pass plays that will complement your present successful passes. These new pass plays must be able to work in areas where you have not been able to enjoy success.

Where do you find these new plays? You must look first to other coaches. Clinics, periodicals, books, conversations with fellow coaches are some of the sources from which you can get new ideas. A college or fellow high-school coach is flattered when you ask him a question, and he may be able to help you solve a particular problem. "Pick the brains" of others in your profession. Experiment with their ideas and ideas of your own. You will not be able to fill all the holes in your passing attack in one season but keep plugging away at it season after season and your passing game will gradually become almost complete.

TEN

# INTEGRATING NEW TRENDS AND IDEAS INTO YOUR ATTACK

Football is a much different game today than it was twenty years ago. Offenses have become more complex and defenses have kept pace. There are so many different problems that arise from these complexities that no one coach is capable of coming up with a solution to all of them. Therefore, it behooves the successful coach to consider himself a student of the game. He must constantly strive to learn more of the game by any means open to him.

## Be a Student of the Game

I have known a coach, in another sport, to make a remark to the effect that it wasn't necessary for him to attend clinics because he already knew exactly what he was going to teach and how he was going to do it. It should be pointed out that no one is obliged to use the ideas of other coaches. You may reject every idea presented to you, that's your privilege. However, a good coach will find himself continually evaluating the ideas of others and integrating some, or many, of these into his own program.

The coach who does not keep abreast of the ever-changing

game of football will one day find himself hopelessly outdistanced by his fellow coaches. He will encounter situations during ball games that he will be unable to cope with and will be at the mercy of his opponent. My biggest fear is that some day an opponent will come up with a new maneuver that I will be unable to counter while a ball game is in progress.

Basically, then, there are two reasons why we must continually research the game. First, we wish to make ourselves and our program ever better by injecting new ideas and methods. We must also learn so as to be able to counteract our opponents who are also involved in this business of research. If the coach of every team in my conference were a diligent student and I were to do nothing, it would not take very long to slide from the top to the bottom. Only the coach who has superior players can afford to be lax. But if he is lax, he is not being fair to his players, and he won't be prepared for the day when his players are not superior.

**Books, periodicals, articles as sources**

I have in my possession a considerable number of books on football. My "library" is in continual use throughout the year. I read them when they arrive and jot down any ideas I think useful. And I find myself continually referring to them for answers to problems I encounter.

I may encounter a team with a rotation type of pass defense and be uncertain as to the best way to cope with it. By referring to my library, I should be able to find at least five or six presentations of how to handle such a pass defense. By using these sources, I am usually able to come up with a better solution to a problem than I would if I tried to work out the answers myself.

Not only must books be a source of reference for you; you should have access to many of the fine coaching periodicals being printed. If you come across an article that you feel may be useful at some time, it is no problem to cut it out and file it away. There is a great deal of writing done by successful coaches on all levels and phases of the game. A coach would be remiss in his duties if he did not take advantage of this wealth of material.

### Attendance at coaching clinics

I believe a coach should attend as many coaching clinics as he can find time for. There are no secrets in football, and successful coaches usually hold back nothing when they present their ideas to you. With the advent of the filming of games, no coach can prevent his strategy from becoming common knowledge.

When you listen to a coach make a presentation, it is imperative that you take notes. Take good notes on his entire lecture rather than only on the areas you think you can use. If you do not take notes, in two weeks you will have forgotten at least 90 per cent of what was said.

I have a large set of clinic notes and every now and then I leaf through them. This sometimes proves to be very fruitful. You often hear a speaker say, "If I can just leave you with one thought, my presentation will have been worthwhile." You should nearly always get at least one thing out of a well-presented lecture. Often you may learn from a negative attitude. That is, you may disagree with the speaker and, knowing of his idea, may be able to develop a corresponding idea of your own.

Considering the number of football clinics now held throughout the country, no coach should have difficulty getting to hear one of the top college coaches in the nation. These gentlemen work on football on a year-round basis. We in high school are part-time coaches, so it is only logical that the new wrinkles originate in the college and professional ranks. We should listen carefully to the top men of the game because they have a great deal to offer us.

A fine source of information at any clinic is the other coaches that are attending. We at the high-school level can learn a great deal from each other because we encounter many of the same problems. An informal "bull session" in a hotel room among five or six coaches can sometimes be as beneficial as the presentations at the clinic during the day. Don't be a snob when talking with other high-school coaches. They have some ideas that can be very useful to you if you will listen.

**Learn from your assistants**

You may not realize it, but your assistant coaches are excellent sources of football information and new ideas. If you have a moment, you might make a list of the names of the coaches your assistants played for and worked under. You will be surprised at the number and prominence of the men that your entire staff has had the opportunity to learn from.

Conduct your coaches meetings in a democratic manner. Encourage the coaches to express their opinions and ideas. If you find that they always agree with you, you can be sure that something is wrong. A good coach doesn't want a parrot for an assistant. Many minds can solve a problem better than one. Of course, as head coach you will have to make the final decision even though the majority may be opposed.

**Learn from your opponents**

I recall a game we nearly lost because a particular pass pattern was giving us a very bad time. After the game, I asked the coach where he had picked up this peculiar pass pattern. He told me that while he was preparing to play Marblehead several seasons before, he noticed that we had this same pattern. We just hadn't used it lately. In preparing for us that year, he had had a terrible time trying to defend against this pattern. So he decided to put the pattern into his own offense, and our own play came back to haunt us.

This instance serves to illustrate what I consider to be a primary axiom of coaching. If your opponent has a play, a defense, or some maneuver that causes you great difficulty; incorporate it into your own set-up if at all possible. If you have great difficulty coping with a particular play, certainly other people should have the same problems when you use the play. You are not stealing plays from an opponent; there just are not any secrets. Some coaches are reluctant to do this because it may appear that the opposing coach knows more football. There is no place for such self-pride in coaching. Every coach should realize that there is much he doesn't know and that other coaches can teach him a great deal.

Our off-tackle pass, the backbone of our passing game, was vastly improved because of the slightly different manner in which one of our opponents ran it. We incorporated this "wrinkle" into the play and now have a much better play.

### Learn from losing

If your league is as evenly balanced as ours, there is no question that you will know what it is to be a loser. The only good thing about a loss is that you learn ten times as much from it as you do from a win. A loss is the greatest teaching device there is for a conscientious coach.

There are many things to consider after losing a game. Second guessing your own moves is extremely helpful for future strategy. Your offense and defense both receive your careful scrutiny and very often changes are made to overcome some weaknesses that your opponent picked you apart on. I review the manner in which I prepared the team and add this to my store of information. Don't hide the films of your losing games in the back of your closet just because you get upset watching them. A loss is in vain if you do not carefully scrutinize the game and attempt to learn as much as possible from the experience.

## The Sprint Series

There is little question that the research being done by the college and professional coaches is continually affecting the play of the game at all levels. When a new technique is developed, the high-school coach who learns of it early, can gain an advantage from using it, or at least be prepared to defend against it. The game is in a continual state of fluctuation.

New ideas are being introduced, others discarded, and quite often old discarded ideas are being re-introduced.

One of the more recent innovations is the sprint series. It employs a new way of running the ends by combining the end sweep with the running pass. On a normal end sweep the on-side blockers, including the end, block down the line. The defensive backs key on the end and the backfield and when they see these blocks being executed, they come up quickly to stop the run. The running pass has always been an excellent play because the on-side receivers put the defensive backs in a dilemma. They want to come up to stop the run but can't leave the receiver to do so. Although the running pass often ended up as a run, it was a play separate from the actual running end sweep.

The one drawback in the running pass as most coaches used to run it is that it is somewhat slow in developing. A good defensive backfield, by rotating toward the play as it develops, can cause great pressure against the run as well as covering the receivers downfield.

Notice that in Figure 76 the end and the corner back can apply enough pressure to stop the run, while the defensive backs have rotated into a good zone coverage. But the defen-

Figure 76

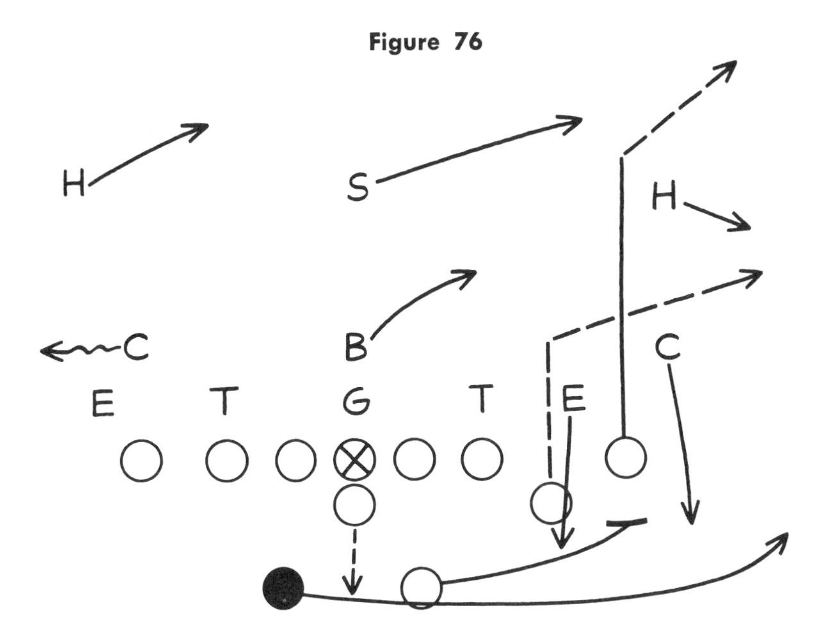

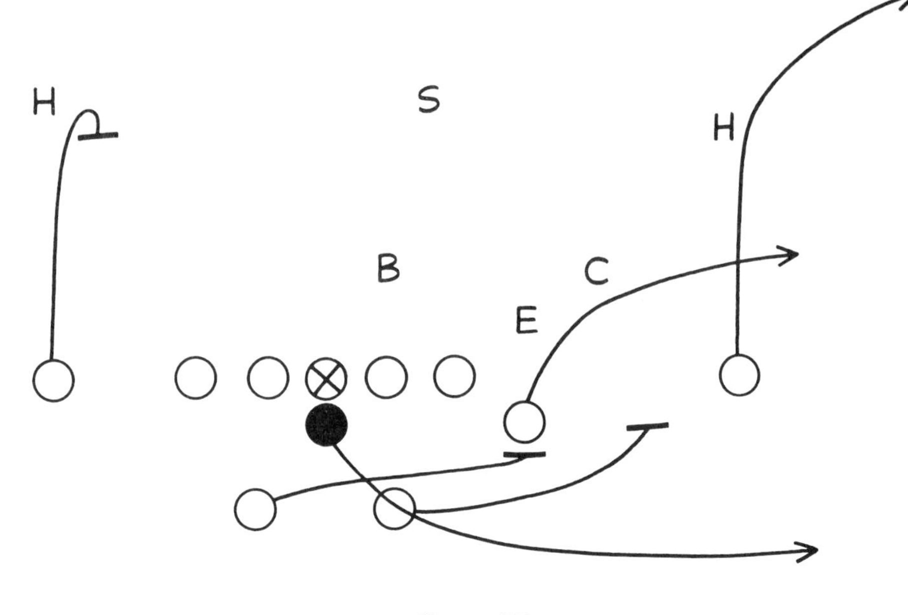


**Figure 77**

sive backfield needs some time to accomplish this rotation. The sprint series is designed to develop so quickly that there is no time at all for this defensive reaction to take place.

In executing the sprint right pass (see Figure 77), the quarterback must move away from the center at full speed along a flatter path than usual. We don't even use a reverse pivot. He just steps off in the direction that he is going and runs as fast as he can. He must be prepared to throw after only three steps. From this point onward he must be prepared to throw at any moment. He looks at the defensive halfback as soon as he can and will pass depending on this man's reaction. If the halfback comes up, the ball must be thrown quickly before the safety man can pick up the end. Should the halfback cover the end, then the passer should look for the slot back. The only man to cover him is the corner linebacker and if this is the case, it should develop into a good running play.

The left halfback can be put in motion on one count so that the quarterback will be able to run a flat path and still have two backs in front of him. You should use this type of motion only if you have good counter-plays coming from it.

We have found that the motion spoiled the play for us by taking away the element of surprise. We now have the left halfback step behind the quarterback and become the inside blocker of the two blocking backs. This means the passer runs right off the heels of the fullback and gets a little ahead of the left halfback. The two blocking backs must block aggressively up on the line of scrimmage so that the passer's path will remain relatively flat. If it develops into a run, these two blockers should get their key from the defensive reaction. Should the defense come up quickly, the blockers know the passer has started to run and should block accordingly.

The path of the right end should be curved toward the halfback and behind him about 15–20 yards downfield toward the sideline. His job is to make the defensive halfback cover him. If the halfback leaves him to come up to the shorter flat area, the end should flatten his path toward the sideline so that the safety will find it even more difficult to rotate over to pick him up.

The slot back must race into the flat 5–10 yards deep by running a flat path. He does not fake and gains depth only as he moves toward the sideline. If he is at all slow or moves downfield before going to the sideline, a middle linebacker may be able to move over to cover him. This will spoil the play. The slot back must be covered by either the halfback or the corner line backer.

The left end hooks about 10 yards deep so that if the passer's rollout is prevented, he can throw back to the left end. This has also proven to be effective. The entire offensive line blocks one man to the right. The blocks do not need to be held as long as usual because the play must necessarily develop very quickly.

You can see that this play is designed to put a great deal of pressure on two defensive men, the outside linebacker and halfback. The passer must be rushed, the slot man must be covered in the short flat, and the end must be covered in the deep outside flat.

## Initial experience with the sprint pass

Prior to this past season, I acquired information on the sprint pass from three sources. The first presentation I encountered was at a coaching clinic. This made me curious to know more and I found additional information in a coaching periodical. I then visited with a local college coach and received a good deal of information from a discussion with him. My sources were three highly successful college coaches and I merely adapted their ideas to fit my own situation. I knew that my offense was in need of a play to exploit further the running passer. The sprint pass seemed to be the answer. After one season there are some wrinkles to work out before it becomes a great play for us.

In nine games we used this play 35 times, completing 13 of 28 passes. We enjoyed modest success with this play, and it was a contributing factor to our seven wins. The threat of this play loosened up the defenses on our slot side, and so our dive play to that side was more successful than ever before. The sprint pass is now part of our offense, and we must now bring the play to its fullest potential.

## Difficulties encountered in sprint series

The sprint pass is designed to be a pass-or-run play. However, it seldom developed into a run although the quarterback should have run many times. Thus the quarterback must be convinced that the sprint pass can also be one of our better running plays. Unfortunately, most high-school boys predetermine, even while calling the play in the huddle, whether they intend to pass or run on an option play. By referring to films, setting up similar situations in practice, and continually haranguing your quarterbacks, you should be able to get them to think quickly and correctly on these option plays.

Also, the two blocking backs would often drift deep to make their blocks, thus forcing the passer back. This removed the run threat and made the play much less effective.

Good passer timing is also essential in the sprint pass because the ball must arrive when the receiver is open. When we first started to use the play, the passers were waiting much too long to throw, and the receivers, who were initially open, became covered. As a result, the play was getting strung out and often the whole pattern was forced into the sideline. We were able to correct this problem quickly. Later in the season the quarterback often passed to the slot back almost immediately and proper timing was the real reason for our success.

I have discussed the sprint pass for two reasons. First, it is one of the new developments of the game, and even if we may not use it ourselves, we must be prepared to defend against it. In addition, I want to emphasize that there are many things a coach can learn from other coaches. We are continually exposed to new ideas, which we should evaluate, accept or reject, and re-evaluate if we decide to include them in our plans.

### The Rollout versus the Pocket Pass

Whereas the professional passer throws from a pocket and the college passer most often from a rollout, the high-school passer often throws from a pocket for the middle-field pass, and rolls out for sideline patterns. The reasons for these different styles of passing at different levels are experience and strength.

Professionals use the pocket pass almost exclusively because the most effective and efficient way to pass is from the pocket. The pocket passer can throw to all parts of the field and threaten a very large area. The rollout passer is effective in only half of the passing area of the field since he throws anywhere from midfield to the sideline on the side that he is rolling to. A "cross-country" pass is difficult to throw and easily covered by one man, and thus is used only when a surprise play is wanted instead of an established pattern.

The defense has only half the field to cover on a rollout,

whereas they must cover the entire field on a pocket pass. Obviously, it is very difficult to defend against a good pocket passer.

The sideline pass run by either end from a "pro" formation is probably the most difficult pattern to defend against. With two receivers split wide, the most the defense can do is to double-team the best receiver. The single defender, who must be ready for the deep pass, is nearly always late covering a correctly timed sideline pattern. If the defender comes up too quickly for the sideline pattern, he is set up for a good sideline fake, and a deep pattern should result in an automatic score. From the pocket the passer can hit either sideline. On a rollout the defensive backfield can rotate and provide double coverage on the end running the sideline pattern.

The professional passer has the experience and the strength to throw from a pocket and practices passing until his timing is almost perfect. Some colleges are running offenses like the pros and I believe the number will increase. However, many colleges employ the running game as their primary weapon. Thus the college passer is quite often not developed enough to become a good pocket passer. Still, many college passers are excellent runners and thus pose a tremendous threat every time they handle the ball.

## The passer is the key

The effectiveness of any team's pocket passing attack depends directly on the ability of the passer. He must have the strength to throw to either sideline from any spot between the hash-marks. On the sideline patterns the pass must be a hard linedrive. The passer's timing must be developed to a high degree of efficiency. Finally, he must have sufficient playing experience to have developed those automatic reactions, such as coolness under fire, that only actual game experience can teach.

How much use, then, can we at the high-school level make of the wide-open attack as developed from the pocket pass?

That depends solely on your passer. Not very many high-school boys have been developed quickly enough to do the job. Indeed, not many college passers have reached this level. Even if you have the passer, there is no assurance that you will have receivers for him. But these difficulties should not prevent you from considering such an attack because such an attack can make your offense nearly unstoppable. By exerting a great effort on the passing game, we have developed many good passers and receivers. With hard work you can quite often develop a passer who can throw effectively to any area of the field from a pocket.

This past season, we had two senior passers, who had had considerable experience and the strength and accuracy to do the job. Because they threw the sideline pass well, we ran most of our plays with both ends split wide. In a 7–2 season, the two boys completed 101 passes in 173 attempts for over 1300 yards and 16 touchdowns. As usual this team had many light boys and at the beginning of the season showed little promise.

## Influence of the College Game

The play of high-school football is most immediately affected by college football. The sprint series is an indication of the amount of stress that is placed on the passer who can run. There are few college quarterbacks who pass only. Some colleges have a reserve quarterback in this category for use when an obvious passing situation arises.

Because college football is so successful in developing ground games, the running passer is the ideal complement to a college team's attack. When defenses learn to stop this type of game, colleges will in turn find themselves being influenced by the professionals. Because of the age and caliber of the boy, high schools are capable of developing strong ground games. The rollout pass or running pass is ideally suited to the offense of a team with a strong ground game.

Ball control, as employed by a good running attack, is one

of the best ways to win ball games. If you are unable to establish such a ground game because of the various limiting factors, then you may find yourself turning to a wide-open style of attack.

## Influence of the Professionals

There is no doubt that the game as played by professionals has affected all of our thinking. All of these teams use the same basic offense—ample proof, I believe, that the pro attack is the most efficient offensive football. All football teams don't employ this attack because not all players are old enough and mature enough. The younger the boy the less effect the pro attack will have on his game.

As pro techniques filter down, they will gradually affect the high school game. They already have. Split ends, flankers, tackle-eligible passes—all are seen in high-school games today. The effective passing attack will become so necessary for teams of average ability that coaches who ignore it will find themselves quite handicapped.

Figure 78 shows many of the patterns that individual receivers may run. By staying in the pocket all of these receivers remain a threat. The whole picture is so complicated an arrangement that a defense can hardly cover everything.

Our present slot formation with both ends split creates the same opportunities for receivers to run the various patterns. Although the slot back enables us to run a reverse, it is at the expense of having less effective blocking from that spot. Eventually we may develop to the point where we will feel compelled to give up the slot back for the tight end. But this may never come about because it may be too difficult to find the proper boy to play the tight end.

### Personnel problems created by the pro attack

The evolution of the various offenses toward the pro attack will cause all of us to think differently about how to fill back-

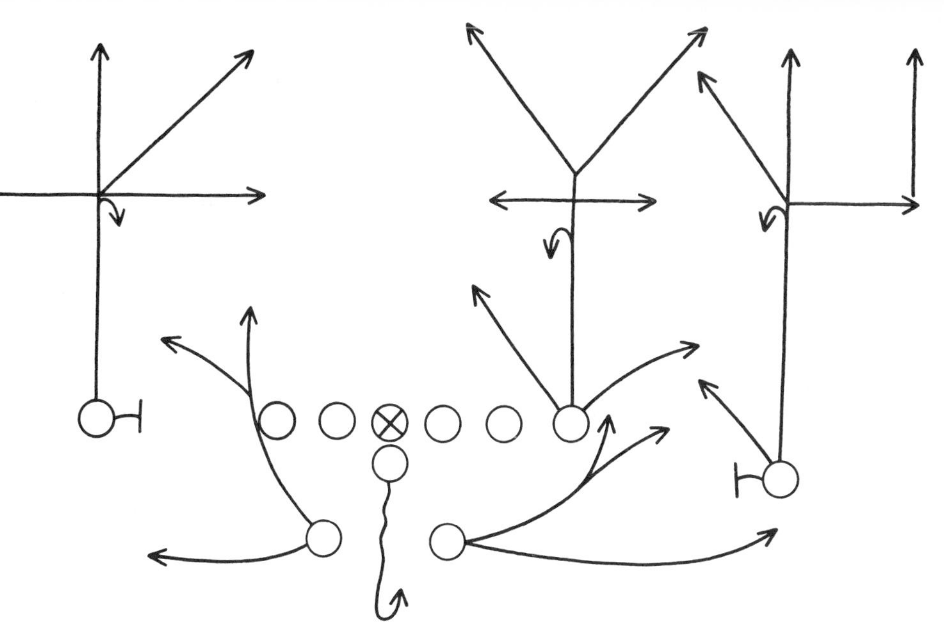

Figure 78

field and end positions. The small, speedy boy who was your scatback before may become a split end or flanker. The two backs must be able to do everything well. They must be big enough to block—one of their most important tasks. Naturally they must be able to run well and fast. They must have pass-receiving abilities. The tight end must be of a good size, be an excellent blocker, and have at least fair receiving ability. He is the hardest type to find because he would probably also make a good back.

It is hard to find just the right boys to fill these spots and have the passer as well. We are faced with problems now in trying to fill the positions in our own offense. Most high-school coaches find that they are forced to compromise and fill several positions with boys who don't have all the desirable abilities. Of course, this is one reason why the high-school game is so interesting.

Your players have a great deal to do with the selection and development of your offense. Because our boys are small, we have been forced into the wide-open game. However, the play of the professionals will continually affect the high-school game and cause it to move toward the wide-open offense.

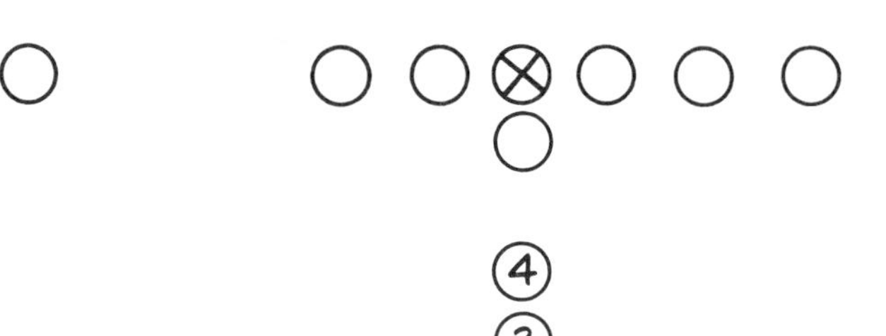


**Figure 79**

## The Tandem Backs

The Pro-style attack tends to eliminate the small, speedy scatback because he cannot block well. At times you may have a small boy who is such a terrific runner that you must use him as a running back. I have just such a back returning next season.

A new wrinkle to the game, the pre-shift formation, can very well be the answer to putting the small speedster back into the backfield.

The team assumes a pre-shift position with both backs directly behind the quarterback, the speedster being the deep back (see Figure 79). This boy can be put in motion as a quick-pitch threat or as a pass-receiver threat. Some of your plays can be run from this pre-shift arrangement. When the backs shift into a formation, the small boy can move up to the left or right of your larger blocking back. The play is run so quickly afterwards that the defense has little time to react to the way your players are positioned.

By carefully planning your offense, you can keep the amount of blocking done by your small back to a minimum. He can run off-tackle or around either end and you can use your bigger back mainly as a blocker and for running your inside plays. The defense will be able to read your offense to some extent by the way you line up, so you must include offensive situations that will counteract defensive keying.

Next season we will be forced to use this type of shifting. I am grateful to the coach that originated this idea. I am sure that I would never have found such an ideal solution on my own.

ELEVEN

# ATTACKING PASS DEFENSES

"When a pass is thrown there are three things that can happen, one good and two bad." That is, it will be complete, incomplete or intercepted. Many coaches who emphasize the running game abide by this cliché. While the bad outweighs the good, if a pass is completed the reward is worth the risk.

There is one important thing a passing team has—initiative. The team with initiative has an immediate advantage. It puts pressure on its opponent, who must spend a lot of time during the week before the game on pass defense. The opponent is forced to concentrate his practice on certain areas because he must be prepared to defend against the passing attack.

## Difficulties of Pass Defense

An offensive team can send three receivers downfield where the defense is using six men to cover, and still outnumber the defenders in a particular zone. In pass defense, not all of the defensive backfield is involved in covering the receivers. This gives a considerable advantage to the passing team. Receivers can outnumber defenders in any area by flooding a zone. The offense can avoid the best pass defender by not running any patterns at him except those intended to decoy him out of an area. Most important, the offense can pit its best receiver against the poorest defender. These three advantages arise from the fact that the offense knows in advance what the pattern will be and the defense does not. This places a great burden on the defense.

Another thing that makes pass defense so difficult is that a pass defender must be very skillful. If you were to take two men of equal ability and use one as a receiver and the other as a defender, you would find that the receiver has a decided advantage. He will nearly always be able to get a two or three yard jump on the defender after making his fake. The receiver knows where he is going and when he is faking, and this puts the defender at a decided disadvantage.

### Pass Defense Alternatives

We are all familiar with the three different ways to counter a passing attack.

1. Rushing the passer
2. Holding up the receivers
3. Covering downfield completely

A defense that attempts to do all of these things at the same time will do none of them well. It is physically impossible to do all three well unless you use 14 or 15 players. To cover downfield completely, the defenders should outnumber the receivers. To rush the passer defenders must outnumber blockers in the area they are trying to break through. If they try to hold up the receivers, they will be delayed in carrying out their second assignment, which may be to rush or to drop back.

### Rushing the Passer

The most effective way to stop a high-school passing attack is to get to the passer before he has time to pass. The high-school passer, particularly if he is inexperienced, will be definitely influenced by a concerted rush. He will get caught for huge losses. He will throw the ball away or throw at the wrong time. He will hurry his pass. His vision will be obscured by the rushing linemen. A pass thrown by a distracted passer is seldom a good one, and if intercepted it can spell disaster.

For these reasons you can expect your opponent to try to rush your passer. He is gambling when he does this because his downfield area will not be well covered. If the rushers do not reach the passer quickly, the odds for a completed pass are much better and it will usually result in a longer gain than normal.

**Protect your passer**

The key to preventing a concentrated rush of your passer is in your passer-protection system. As long as your opponent rushes with no more than seven men, your blockers should be able to adjust to the rush. In Chapter 7, on protecting the passer, these situations are presented in detail. If your passer still has sufficient time to pass while being rushed, then the success of your passing attack will force your opponent to hold more men back to help cover the passing zones.

**Passes to use when rushed**

We have been very successful in passing in the four shorter passing zones. For this reason teams have been reluctant to stunt or overload an area in order to provide a good rush on our passer. This suggests that the most effective way to discourage a team from stunting or overloading is to pass successfully in these four short zones. If the defense bothers you with these tactics you should immediately go into your short passing game. The passer will have less time, but there should be a receiver in an uncovered short zone much sooner than he would be in a longer zone.

A team that wants to put extreme pressure on the passer must use extra men in order to outnumber the blockers in a given area. If the defense is successfully rushing your passer without using extra men, then you're not going to win because his men are more determined than yours. These extra rushers will be linebackers, and this means that some of the shorter passing zones will be sparsely covered. Throw your short passes quickly into these areas. Throw passes that require less time and that take advantage of the four short passing zones.

In this situation we throw our pro-left and pro-right passes, hitting either the end or the swinging halfback, both of whom are normally covered by a linebacker. This has been the most effective pass in stopping the "big rush." We also go to our action pass plays and their companion running plays. If the defense has trouble determining pass or run, they will be slower in starting their rush.

### Tight-covering halfbacks

Some teams play their defensive halfbacks tighter in a rushing defense so that they can move quickly into the short zones to cover short passes as well. In this situation we try to throw the long pass. First we roll out to offset the rush and to allow the passer and receiver enough time to maneuver for the long pass. We usually run individual pass patterns that fake a short pass first, and then develop into a long pattern. Rolling out to either side, we use Roger or Louie, out-and-down, hook-and-go, stay-and-go, and go patterns. Sprint-right or sprint-left pass is also very effective against such a rushing defense.

### The rush from one end

Some teams may decide to rush with a tough defensive end or with the end and corner linebacker from one side. In this case we can throw our pass patterns by rolling out away from the rush. We also run screen passes, and fall-off passes to the side of the rush.

## Holding Up the Receivers

Many coaches will not let a receiver get downfield without having someone striking him first on the line of scrimmage. There is a great deal to be said in favor of this tactic. If a receiver is contacted on the line of scrimmage, he is not only delayed in getting downfield but he is usually forced to run his intended path differently.

The ends may be delayed by the defensive ends. Linebackers can be used to hold up receivers, and tackles can hold up receivers from a wide-tackle six-man line. There are some disadvantages to holding up receivers. The man doing the holding will be more vulnerable to a block from the end. The defender must be taught to treat every move of the end as an intended block and that he must first defeat that block. The defender is also delayed in getting to his other assignment, which for a linebacker may be to drop back and cover a flat area.

If a good receiver splits out very wide, some coaches put two men on him, one to hit him on the line of scrimmage and the other to cover him downfield. In this situation the defense in the middle of the field is shy one man and can very well be hurt by a run.

The most successful pass defense our opponents have used against us has been to hold up our receivers on the line of scrimmage. We have recently been able to defeat this strategy so that we no longer are bothered by it. We have run more often to the area in which the holding-up has taken place—usually off-tackle or around the end. We give our ends a good deal of practice on blocking a man who is trying to hold them up. The block is a simple one because the defender is in a higher body position and has more weight on his heels for body control. It is very difficult for a defender to try to delay a receiver and also stop a power running play that is coming right at him.

### Overcoming the delaying of receivers

Another way we have overcome this pass defense is by splitting our receivers wide. The best right end we ever had used to be double-teamed. We would split him real wide, and a linebacker and halfback would both go out with him to delay him at the line of scrimmage and also cover deep. Figure 80 shows the way one team handled this.

We were very successful running our off-tackle play to

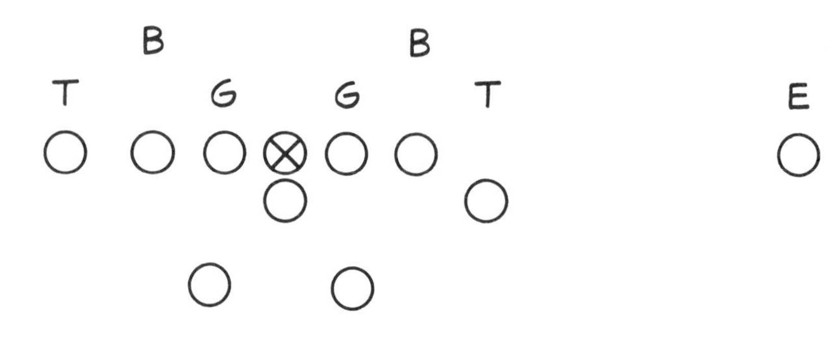


Figure 80

the right and our 46–0 pass to our halfback in the left flat. These two plays accounted for our scoring that day. When the defense began being hurt too much, they would only send out one man with our right end and this is exactly what we wanted. We feel that chances for success are excellent when the defense covers our best receiver with only one man.

We also split both ends real wide, and no team has yet sent two men out on each split end. They may do it on one side, but they would be spreading themselves too thin by using a man to hit each receiver on the line of scrimmage and then another man to cover him deep. If both ends are split wide, at least one of them will no longer be delayed on the line of scrimmage, and we can then run individual pass patterns to this receiver.

## Complete Downfield Coverage

The professionals cover downfield completely and usually rush with only four men. They are compelled by the caliber of the passing to do this. Even the most unknowledgeable fan recognizes that it is very hard to have a good rush on the professional passer. In complete downfield coverage the defensive linemen must be at least as capable as the offensive linemen.

They will have to defeat one blocker, or perhaps two, before they are free to rush the passer. They must put some pressure on the passer. Downfield defense is usually a zone defense, with each defender having an area to cover. A typical defense which gives such coverage is the Oklahoma 5–4 (see Figure 81).

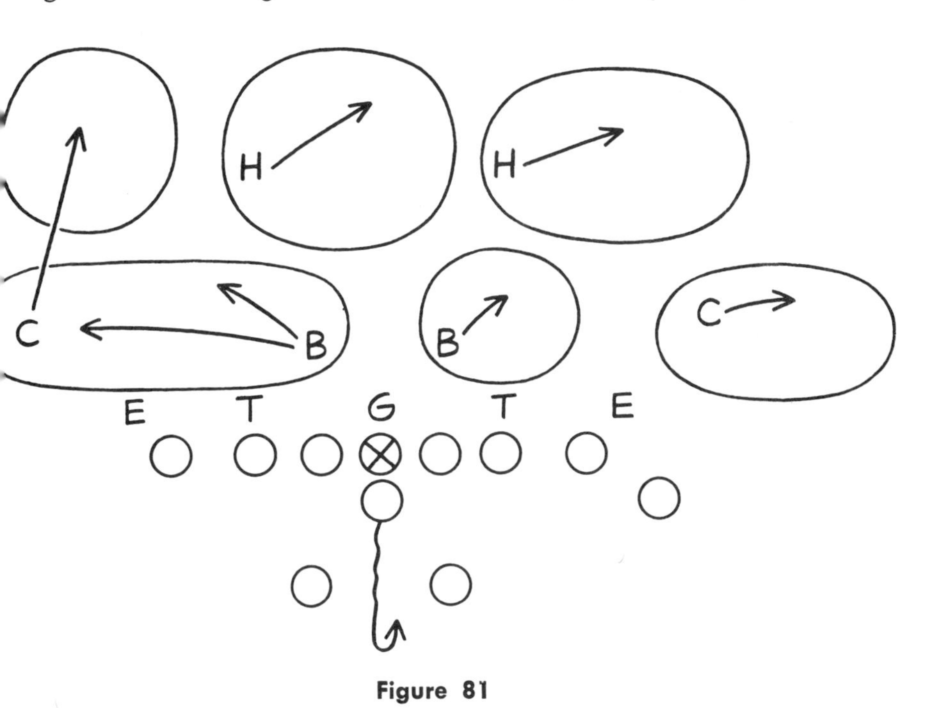


**Figure 81**

In this situation the rotation is predetermined. One corner back takes a deep outside zone, while the halfbacks take the deep middle and other deep outside zones. Note that in the shallow areas the linebacker on the side where the corner back has dropped back now has a double assignment. He must cover the hook area and also the flat area. To actually get complete coverage the defensive right end should drop back into the outside flat area, leaving only a four-man rush. In either a four- or five-man rush the amount of pressure that can be exerted is directly dependent on the caliber of the linemen.

## Passing against full coverage

Should your opponent present you with a downfield coverage of this type, the first thing you should do is to be grateful. As a passer the thing I appreciated most was ample time. There were plays, though not very many, in which I was able to throw to the third receiver I looked at. To combat complete coverage you must have a good passer, a few good receivers, and an adequate line to protect. The key here is the passer. He must have a good sense of timing. We assume he will have ample time and an open receiver. It is the passer's job to see that the ball arrives on time.

Your passer can help by not looking at the intended receiver first. Defensive personnel are trained to watch the passer's eyes for an indication of where he intends to throw. He will have sufficient time to look elsewhere and even to make a fake in another direction before looking at the intended receiver. If you have a passer who is a fair runner, only a very poor defense would drop all the way back. We encourage our passer to drift out of his pocket if he feels no pressure from one side or the other. Some of the longest runs in a ball game are often made by the quarterback who has decided to take off on his own on a pass play.

## Type of pass

No matter what pass you try against complete downfield coverage, a defensive man will always be in the area of the receiver. You will find a receiver in the clear only if the defense is fooled by an action pass. If you split your ends wide, each defender's zone will be widened and you will force the defense to use man-to-man coverage. You can also line up your best receiver against the poorest defender and run an individual pass pattern. Flooding a defensive zone is also very effective against complete coverage. Your action passes should be very effective if properly executed, and both running plays and pass plays of your action series should be successful. To defeat complete coverage, therefore, you can spread, flood zones and run action passes; but the key to success will be the accuracy of your passer's timing.

## Defeating Man-to-Man Coverage

Man-to-man coverage requires a defender to be assigned to each potential receiver and to cover him no matter where he goes. It is a very easy pass defense to use but requires superior personnel for effective execution. The linebackers responsible for running plays and for covering halfbacks on pass plays have very difficult tasks to perform and must be very capable football players. A linebacker needs to be deceived only once into thinking a pass is a running play and you have a touchdown.

Figure 82 shows a typical man-to-man defensive alignment. Pro-left pass is diagramed to show the type of pattern we would want to run. We try to clear a deep defensive zone by running the deep defender out of it and then sending a halfback down into this zone. This results in the man-to-man coverage of a halfback by a linebacker.

**Figure 82**

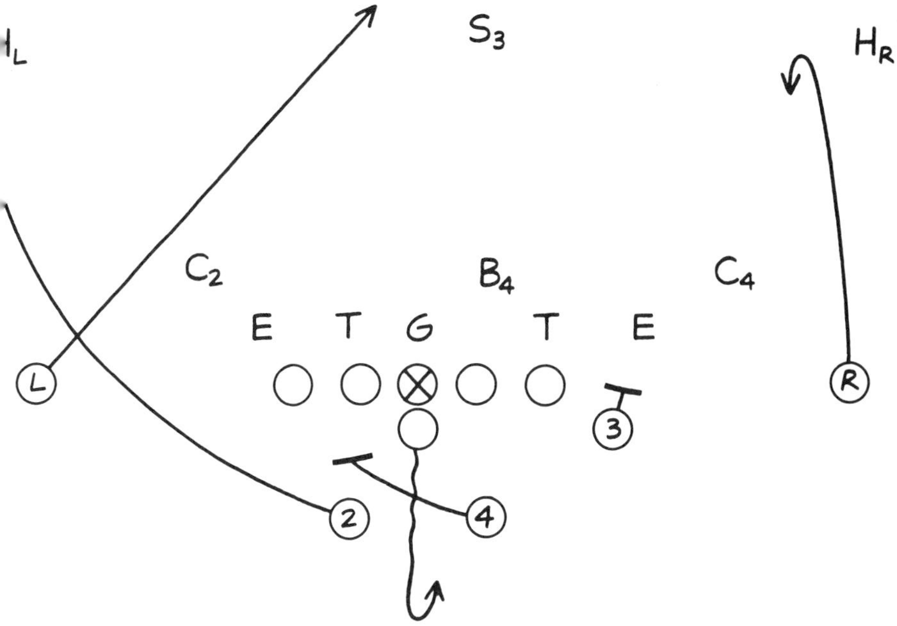

It would seem that the only advantage to employing a man-to-man pass defense is that the coach will know which defender to blame when a pass is caught. Since there is too great an opportunity for a defender to make a fatal mistake, we seldom face a strictly man-to-man defense. Many of our opponents do cover a few of our receivers man-to-man, particularly backs running patterns from the deep set position in our backfield. Whenever possible we split our receivers real wide in an attempt to force our opponent into man-to-man coverage.

### Type of pass

Any pass that will pit a good man against a poorer man should be used against man-to-man defense. Your decoy receivers should clear their defenders from a zone so that the intended receiver will have only one man to beat in this zone.

For split receivers, we run our Roger and Louie individual passes. These patterns include sideline, hook, stay, go, out-and-down, hook-and-go and any other moves that the receiver feels can defeat his opponent. For our backs we run pro passes, screens, fall-offs, and off-tackle action passes. We hit our slot back on the sprint pass, trail-out, trail-in, hook-go and the cross pass. If we find man-to-man coverage on only one receiver, such as the left halfback, we improvise pass paths for him to take proper advantage of the situation.

While man-to-man coverage is the easiest pass defense to teach, it definitely is the poorest type at the high-school level. It requires superior defensive personnel to be effective. A high-school boy is just not experienced enough to properly execute his part.

## Zone Coverage

As zone pass coverage is used almost exclusively in high-school football, it seems to be the best method. Perhaps it would be more precise to say, zone pass defense is the least poor of all pass defenses. The only way to have a perfect pass defense is to use more than eleven men. However, a pass defense can be made excellent by the people playing it. They must know their assignments thoroughly and be very alert and aggressive in carrying them out.

**Weakness of zone defense**

Zone pass defense has so many obvious weaknesses that it is a wonder it is used at all.

1. Unless the defense rushes with only four men not all of the zones will be covered. One man, usually a linebacker, is often assigned to cover both a hook and a flat zone.
2. The receivers are not continually covered as they pass from one zone to another.
3. Coverage deep downfield can become confusing when a deep receiver is running diagonally from one zone into another.
4. Offensive pass patterns will attempt to flood a zone and outnumber the defenders in a given area.
5. By splitting wide on one or both sides, the offense can spread the zone and give each defender a larger area to cover.

**Advantages of zone defense**

The advantages of zone defense are also many.

1. It is easy to teach.
2. Every receiver if not actually covered will find a defender close by.
3. It is the most effective defense for preventing the long touchdown pass.
4. When a pass is caught, the defenders closing in should be many and should quickly cover the receiver.
5. Linemen do not have to chase speedy backs deep downfield.
6. Most high-school passers are of only average ability.

They will look where they are going to throw. On long passes the ball will be in the air a long time, and the passer's accuracy and sense of timing will not be very good.

7. On a long pass several defenders should be at the point of reception by the time the ball arrives.
8. Blocking on interceptions can quickly be formed from a zone defense.

## Normal zone coverage

Most zone defenses employ a 3–3 type of defensive coverage. Three men are assigned deep outside, deep middle, and deep outside. The other three men are assigned the four shorter passing zones, the two hook areas and the two flat areas. The linebacker who is assigned two zones to cover is usually given a key or some sort of rule to help him do the job. This leaves five men to rush the passer and an occasional linebacker to rush by stunting.

Figure 83

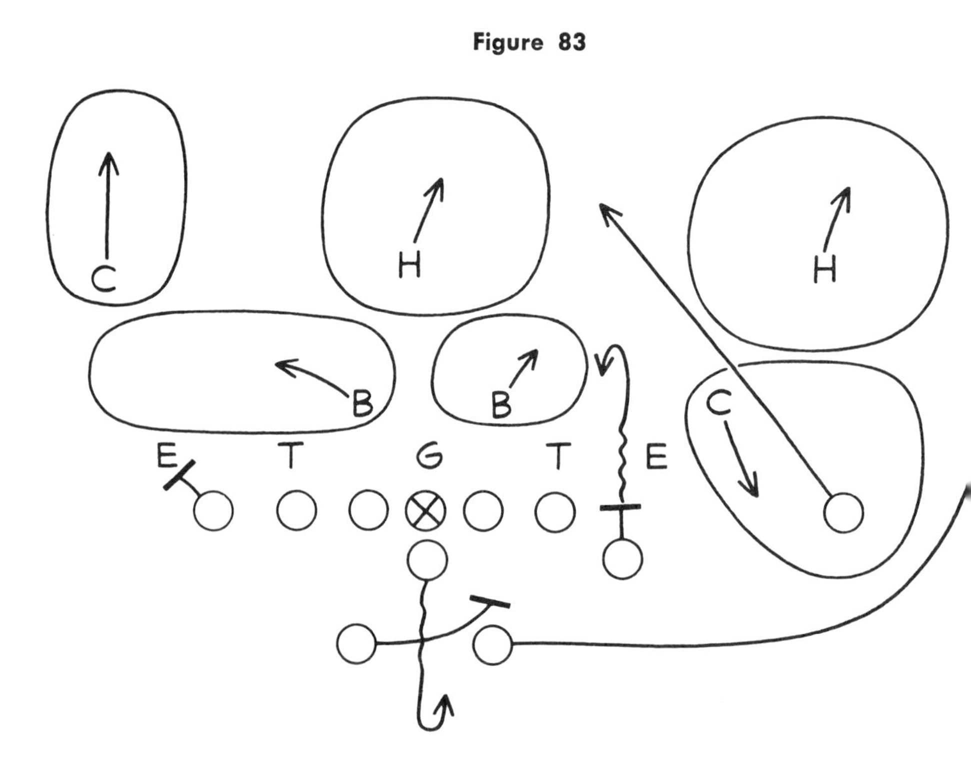

Although a defense may not always look like 3–3 coverage, it will usually end up that way. The umbrella defense, which has a two-deep appearance will, by predetermined rotation or rotation by keying, end up with three-deep coverage. Figure 83 shows the way this zone would cover our pro-right pass.

## Defeating a Zone Pass Defense

### Force some man-to-man coverage

The one thing we don't want to happen to our own zone pass defense is to have it forced into some man-to-man coverage. Therefore, the first thing we try to do is force our opponent into man-to-man coverage by splitting a receiver, or preferably two receivers, real wide. The defense is forced either to stretch their zones and leave large gaps, or to use some man-to-man coverage.

Splitting both receivers real wide will really open up the pass defense and complicate your opponent's job of pass defense. In Figure 84, the defensive halfbacks are forced to cover the split ends man-to-man if the ends start by running a deep outside pattern. It is then difficult for the defense to cover a shallower outside zone as on our Trail-out pass. If the corner tries to cover the slot man, the slot runs his flat pattern a little deeper. If the safety man attempts to cover the slot back in the flat, we will have forced the defense into deep man-to-man coverage.

On the Trail-out pass, if the coverage becomes strictly man-to-man, the left end has only one man to beat for six points. With our receivers split real wide, we run our Trail-out pass, sprint-out pass, and pro passes. Our Louie and Roger individual passes are used a great deal with the patterns that exploit the outside passing zones; that is, the stay, stay-go, hook, sideline, out-and-down, and the hook-go patterns. Also, to complicate the defense's problems, we run our tackle-eligible pass from this formation.

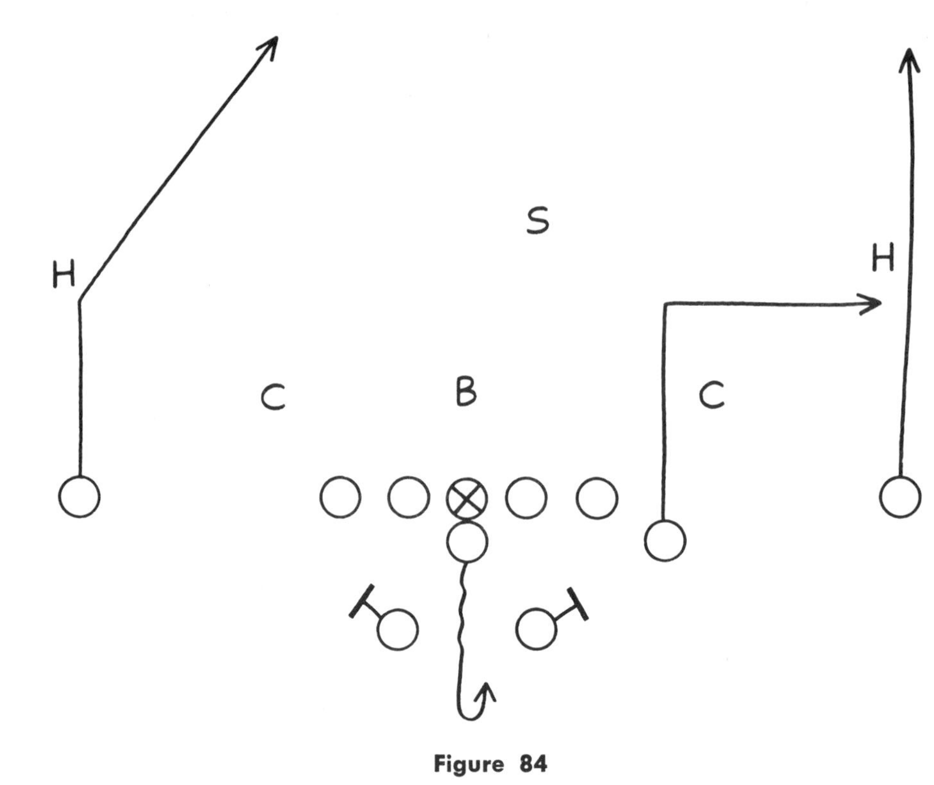


**Figure 84**

## Flooding zones

A very effective way to defeat a zone pass defense is to flood defensive zones with a surplus of receivers. A rollout pass can do this quite effectively (see Figure 85). This is normally done by running three receivers into two defensive zones. Trail-out pass—fall off right will place three receivers down the right sideline, one shallow, one in the deep flat, and one deep outside. Pro-right pass thrown to the slot back on a delayed hook will effectively flood the inside hook zone. In addition to these two passes, we will flood zones by slipping one of our two deep backs into one of our standard pass patterns.

When you flood a zone, there should be at least one receiver in the clear. There will be defenders nearby, however, who will begin to move toward the receiver once the ball is thrown. To be successful in flooding areas, your passer must be accurate, throw hard and have good timing.

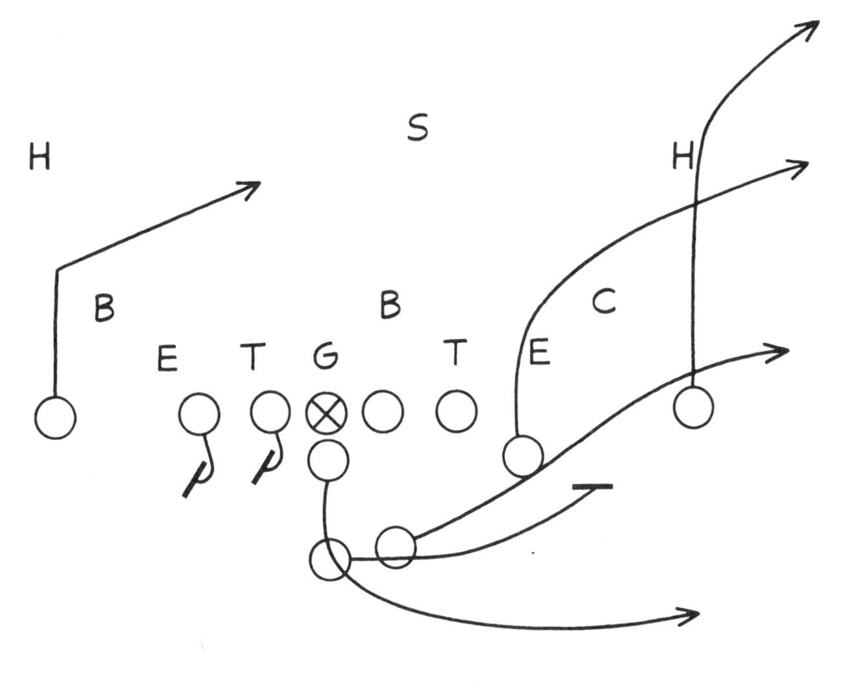


**Figure 85**

### Pass into "in-between" areas

In attacking a zone pass defense we try to take advantage of its inherent weaknesses. Receivers passing from one zone to another will be momentarily open. Our Trail-in pass is our most effective pass because it is designed to hit our trailing end in the defensive "blind" spots; that is, hit him when he is between zones. Figure 5 in Chapter 2 demonstrates this quite well. Our hook-go standard pass pattern is executed so that the paths are run dead between defensive zones. This greatly confuses the defense because they don't quite know who is to cover which receiver. By confusing the defense momentarily, your receivers will break into the open for a short period of time.

### The passer is the key

The secret to passing successfully against a zone is to have a good passer. The more time and coaching you devote to your passer, the better your chances are for a successful passing game. Zone defense relies a good deal on the inadequacy of the passer, particularly with respect to his timing and accuracy. Pass patterns are secondary. Develop an outstanding passer along with capable receivers and any well-conceived pattern should have reasonable success. The best way to beat any pass defense is to have a good passer and the best way to beat a good passer is not to give him enough time to pass.

## Perfect Your Own Pass Defense

Because we are basically a passing team, one of the hidden benefits of the time we spend on our passing offense is that defensive skills are being developed at the same time. When pass-protection blocking is being taught to a lineman, the defensive lineman is also learning how to avoid a block and how to rush the passer. We throw our pass patterns a great deal in dummy scrimmage and there is no better pass defense to throw against than your own. Our passing attack is varied enough so that our own defense is put to a real test in this situation.

### Become a pass defense expert

The best way to attack any pass defense is to become completely familiar with all of the various types of pass defense. If you employ a certain pass defense yourself, you are well aware of its weaknesses. If your opponent uses the same defense, it certainly is going to have the same weaknesses. Because we spend considerable practice time on our pass offensive, we also spend an equivalent amount of time on pass defense. We have learned a great deal about pass defense in our own practices. All the information we can absorb on pass defense will be extremely helpful in attacking our opponent's pass defense.

TWELVE

# THE WEEK OF THE GAME

A football coach today has the opportunity to do much creative and original thinking. The day of the standard situation is gone forever. There are really no standard solutions to the many problems that confront a modern coach. The only bounds and restrictions placed on the maneuvers of offensive and defensive play are the rules. Coaches today do not restrict themselves to any set offense. Unbalanced lines, split ends, flankers, motions, spreads and "mongrel" formations are now used to such an extent that most offenses could be termed "multiple." Using one defense for an entire season also belongs to ancient history.

The fact that coaches are now so flexible in their thinking and planning has introduced a quantity into the game that the average football fan is not really aware of. The outcome of a game is very often decided by the abilities of the coaches on the sidelines to think and react quickly. A coach is therefore compelled to think hard both during the game and in the preparation for it.

I consider each game a battle of wits between myself and the opposing coach. Since I expect my team to think that they are the better team and can win, I must in turn feel confident of my own ability to outthink my opponent. Just as a team can't win all the games, neither can a coach win all these intellectual struggles. I have been outfoxed often enough, but that does not dampen my spirits. To be so outwitted teaches us a great deal and should drive us to greater efforts to improve our knowledge of all aspects of the game.

## Be Prepared for Anything

I recall speaking with a coach the night before his team was to play. I asked him what he expected his opponent to do and how he planned to defend. He expected his opponent to run a wing "T" formation from a balanced line. I was quite surprised because I knew that this team often ran from an unbalanced line in the past. I then asked him how he intended to adjust should this team come out unbalanced. He said he would be "done for" if this happened because he had not prepared for it. One of our scouts who watched the game reported that the opponent ran unbalanced all day. This coach not only lost what should have been a close game by over 40 points, but he is no longer coaching today.

You must never be so unprepared for your opponent. The fact that a certain team "always" runs from a single wing does not permit you to overlook the possibility that they may change for your game. This means that you should prepare yourself and your team to meet certain general situations regardless of who your next opponent is.

## Combating Various Offensive Formations

We have two systems of defense for the entire season upon which we base our defensive planning. In addition to these basic systems, we often have a special defense for a certain opponent. If this special defense fails, at least we have adequate defenses to fall back on. Our basic defenses must therefore be taught in such a way that adjustments to any reasonable offensive formation a team might use are automatic. Our team is taught to line up each of the two basic defensive systems against unbalanced lines, overshifted backs, split receivers, spreads and other offensive set-ups that any team could run against us. Although a team may surprise us with a new formation, at least we can quickly adjust so that we won't be outmanned in any one area. This ability has come to our rescue more than once.

We have an excellent drill for teaching our defense to recognize and adapt to these different formations. We have our junior varsity team huddle up and then quickly come out of the huddle into a formation and quickly snap the ball. The defense must immediately recognize the formations and adjust to each. At the snap of the ball the defenders take only the first several steps of their moves. The offense does not run any plays in this drill, just formations. This enables you to practice lining up on a great many situations in a very short time. We use this drill twice a week for 15 minutes each time. Our primary concern is that the boys can line up properly when confronted by an unexpected formation. If they line up correctly and are good players, they should be able to do the job. Keep in mind that your opponent cannot perform as well from a new formation. The main reason he would use it is to attempt to outmaneuver you.

Because an opponent may try so many offensive formations and tricks, it is necessary that your rules for adjustment be relatively simple. Your defensive system must be well conceived and its rules formulated for the various adjustments before you present it to your squad. We find that developing a defensive system is a very complex and time-consuming task. But it is imperative that your completed defense be uncomplicated. Coaches must examine all the possibilities of the defense but should present only the simplified conclusions to their players. The simpler the rules are to remember, the more a boy will be able to concentrate on performing his defensive duties.

## Combating Various Defenses

No defense should take a team by surprise. The old standard type of defense is no longer with us. There seem to be no rigid rules for setting up defenses, and so we are faced with various types of multiple defense. Therefore, we all spend much of our time teaching the blocking assignments against various defenses. We divide our work on odd and even defenses about equally. Because we emphasize offensive blocking rules, we should automatically be able to handle the majority of defenses that are presented to us. However, there are special defensive maneuvers we should be prepared for.

A passing team must be prepared to handle shooting linebackers. The thing that will hurt a passing game most is a concentrated rush. By splitting the ends, we can tie up five men, the three deep men and the two corners, and keep them from rushing the passer. Therefore, the rush will be a six-man rush or if the defense really gambles, a seven-man rush at the most. We must be prepared for such rushes. The entire team practices defending against such stunting, both dummy and live. We take seven men and put them on defense with a coach directing them. Then they are lined up in a 5–2 or a 4–3, an overloaded, and any other formation that the coach can come up with. All kinds of stunts are tried and each offensive man must pick up one defensive man. In spite of this preparation, at times a team has been able to rush us because our blockers have made mistakes such as two men blocking one man.

**Figure 86**

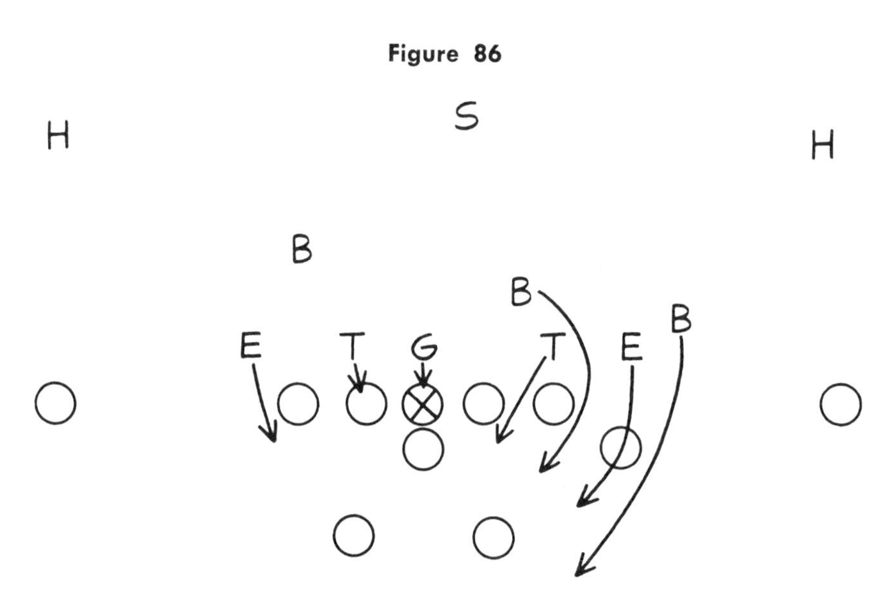

Such a problem is illustrated in Figure 86. With a seven man rush in progress, we quickly held in our slot back in order to have eight men blocking. Pressure was exerted from the right. Our right tackle, an experienced boy, blocked the tackle who was also being picked up by our guard. The tackle should have area blocked and thereby picked up the linebacker. This stunting shut off our pocket pass for the day. We started rolling out and throwing pro passes, and had a respectable 16 for 30 completion rate for the day. Our tackle had practiced enough so that he should have adjusted immediately. But, I, too, was at fault because I was unable to make the proper adjustments during the game. Coaches as well as players have their bad days.

Gap and stunting defenses are also apt to be used against you, and your team must have had practice time in working against them. An 8-gap goal line defense is easy to block because your blockers have excellent blocking angles. But you must practice running against such a set-up because it is so easy to leave one vital defender unblocked.

One more consideration that should be mentioned is that both you and your signal callers should become very familiar with the general weakness of the various defensive set-ups. A four-man line is usually weak on the outside. Slanting defenses usually are called toward the wide side of the field. You can impart some of this information to your signal caller, but you must be an expert in this area. No defense should stop your offense, all things being equal. Every defense has a weakness, and you must be adept at spotting it and quickly attacking it. Although we are a lighter team and a passing team, a large number of our games have been won through our ability to pick apart the defense.

## Knowledge of the Rules

So many important things must be taught that it seems impossible to find the time to do all we wish. One area that must be well covered is the rules of the game. The coach must be an expert on, and the boys must be conversant with, the rules.

At unexpected moments in a ball game, knowledge of the rules can directly affect the outcome. An offensive player should know that the kickoff is a live ball after it goes 10 yards; yet how often does a defensive man come down and recover the kickoff in a good field position, perhaps for a score? A quarterback should know all the ways of stopping the clock. Coaches are often penalized for making illegal substitutions. A coach can never look worse to the spectators than when he or his team makes a mistake because of not knowing the rules. More important, such mistakes often decide the outcome of the game.

This is one area where our midget and junior high-school program make a large contribution. A great deal of the basic rule teaching can and should be done at the lower levels. By the time these boys are in high school, they should have a good knowledge of the basic rules to build on. By keeping yourself and your team abreast of the latest rules of the game, you should be able to meet any unexpected situations promptly, perhaps to your advantage.

## Game Week Preparation—Coaches Meetings

The week of the game is indeed a busy one for us all. The hours spent in practice and preparation never seem to be enough. This means that considerable planning is necessary if every minute of practice time is to be wisely used. The coaching staff has much to do and coaches meetings take up much free time. Any successful coach devotes nearly every waking hour to football during the fall, and his wife knows how little she will see of him during this time. Once the season starts our coaches meetings run something like this: Some of the work is done during one free period we have together each school day, but most of it is done in the evening.

1. *Sunday night.* Go over previous Saturday films, compile statistics. Begin planning for next week's opponent.
2. *Monday night.* Finish planning for coming game. Lay out week's practice schedule.
3. *Wednesday night.* Review defensive and offensive plans and make necessary changes.
4. *Friday night.* Go over last year's film of the opponent to be scouted with our scouts. Discuss our personnel and our game plans for Saturday.

**Preparing your defense**

From scouting reports, films of previous seasons, and our knowledge of the opposing coach, we have a pretty good idea of what to expect on Saturday. We are nearly positive of their basic offensive formations, although as previously pointed out, we must be prepared to meet the unexpected. As far as defense is concerned, a study of your own offensive abilities along with a review of the opposing coach's ideas may enable you to make a good guess about the defense you will see.

During the coaches' meetings Sunday and Monday nights, you and your coaches must hammer out your defensive plans for the game. You know what your opponent does offensively and know his strengths and weaknesses. You must then consider your own defensive alignments and your players in order to adapt them to your opponent. During this time you may also wish to put in one special defense, which is often the case with us.

Our coaches meetings on these occasions run something like this:

1. Look at films of last year's game.
2. Look over play cards made up on opponent from last year's film.
3. Listen to presentation of scouting report on the offense.
4. Make up play cards of opponent this season.
5. Set up defensive systems against this offense and make necessary adjustments.
6. Set up a special defense if desired.

7. Write up defenses on cards for presentation to the team.
8. Examine old films and scouting reports for opponent's possible defenses.
9. Plan tentative offensive attack against opponent.
10. Discuss and list possible unexpected developments and how we as coaches will react to them.

Everything looks neat and clear cut when put in outline form, but we are all aware that a good coaches meeting is not a cut and dried affair. We have a procedure to follow, necessarily, but we often get bogged down in certain areas. Items one through four are straightforward enough and are easily accomplished. Then the fun begins.

In lining up our defensive system against our opponent's attack there are quite often apparent weaknesses in the defense. Usually a simple adjustment will correct such a weakness. However, every time a simple adjustment is made, the coaching staff must refer again to the entire defense to reconsider its soundness. Fitting your defense to your opponent usually turns into a very time-consuming job.

If you encourage your assistants to be students of the game, they should be able to make a large contribution in this work. You may not be able to see any fault in a defense because you are quite prejudiced in its favor. An alert assistant will often spot the error immediately. Value highly the opinions of your assistants. Be critical of them only when they fail to seek to improve themselves or to make an effort to try to outthink your opponent.

Coaches must spend much time preparing the defense. There may be as many as twenty ways to combat a particular offense, and the coaching staff must explore the pros and cons of each way. Your final defensive solution will probably contain a combination of several of these ways and be a composite of the ideas of members of your staff. It would be a foolish coach indeed who did not take advantage of the brain power of his assistants.

A particularly enjoyable part of this defensive planning is the consideration of a special defense. Each coach takes his work to a separate corner and diagrams a defense that he feels will work. Any ideas that can be defended are considered. One season, we used a three-man line in our biggest game as a result of this kind of collaboration. The defense helped us to win and was used considerably during the game because the coaching staff could find no real reason why it wasn't the best defense to do the job. This encourages your assistants to do a good amount of original thinking because if a coach's defense is selected, he feels great pride and has the good feeling of making a contribution. Win your coaches' assistance by using them.

**Preparing your offense**

We usually know the defensive philosophy of the opposing coach. This information is considered in relation to our offensive capabilities and the strengths and weaknesses of the opponent's personnel. Our pre-game plan of attack is tentative and the course of the ball game will determine what we do offensively. We may put in a special play in order to exploit some weakness, but the offensive practice during the week is distributed quite evenly on all our plays.

One of our opponents has been notoriously weak in pass defense. Every year we consistently beat this bigger, stronger team by immediately going to the air. We hardly bother with our ground game because we know from previous experience that this team has to stop our passing to beat us. Another opponent always has his big linemen in a four-point stance and pinching very hard. One year he didn't do this and we beat him badly. We have come to expect this type of defensive play from this opponent.

In investigating our opponent's personnel we are most directly concerned with the abilities of the defensive halfbacks and the linebackers. When we uncover the weaker pass defenders, our plan of attack includes pitting our best receivers against these men.

## Introducing Your Plans at Practice

### Offensive plans

Integrating your offensive plans for your forthcoming opponent into your practices involves little difficulty. We make up cards of several possible defenses we think our opponent may use. We then use these cards for our junior varsity team to run against our varsity in both dummy and live scrimmage. During these offense drills we constantly emphasize the tactics we want to exploit on Saturday. Our passing drills emphasize the patterns we plan to run. If we feel that our opponent will stunt or shoot linebackers, our line coach spends more time than usual on these tactics. Throughout this offensive preparation, don't forget to work on your over-all offense. You are trying to outguess your opponent but you will not always be able to. Your entire offense should be continually practiced so that any part of it is ready when called upon.

### Defensive plans

Incorporating your defensive plans into practice is quite different from working the offensive plans. Our plans must be completed and ready for Tuesday's practice. The defense is introduced and explained to the team and then is practiced dummy. Our jayvees will come out of the huddle in the various offensive formations of our opponent and just snap the ball as in the drill previously explained. They will then run our opponent's plays against our defense with the defensive men not making any movements at all. This is done so that the defense will see how they will be blocked on the various plays and how each play develops. We have found that our personnel receive no benefit from defensive dummy scrimmage if they exercise their defensive maneuvers. They are made to stand still and watch after they adjust to the formation. This defensive work on Tuesday takes no more than thirty minutes to run. We spend most of Tuesday working on the offensive.

On Wednesday, the backs spend ample time working on pass defense. We try to use our first team passer and receivers against our defensive backfield so that our defenders will be working against good personnel only. In addition, the offensive men have the opportunity to work on their passing game. Our opponent's patterns are on play cards, and for the benefit of our offense, our own pass patterns are integrated into this drill.

A good portion of our scrimmage on Wednesday must be devoted to the defense. The team running the opponent's plays must have good personnel so as to be able to test our defense. This is a very big problem for us as is any inter-squad scrimmage. We just don't have enough capable players to make these scrimmages a true test. When it is time to scrimmage, we use our first team reserves and our second team to run our opponent's offense. You will need all your coaches with you for this work. Two coaches must work with the defense, and there must be coaches pushing the offensive team and directing the plays.

Should your defense prove vulnerable to any particular play in scrimmage, you must make a defensive adjustment. If your second team can make yardage on a play they've never practiced, you can be positive that your opponent will do considerably better with it. Sometimes, it seems amazing that all of this careful planning can be made to look ridiculous during a Wednesday scrimmage. Plans often look wonderful until they've actually been put into practice. You have to test your defense during the week and make adjustments to keep your opponent from finding these weaknesses and exploiting them on Saturday.

In your coaches meeting after Wednesday's practice, you must take a hard look at your defense. If second team personnel were able to make progress against it, there is no question that some changes have to be made. Some adjustments can be made during scrimmage. Others may have to be thrashed out at the coaches' meeting. The changes are introduced in Thursday's practice when the defenses are run for formation line-ups and in dummy scrimmage. If we are particularly concerned, a short defensive scrimmage will be run to test the adjustments and to help arrive at a final defensive plan.

Seldom have we had to throw out the entire defensive plan and start from scratch. We wish to avoid this as the "unlearning" and re-teaching problems would make any new defense difficult to learn and execute. Should you be compelled to introduce an entirely new defense on Thursday, you must wait for Saturday to test it. At times it is necessary to make such a change but a last-minute change of the whole defense should be avoided.

The defenses must be complete by the end of Thursday's practice, and you and your staff must be completely satisfied with your defensive plan. Your team must feel the same way. If you lack confidence in your defensive plan, your team will sense it and lose its confidence. A defense employed without confidence and enthusiasm is doomed to failure.

## A Practice Schedule

Our practice schedules are flexible because many of the things worked on are dictated by our play in last week's game as well as by a consideration of our forthcoming opponent. If we tackled poorly, more practice time is devoted to tackling the following week. However, a typical week's practice would be much like this schedule we used in preparation for a game with Gloucester High School, the fourth team on our schedule.

MONDAY

| | | |
|---|---|---|
| 3–4 | Entire team, go over Saturday's films of game with Andover High | |
| 4–5 | *Linemen* | *Backs and Ends* |
| | 1. Another look at Andover film | 1. Work on passing and receiving techniques |
| | 2. Look at last year's Gloucester film | 2. Run pass patterns |

TUESDAY

3–3:10 Light calisthenics or, preferably, a good loosening up drill

3:10–3:30 One-on-one hand-off drill, live

3:30–4:00

| *Lineman and Ends, Live* | *Backs* |
|---|---|
| 1. Trapping | 1. Pass defense drill |
| 2. Near-shoulder block | 2. Plays for timing |
| 3. Reverse-shoulder block | |
| 4. Double-team block | |

4:00–4:30 Introduce defense and run it dummy

4:30–5:15 Scrimmage offense

5:15 Sprints and in—kickers stay out 10 min.

WEDNESDAY

3:00–3:45

| *Linemen* | *Backs and Ends* |
|---|---|
| 1. Light cals or a loosening drill | 1. Passing skills |
| 2. Dummy blocking for pass protection against live stunting and shooting line backers | 2. Pass defense |
| 3. Live pass protection, one-on-one | 3. Protection pass drill, semi-live and live |
| 4. Defensive stunts, dummy | |

3:45–3:55 In and out of huddle—hit seven men sled for offensive timing

3:55–4:15 Offensive dummy scrimmage—running versus standard defense

4:15–4:30 Team scrimmage for protecting passer, live

4:30–5:15 Scrimmage our defense for Gloucester

5:15 Sprints and in—specialists stay out 10 min.

THURSDAY

3:00–3:30 Entire team look at some of last year's Gloucester films

3:30–4:00

| *Linemen* | *Backs and Ends* |
|---|---|
| Offensive assignments, dummy | Pass offense versus pass defense |

4:00–4:15 Tackle, live

4:15–4:30 Kicking game

4:30–5:00 Offense versus anticipated Gloucester defenses, dummy

THURSDAY (cont.)

| | |
|---|---|
| 5:00–5:15 | Final defensive adjustments |
| 5:15 | Sprints and in—specialists stay out |

FRIDAY

| | |
|---|---|
| | No Pads |
| 3:00–3:45 | Go over last year's Gloucester film |
| 3:45–4:30 | 1. Running under punts<br>2. Kickoffs and returns<br>3. Defensive lining up<br>4. Punts and punt return<br>5. Run plays up and down field |
| 4:30 | All in but specialists—passer and receivers work on individual pass patterns for 30 min. |

Don't be too critical of our schedule. We have omitted much from our practices but these omissions could very well be included in the next week's work. Pre-season work has also covered in detail many areas we touch upon only lightly during the season. There are too many phases of the game for all of them to be incorporated into one week's practice. Decisions must be made as to where you need the work the most.

We're all familiar with the expression: "Jack of all trades, master of none." By referring to this schedule, you will see that we obviously set out to master the passing game. In doing so, our biggest concern is that work on fundamentals does not suffer.

By thinking, planning, teaching, and evaluating, a coaching staff can do a great deal toward helping to win the game on Saturday. A football coaching career is ideal for all of us "frustrated" players who are "over the hill." We are no longer able to enjoy the thrill and enjoyment of playing. But this loss is more than compensated for by the thrill of matching wits with our opponent in a game that, once it touches your life, will always be a part of it.

# THIRTEEN

# CONDUCTING THE GAME

Once Friday's practice is finished, some coaches feel that they have done all they are able to and that the fate of the game is in the hands of their players. To some extent this is true in that your team's preparation is completed and it is up to the boys to put all this hard preparation to work. They will be doing the playing; you cannot do their blocking and tackling for them. After Friday's practice your team must be completely prepared, and there is nothing you can do about it if they are not.

The fate of the game, however, is more often in the hands of the coach, particularly if the teams are evenly matched. Football is played by only eleven men on the field, but the twelfth man, the head coach on the sideline, handles the strategy. He must be thoroughly prepared, not only by having carefully planned his strategy, but also by coming to the game with the proper attitude. For he too has a game to play. He must continually match wits with the opposing coach and will constantly be called upon to make key decisions. Your team can play a good game and still lose if you have "played" a poor game. It is therefore our duty to our players that we have ourselves "up" for the game; that we conduct the game to the best of our ability.

I'm sure that all of us are often asked if we enjoy watching the game. My reply is that I don't watch the game but that I work the game. The one drawback to coaching is that you can't watch a game on Saturday afternoon. I become completely engrossed in the conduct of the game and never have time to be a spectator.

Because coaches play such an important role in the conduct of a game, it is unfortunate that they are subject to human frailties. You will have your good days and your bad days. Players aren't the only ones who can "choke" at the critical moment; coaches can "choke" too. Being human we all make our mistakes. Second guess yourself only in so far as it helps you to learn from your errors. After you have made a bad decision, chances are that if you could go back to that moment, you would make the same error again. After all, we can't predict the future. Had your decision proved correct, you would have been a hero.

### Believe You Can Win

I recall going into a game against a very strong opponent at a time when our team was showing less promise than average. Unfortunately all I hoped for was a good showing and an injury-free game. I felt we had very little chance of winning, and there is no doubt that the boys of the squad can sense your feelings no matter how you may try to hide them. We gave away two touchdowns in the first half. With the score at 12–0, both the team and I found out that this team could be beaten. However, it was too late to undo the harm caused by my unfortunate attitude. We lost the game and looked respectable in doing so, just as I had wished for. Had I convinced myself that we could win, I'm sure the team would have sensed this and played much better. Having learned this lesson, two weeks later we defeated by a considerable margin, the only team that was able to beat this much dreaded opponent.

You must sincerely feel that you are capable of beating every team you play, no matter how weak you may be and how strong they are. There is nothing wrong with considering yourself the underdog as long as you are convinced that you can win. *Can win,* not *will win,* is the key to the proper feeling. Convincing yourself that you *will win* is one step away from over-confidence. The only other game we lost that season was the last game, which I had felt certain we were going to win.

## Your Written Preparation

During a game I always carry a clipboard with me. Although nearly everything that I have planned is committed to memory, I think it is necessary to have certain key information at my fingertips in case my memory should fail me.

### Personnel charts

It is necessary for me to have offensive and defensive charts listing all the personnel who will play, and those who may play, in the game. The chart is made up in the formation we are using and under each position are listed the boys who will fill that position. Because we have only a certain number of capable players, quite often a boy will be listed as a starter in one position and as substitute in several other positions. This can lead to a complicated substitution problem if a boy has to be replaced. Any coach wants his eleven best players on the field, so a personnel chart is necessary for a situation like this. If your left tackle is injured, you may replace him with your second-team safety man. The safety man moves to defensive halfback, while the halfback moves up to left end so that the left end can now play left tackle because he is the second best man in that position. Is it any wonder that high-school coaches often have ten or twelve men on the field? My biggest substitution blunder was to have a field goal nullified because twelve men were on the field.

### Offensive plans

I also jot down the basic ideas of our offensive planning.

If we have developed a special play for a game, it would be a shame if we forgot to use it. This information is at my fingertips to insure that the offensive planning of the week before plays a part in the conduct of the offense during the game.

### Defensive alignments

The charts showing our various defenses are also carried with me. If our opponent is successful against a certain defense, I have a picture of it in front of me and am able to adjust much more quickly. Also, I use these defensive charts to refresh the memory of a substitute before putting him into the game.

I carry the opposition's lineup as listed on the program for immediate reference. Finally, I have some blank paper, which I use to sketch defenses, improvise pass patterns, instruct players, and jot down anything else. Adapting the passing game to take advantage of defensive weaknesses is an important part of the coach's job during a game and will be discussed in detail later in this chapter.

## Role of the Assistant Coaches

If you are like me, you don't have enough assistants. I don't have very many assistants to begin with, and several of them must handle the scouting chores. I would like to have four coaches working the game with me: two coaches in the press box with a phone, one coach on the phone at the bench, and my chief assistant "prowling" the sidelines and assisting me during the game. However, I don't have all this help and I have found that I can get along with two coaches. Both of these men must be capable and must have a thorough knowledge of my football system as well as my current game plans.

### Work of the assistant coach

The second assistant's job is to continually analyze and report on the actions of the opponent. He has nothing to do with substitution or strategy. He concerns himself with our offense or defense only if he thinks a certain play or move on our part would exploit a weakness of our opponent. Once the game is under way, I expect this coach to furnish me with a diagram of their defense and to continue to give me information during the course of the game.

Most head coaches assign this coach to the press box where he has the best possible view of the field. For us such an arrangement is not effective principally because communication is poor. I refuse to spend the afternoon on the phones because I would then neglect my other duties. The same is true for my chief assistant. To place a high-school boy on the phone would be a waste of the valuable assistance of the coach in the press box. If he is on the sidelines, this coach can supplement his information by talking with players when they come out of the game. By moving in the legal coaching area, he can usually obtain a fairly good view of their lineups. During halftime we look to this coach for detailed information on our opponent. Since it is his only job, we expect him to have it.

### Work of the line coach

The role of your chief assistant is determined by both his abilities and yours. My coaching abilities and experience are with the backfield, so naturally my chief assistant is my line coach. My present line coach has been with me for four seasons. By working with me for several years, he has become my complement and has come to share my responsibilities. As a result, we have achieved a remarkably high degree of efficiency in working a ball game together. But good assistants don't remain assistants long. They move on, with your help, to become good head coaches. Teaching and training new assistants is therefore a continuous job for a head coach.

My line coach is completely responsible for the line. It sounds like a simple task, but it certainly is not. As he mainly determines who will be in the starting lineup, it is his job to replace them if they are not doing their job or need to be rested. I interfere in this responsibility only if the strategy at the moment does not permit this substitution. Because the rules regarding substitution are strictly enforced, it is necessary that whenever the line coach makes a substitution, he sends the boy to me and I put him into the game. Only one coach, the head coach, should make substitutions.

The offensive and defensive play of individual linemen are closely observed by the line coach. Often a boy who makes a mistake on his charge or on a blocking assignment is removed from the game by the line coach, who then tells him how to correct his mistake and returns him to the game. It is obvious that the line coach often teaches and gives individual instruction during the game. He should therefore know a good deal about the way that you think so that his actions blend into your way of conducting the game. Because I have a capable line coach, I know that the play of the line is being well handled and can concentrate my attention elsewhere.

Last season we had a very successful passing attack but were unable to run because we had small linemen. Most teams would attempt to stop our passing game by "red-dogging" linebackers. As I have previously mentioned, we work on this considerably during the week. During many of our games, our passer would be caught for a loss at the beginning of the game. Our line coach would make the proper blocking adjustments and the passer would have sufficient time for the remainder of the game. Since I knew that the pass blocking assignments were being taken care of, I could focus my attention on the downfield coverage and concentrate on picking apart their pass defense. With the coaches working together in this way, we were able to exploit our passing abilities quite early in the game.

Because he is concerned with both offensive and defensive assignments, the line coach can make a real contribution to the game strategy. He may advise rollout passes because of a particular defensive rush or recommend certain running plays because of good blocking angles or because you have better personnel in a certain area. His role in the development of strategy is advisory, and his information will be a valuable aid to you in conducting the game.

## Coaching Teamwork Is Required

Directing a game is too big a job for one man to do effectively. There is as much need for teamwork among coaches as among players. You must assign responsibilities to your assistants that complement your own over-all responsibilities for the conduct of the game. Then you must see that these men conscientiously meet their responsibilities. A caution: *never permit an assistant to exceed his authority.* If you permit just one encroachment by an assistant into your work, your organization may disintegrate. Every coach may think he is the head coach on the sideline. Then you may have three coaches telling your quarterback what play to call, and substitutions going in and out of the game like people changing trains during the rush hour in the subway. The head coach conducts the game and is only aided by his assistants, though their aid may be considerable.

## The Job of the Head Coach

The head coach must coordinate his own tasks with those of his assistant and produce a total policy of game conduct which emanates from one leader. He is the leader and everything should be done by his direction, all orders coming through him. Team effort is essential to winning, and the primary job of the head coach is to coordinate the efforts of everyone into a smooth working team.

### Substitution

The head coach is responsible for all substitutions although he may be aided in some areas by his assistants. Substitution is a tricky business for us and requires constant alertness. As I have already said one substitution may often involve several position moves on the field. Substitutions must often be made for the purpose of instructing players. If you are a passing team, certain players must be in the game in specified places in order to run a particular pass pattern. Add to this the fact that a coach often sends in plays and it is easy to see that substitution can be a complicated business.

Of course, we do have some automatic substitutions that ease this burden a little. First of all some players play only one way and are available for instruction throughout the game. At Marblehead we do not like to play linemen both ways for the entire game because they should be periodically rested. We try to develop three first-team guards and three first-team tackles. Two play while the third rests. Every time the ball changes hands, the boy who has been resting automatically goes into the game so that another boy can rest. This process continues throughout the game and is handled by the players themselves. With such automatic substitution, most of our players get some rest during the game.

### Observe backs and ends

I assume responsibility for watching the backfield and the ends. Our backs are required to do a good deal of blocking and when they fail in this our offense fails. They can miss assignments, run the wrong hole, or have a bad day, just as any lineman. They are easier to watch than linemen, however, and I find it easy to keep track of the job being done by both offensive and defensive backs and ends. If a back is making a mistake and I don't pick it up, there is a good chance that it won't be uncovered because the other coaches are concerned with other areas. Sometimes they do notice errors that I miss because I am preoccupied with something else.

## Defensive Strategy

Over-all defensive strategy is my responsibility and I am directly aided by my two assistants. Our basic axiom of defense is that you should never allow the offense to get away with the same play more than once. If a play starts to hurt us, we make some adjustments. So that we won't make too hasty a move, we have to discover why the play is working. So we first examine our own personnel. Are they carrying out their assignments? Are they being defeated by superior ability at the point of attack? Perhaps a player is having a bad day and must be removed until he can be "fired up." By substitution and instruction we are often able to stop a successful play without changing our defense.

We often find that a play is successful against us because we are outpositioned in an area. This requires a defensive adjustment or perhaps an entirely new defense. As long as we have defensive systems, there is always a defense that we can change to. Certain defenses are stronger against end runs, while others are more effective against a trapping offense. If our new defensive alignment is no more successful, it must be examined and some new action must be taken.

Our defensive strategy is developed along these lines:

1. Adjust to stop any successful plays
2. Have alternate defensive plans in mind
3. Have sufficient defenses in your systems in the event you must change
4. Be as prepared for the unexpected as possible.

## Offensive Strategy

In order to win, your team must be able to move the ball consistently. The defense is naturally aware of this and will spare no effort or device to prevent it. You must face each game realizing that you will have to solve a defense. The earlier in the game you can do this, the better chance you have to win. If your opponent always adjusts to your success, your task becomes even more difficult.

In the opening moments of a game, you are often too busy to be able to observe very much of your opponent's defense. Remember that you have a coach who is observing it, and by the end of the first series of plays he should be able to give you a preliminary diagram of their defense. The players who rotate in on offense can help your coach diagram the defense. Do not rely too heavily on your players' information because they often do not really know what is going on out there. They are nervous and are making contact. I have often found that the information they give is incorrect. They are often not experienced enough to know just where the man opposite them is lining up. If you lined up men everywhere your players said they were, you would often find the opposition using 12 or 13 men. If the information received from your players does not contradict your other information, chances are that you have the correct story.

**Uncover defensive weaknesses**

"A chain is only as strong as its weakest link." Discover the vulnerable spots in your opponent's defense and attack these without mercy. If you have superior personnel, you may want to defeat your opponent at their strongest point since this would quickly demoralize them. We run our plays at the poorest lineman or to a place made vulnerable by the way they line up. If you discover these weak points and exploit the plays that are working for you, your opponent will be forced to improvise defensive adjustments. Once you have forced him to change his pre-game defensive strategy, you have him on the run.

When he adjusts to your successes, new weaknesses will appear, and it is up to you to spot them and attack them immediately (see Figure 87). Let us assume that our opponent is so concerned about our inside trap play that he pinches the

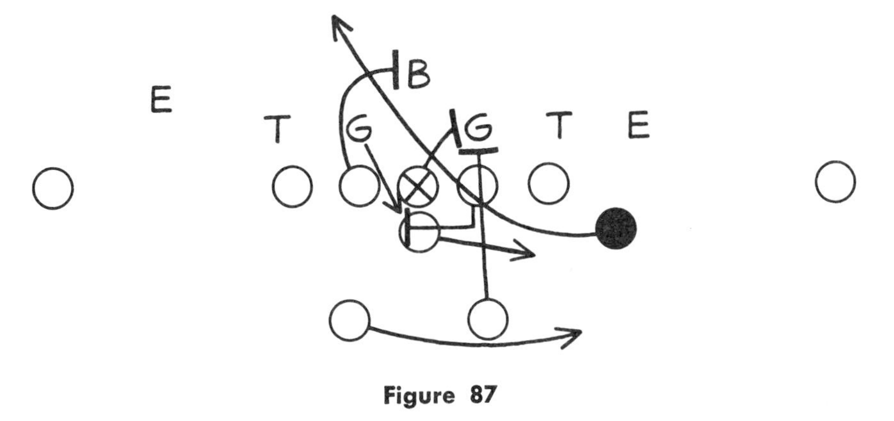


**Figure 87**

guard who is away from our slot man. It is obvious that if we run this trap, the chance for success is rather dim. Our left guard now has a good angle to drive his man in. We have several plays to exploit this hole. We should begin to have success running between the guard and the tackle. Once we do, the defense will adjust. If the guard stops pinching, our trap will work. If they pinch their tackle, the end will be forced to line up on the line of scrimmage. The pro-left pass would then be wide open. Once we start hitting our end for short yardage, the defense will be forced into another adjustment. And so on, throughout the game. The fact that your trap play was successfully defended against at the start could lead to an over-all offensive success for the day. Find the key spot in the defense. Once you have, it is just like having found the key piece of yarn in a sweater: all you have to do is pull it and the whole business will unravel.

**Stay with Success**

Sometimes we fail in that we don't get enough out of a play that is working for us. We shouldn't run such a play three times in a row but should keep coming back to it until the defense can definitely stop it. We should also be running the companion plays of any successful play so as to exploit our success even more. If our off-tackle play to the right, 27–0, is working we should also use the 27–0 pass at the right moment. In looking back at a winning game, we can often credit the success of our offense to just one or two of our plays.

## Fooling the Defense

Every offense has plays that are designed to fool the defense. Be certain to set up your key plays so that you can be reasonably certain of the chance for their success. If you intend to throw a screen pass from your draw play, run the draw play several times first. Then when a similar situation develops, fake the draw play and run the screen pass.

I witnessed an Ivy League game this past season and was quite surprised to see a team run a so-called surprise play when everyone in the ball park knew it was coming. This team was behind by two touchdowns, two minutes left in the game, fourth and ten at midfield. They came out in punt formation, faked the kick and then threw a pass. I don't know why a kick was faked because it seemed obvious they couldn't afford to punt.

In my opinion, if you attempt to fool your opponent, you must take a calculated risk. A fake punt should be tried only in an obvious punting situation. We have had a great deal of success passing on a fourth and one situation. The defense gangs up to stop our power play. We don't have the size to insure the one yard. Sometimes we fake a running play and throw the pass that comes off it. In one game our left end was standing completely alone in the end zone because the defensive halfback came charging up to help stop what looked like an off-tackle play.

Set up your surprise plays and use them only when they will surprise. But remember, there is an element of risk involved. We have lost some games, but have won many more, by using surprise plays. When you are always smaller than your opponents, you have to take chances and play a wide-open brand of ball.

## Making Your Passing Game Go

To make our passing game go, I really have to hustle during the course of a game. We have the reputation of being a passing team, so we are continually being confronted with new situations. It is imperative that we discover as soon as possible just how our opponent intends to stop our passing game.

**Your passer will be rushed**

Many coaches consider that rushing our passer is an excellent way to stop us and we must therefore be prepared to counteract defenses that intend to put the pressure on the passer. We continually practice adjusting pass-blocking assignments. In addition we can hold in our slot back to help with the blocking and just run two-man pass patterns.

We realize that our passer will be rushed at the beginning of the game. When you complete a pass against a rushing defense the receiver has a good deal more running room than is normal. Therefore, your completions should go for considerably more yardage. This has forced our opponents to hold back some of the rushers and thus give our passer more time. We feel that we can exploit either rushing or non-rushing defenses. This is particularly true if our passer can run.

**Breaking down downfield coverage**

Since my line coach is watching the pass-protection blocking, I am particularly concerned with how our opposition intends to cover our receivers. Old films of our opponents do not usually tell us this because we usually have had success in passing against our opponent in the past, so chances are that he will try something new.

Our first play on offense is usually a run and the second is a pass. I look at the opponent's lineup on the first play and then send in a pass play that I think will be successful against it. I believe we might as well find out from the start how they plan to handle our passing attack. We are usually quite successful with our passing attack this early in the game. As long as passing is our game, we might as well start with it right away.

Some defensive lineups are quite spread out at the start for fear of the pass, and this gives our running game a real chance to shine. Quite surprisingly our best running play against such a spread has been the straight dive. In one game our split left end was double-covered. A linebacker would hit him on the line of scrimmage and then a halfback would pick him up downfield. We split him to the very edge of the field and played a ten-man offense against their nine-man defense. By making your opponents fear your passing attack, you create opportunities to do some creative thinking on game strategy.

**Example of exploiting a pass defense**

Perhaps, breaking down a pass defense can be most clearly illustrated by some examples. Figure 88 shows a man-to-man defense we faced in a game last season. The defensive players are marked so as to show who they were covering. We went quickly to work on the left side. The successful paths of the receivers are drawn in.

In our previous game we had considerable success hitting our number two back in the middle or down-and-out toward the sidelines. In this game we exploited our left end who was our best receiver and was considerably better than the man defending him. Our number two back gained considerable yardage on the swing path from the pro-left pattern. The diagonal movement of the left end would freeze the safety man for a moment and he would be late covering the swinging number two back. On the right we were successful with the Roger

**Figure 88**

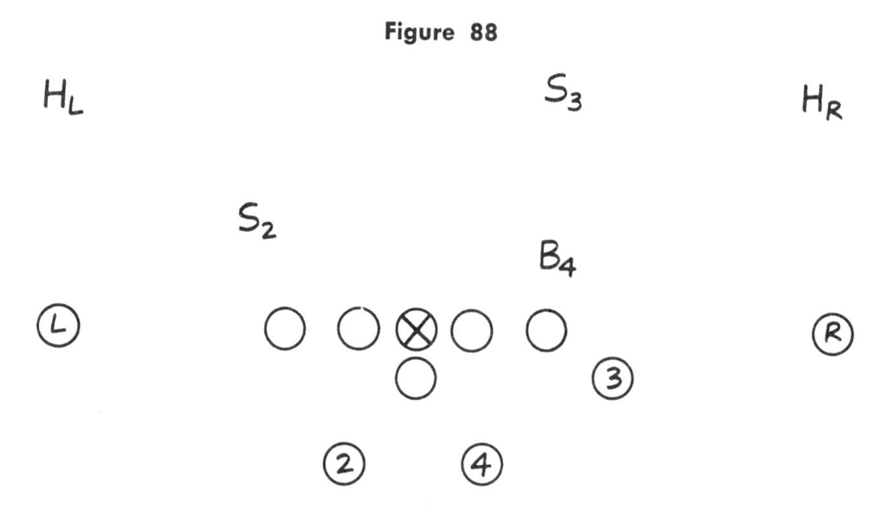

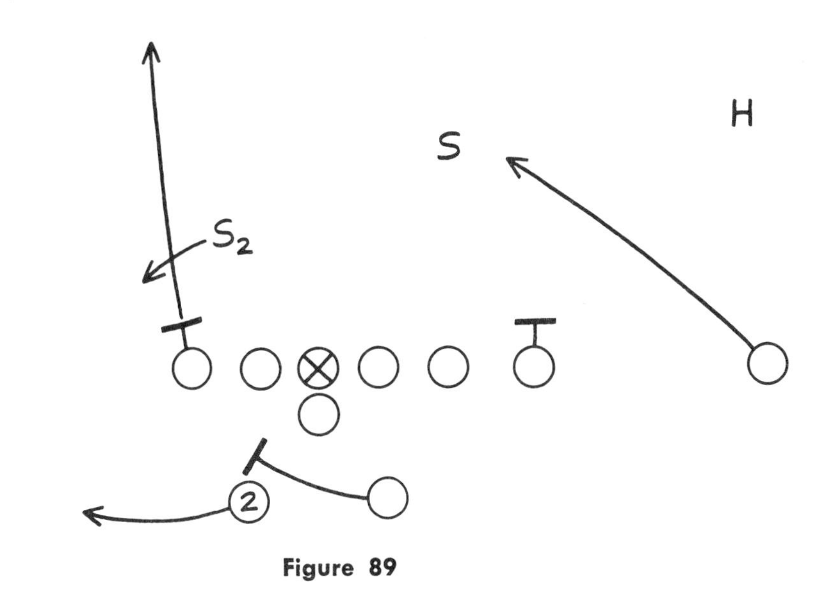


Figure 89

sideline pass, and we also hit the slot back quickly on sprint-right pass.

The play that broke down this defense was our tackle-eligible pass (see Figure 89). We dropped the left end back and put the slot back up on the line of scrimmage. The left end ran a sideline pattern and the number two back swung to the left, taking the safety man with him. Our usual pattern on this play has the number two back remain in as a blocker, but we quickly made a slight change. The tackle would hit his man and then run a pattern right through the spot the safety man left. Our passing record for the day was 11 for 15, and we made 156 yards and three touchdowns. The score midway through the third period was 37–6 and we put in our reserves to finish the game.

If you have a passer with strength, accuracy and good timing, and receivers with good hands, good faking moves and speed; there is not a pass defense in the world that you can't tear apart. We spend a great deal of time developing the talents of our passers and receivers. Our passing attack is well rehearsed. But finally the success of our passing game depends upon whether we exploit it during the course of the game. We must be alert and use our imagination to make our preparation worth-while.

## Originating Plays

In some games the defense may show a weakness that you do not have a play to properly exploit. Our tackle-eligible pass came into being this way. We were playing a team that had no deep middle coverage of the side away from our slot back. We were not able to pass into this area. At halftime we very quickly diagramed a tackle-eligible play and scored two touchdowns in the second half with it to break a 0–0 deadlock. Afterwards this pass play was incorporated into our offense. Don't be afraid to invent a new play, which you can put in at halftime. Your players are intelligent enough to be able to run one play without practice. Do not be afraid to originate. The coach who is afraid to make a move is the one who stands to lose the most.

### Halftime opportunity

During the halftime break you have only about ten minutes to work. Though your team is resting, you must give them instruction. One warning, do not try to accomplish too much at halftime or you will accomplish nothing. At halftime we discuss only the areas that are causing the most trouble. That is why we have no set schedule. One game we may put in a special play; another time we may change some blocking assignments to make a pet play work. Because we have to scramble on defense, many halftime sessions are devoted to stopping our opponent's offense. When halftime is over not only should the boys be rested, but they should have received some instruction to help them during the second half.

## Making the Big Play

In every ball game, there seem to be crucial times when an important play is needed. The entire game may hinge on calling this play, and it is up to you to call it. I don't believe your quarterback should call it because there is too much pressure on him. Let the Monday morning quarterback blame you and not a boy. This is the point where you are put to your severest test. Everyone in the stands is second-guessing you and in a moment you'll be either a bum or a hero, until the next time that is.

In making the call in such a situation, there are certain things you should do:

1. Consider what plays have been working
2. Use your most dependable performers
3. Outwit your opponent by not doing exactly what you think that he thinks you will do.

The fact that we are not a conservative team is helpful in this situation. Because we are quite unpredictable, the defense is less apt to gang up on us in a specific area. This gives us a better choice of plays to call.

We do not change plays on the line of scrimmage because all eleven men have proven unable to catch the change at the same time, and we do not wish to spend the time practicing this skill. One rule our quarterback must follow when running "the big play" is that he must look over the defense. If the defense is ganged up at the point of attack, he is to call time out. The quarterback and I then discuss a change in the call and decide upon another play. This has worked quite well for us.

Under your leadership the coaching staff also has a game to play. If the coaches conduct the game well from the sidelines, there is little question that the chance for success on the field has been greatly increased. Don't be afraid to think and to make changes. Don't "stand pat" with something unless it is working for you. Your ability to conduct the game has a great effect upon its outcome.

## Be Predictably Unpredictable

You may be surprised to find out how predictable your own strategy is in certain situations. You may not feel this to be true of yourself but you probably have a pretty good "book" on your opposing coach's strategy. The strange thing about this is, the predictable coach doesn't think that he is. Only by reviewing your own offensive strategy in an impartial manner could you find out the truth. Other coaches are certainly not going to tell you.

Some coaches have a favorite play for short yardage. Although their teams may execute this play very well, the advantage may be offset by the fact that the defense knows it is coming and is set up to stop it. If your offensive strategy is predictable in a certain situation, defending against you is much easier and the defense can be much more effective.

## Passing Strategy

When and where to pass is a subject upon which there is a great deal of written material. I believe that you should pass at any time and at any place within reason and this will vary with each coach. Because we pass a lot, it is easier to consider the times when we will not pass. Down and distance, and field position have little to do with our deciding not to pass. The score of the game at the time, the weather and perhaps the limitations of personnel on a particular day are the main considerations in determining whether or not to pass. In addition, if we are fairly certain that the running game will do the job, we use it.

We lose possession of the ball more often by fumbles than we do by interceptions. For this reason, fear of interception is not a consideration in determining whether to pass.

The time and the score are really the most influential factors in deciding whether or not to pass. In some games we have gone into the final quarter with a slight lead and failed to continue passing. We have had success during the entire game with our passing, and at the end we have gone to the running game only to try to run out the clock. At times it did not work. We wouldn't make even one first down and would have to punt and relinquish the ball. We have made this mistake several times and as a result now treat this situation differently. If we need first downs near the end of the game, we continue to pass if the passing game has been going for us. We use running plays to run out the clock if we are reasonably sure of their success or if we are sure that four running plays will use up all the time remaining in the game. None of these rules are absolute. The decision should take into account the various factors of the moment. Our general rule is that we do not change our style of play toward the end of a game unless we can run the clock out in one series of downs. We have directly lost one game because of this rule but have saved many more. If you play the wide-open game, you should realize that you must take many calculated risks. You cannot always be right.

Whatever your strategy, don't be a run–run–pass–punt team. Your chances of being successful on a pass play are much better on a first and ten situation than on a third and ten. Call your plays so that your opponent can never be completely sure what the next play will be. Our opponents know we may pass on a fourth and one situation. This fact will give our running play a better chance of making the first down because the defense must be a little cautious. If you have a reputation for doing the unexpected, you have a better chance of succeeding. Our strategy is to keep our opponent in the dark about our intentions so that his defense must be geared to stopping all of our offense all the time.

## Conclusion

The forward pass is the most powerful weapon in football. It is explosive in nature; the entire complexion of a ball game can be quickly changed by it. Trying to contain a good passing offense is like holding a tiger by the tail, whether it is on the professional, collegiate, or high-school level.

# INDEX

# INDEX


A

Ability of receiver, 57–59
Accuracy, loss of, 52–53
Action passes, 105–109
Age of boy as passer, 2–3
Aggressive backfield blocking, 124–125
Aggressive blocking for linemen, 117–118
Agility of passer, 20–23
Attacking pass defenses, 181–196

B

Back as receiver, 57
Backfield pass blocking drill, 125–128
Base, using right foot for, 37
"Big play," 226–227
Block fake, 69–71 (*See* Chap. 13)
Blocking, 113–140

C

Catching a football, techniques for, 60–73
Characteristics of receiver, 57–59
Coaches conducting game, 211–229
Coaching, 1–11, 20, 22–23, 49–51, 55–56, 73–74, 113–115, 166–180, 197–210, 211–229
Compiling and keeping records, 141–155
Concentration of receiver, 61–62
Conducting game, 211–229
  "big play," making, 226–227
    decisions to be made for, 227
Conducting game (*cont.*)
  coach, 211–214
    "can win," attitude, 212–213
    key information on hand when, 213–214
      defensive alignments, 214
      offensive plans, 213–214
      personnel charts, 213
  coach, assistant, 214–216
    as line coach, work of, 215–217
    capabilities of, 214
    knowledge of, 214
      current game plans, 214
      football system, 214
    work of, 214–215
  coach, head, 217–219
    as leader, 217
    backfield and ends, responsible for, 218–219
    substitution, responsible for, 217–218
      automatic substitution, handled by players, 217–218
  defense, fooling, 222
    fakes, use of, 222
    key plays, use of, 222
    surprise plays, use of, 222
  defensive strategy, 219
    development of, 219
    head coach and two assistant coaches, responsible for, 220
  offensive strategy, 219–221
    defensive weaknesses, uncover, 220–221
      key spot, find, 221

Conducting game (*cont.*)
defensive weaknesses (*cont.*)
trap play, use of, 220–221
originating plays, 226
courage for, 226
halftime, during, 226
passing game go, making, 223–225
downfield coverage, breaking down, 223–224
pass defense, examples of exploiting, 224–225
left end, 224–225
man-to-man, 224–225
tackle-eligible pass, 225
with rushing or non-rushing defenses, 222–223
passing strategy, 228
time and score, important factors, 228
personal strategy, 227–228
summary, 229
Control of ball, 12–15
Cross series, 105–107

D

Deep cross pass, 85–86
Defensive adjustments and variations, 102–105
Defensive strategy, 219–220
Developing a depth of passers, 3–8
Development of good passer, 49–56
Direction of throw, changing, 28–30
Double wrinkle fake move, 65
Downfield coverage, 186–189

E

Evaluating present passing game, 156–162

F

Fake block, 69–71
Fake moves, 63–72
Fall-off pass, 87
Fan series, 107–109
"Feel" of throwing while moving in any direction, 44
Films, 36, 42, 73, 143–145
Fooling defense, 222
Fullback blocking, 121–122
Fundamentals of teaching game, 11–19
Fusia, Vic, 142

G

Game film analysis, 145–151
Game week, various duties of coaches during, 197–210
defenses, combating various, 199–201
procedures for, 199–201
general situations, prepared to meet, for self and team, 198
meetings, coaches, 202–205
defense, preparing, 203–205
offense, preparing, 205
offensive formations, combating various, 198–199
practice, introducing plans at, 206–208
defensive, 206–208
offensive, 206
practice schedule, 208–210
outline, 208–210
preparation for, 199–201
rules, game, 201–202
summary, 210
"Giving with the ball," 58
"Gun shy" passer, 55–56

H

Halfback blocking, 122–124
"Heavy" ball, throwing a, 54–55
Holding up receivers, 184–186
Hook fake, 67–68
Hook-go fake, 68–69
Hook-go pass, 85

I

Individual passes, 93–95
Integrating new trends and ideas into your attack, 166–180
Integrating a passing attack into any offense, method used for, 156–165
evaluate your present passing game, 156–157
film, study, 161–162
for all passes in game, 161–162
forms used, 162 (*See* Chap. 8)
memory list, 162
present pass plays, diagram, 157
record of passes, compile, 157–159 (*See* Chap. 5)
standard and action, 158–159
test your memory, 159–160
by listing passes in areas, 159–160
for setting up passing game from year to year, 160
findings, collect, 164–165
passing needs, determining, 162–163
list objectives for, 163
surprise, element of, 163–164 (*See* Chap. 13)
Intelligence and eligibility as passer, 6–7

L

"Lead" on ball, 39
Leadership ability of passer, 7–8
Loss of accuracy, 52–53
Loss of lateral accuracy, 53
Loss of spiral, 54

M

Making passing game go, 223–225
Manning, Tom, 3, 33, 36, 42, 46, 47, 50, 90 151
Man-to-man coverage, defeating, 189–190
Method to improve releasing time of ball, 34
Moves, fake, 63–72
Moving back to pass, 12–13
Moving position, 36–48

N

New trends and ideas into attack, integrating, 166–180
backs, tandem, 180
coach, duties of, 166–180
ideas of others, 166–167
lectures, give and attend, 166–167
material, research for, 166
in old and new books, periodicals, and articles, 167–168, 174
on new techniques, 166
methods, inject new, 166–167
new techniques, learn from assistants, opponents, and from losing, 169–170
student of game, constant, 166
high-school football, 177
influences on, 177–179
pro attack, personnel problems created by, 178–179
rollout versus pocket pass, 175–177
ability of passer, 176–177
styles of passing, 175–176
college, 175–176
high-school, 175–176
professional, 175–176
sprint series, 170–175
difficulties in, 174–175
right pass, executing sprint, 172–175
factor, contributing, 174
running ends, new way of, 170–172
Normal backfield blocking, 120–124

Normal blocking for lineman, 115–117

O

Off-balance position, throwing from, 36–48
analyze your films, 36, 42
pass-or-run option technique, 46
fake moves, 46
pass-or-run situations, 48
pass-or-run skills, teaching, 47
protect quarterback at all times, 47
use films, 47–48
practice, 36
"right-handed factor," 37–38
advantage and disadvantage of, 37–38
use left-handed game, 37–38
running pass drills, various, 44–46
summary, 48
use right foot as base when, 37
while moving backwards, 43–44
disadvantages, 44
limitations, 43–44
while running forward, 42–43
procedure, 43
while running left, 39–42
tactics, 39–42
while running right, 38–39
tactics, 38–39
Offensive passing, 75–112
Offensive set-up, 78–94
Offensive strategy, 219–221
Offensive system, 96
Off-season passing practice, 49–56
"Off" side blocking, 134, 136
Off-tackle pass, 98–100
Off-tackle run, 97–98
"On" side blocking, 134–136
One-on-one drill, 119–120
One-on-one fake move, 68–69
Organized football at Marblehead, 1–2
high school level, program for, 1–2
junior varsity team, 1
ninth grade team, 1
varsity team, 1
junior high school, program for, 1–2
seventh and eighth grade level, 1
midget, program for, 1–2
fifth and sixth grade level, 1
Originating plays, 226
Overhand motion, 15–19

P

Pass defense, breaking down, 73
Pass defenses, attacking, 181–196
alternatives used, 182
difficulties, 181–182
downfield coverage, complete, 186–189
pass, types of, 188–189
passing against, 188
professional, 186–187
man-to-man coverage, defeating, 189–190
pass, type of, 190
requirements for, 189–190
passer, rushing, 182–184
from one end, 184
halfbacks, tight-covering, 184
passes used, 183–184
protection of, 183–184 (*See* Chap. 7)
receivers, holding up, 184–186
disadvantages, 185
manner of overcoming, 185–186
tactics for, 184–185
zone coverage, 190–193
advantages, various, 191–192
normal, 192–193
weaknesses, obvious, 191

Pass defenses (*cont.*)
zone coverage, methods of defeating, 193–196
flooding zones, 194
forced man-to-man coverage, 193
having good passer, 195–196 (*See* Fig. 5, Chap. 2)
passing into "in-between" areas, 195
Pass drills, running, 44–46
Pass protection, 113–140
aggressive backfield blocking, 124–125
aggressive lineman blocking, 117
advantages of, 117
disadvantage of, 117
pro, action, and rollout passes required for, 117
techniques for, 117–118
uncovered blocker, 118
backfield blocking, 138–139
fullback, 138
halfback, 138–139
backfield pass blocking drill, 126–127
aggressive, 127
dummy, 126
live, 127
semi-live, 126
blocking, methods of, 115
aggressive, 115
normal, 115
waiting, 115
blocking outstanding defensive end, 124 (*See* Chap. 6)
concentrated rush, methods used for, 132–134
holding one receiver to block, 132
rolling out, 134
throwing a short quick pass, 132–133
developing good, teamwork for, 113–114
normal backfield blocking, 120–140

Pass protection (*cont.*)
normal backfield blocking (*cont.*)
situations faced by, 121–124
blocking end who rushes from outside, 121–122
halfback block of end on inside path, 122
halfback blocking, 122
non-rushing end, 124
techniques used for, 120–121
normal linemen blocking, 115–117
ability of lineman to execute, 115
pocket, action, or rollout passes, used for, 115
uncovered blocker, 117
with defensive man head on, 115–116
withdrawing pressure, 116
one-on-one drill, 119–120
players used for, 119–120
pocket, 128–129
tight linebacker, 129
pocket protection, 128–129
rules, blocking, 128–129
rollout, 134–136
by blocking off side, 136
by blocking on side, 135
rollout right, 136–138
center, 137
left guard, 137
left tackle, 137
right guard, 137
right tackle, 137–138
rushing high-school passer, 113–114
stunting and red dogging defenses, handling, 130–131
shooting or red dogging linebacker, 131
stunting, methods used for, 130
summary, 140
time, sufficient, 113–115
for blocking, 114–115
for pocket, 114–115

Pass protection (*cont.*)
time (*cont.*)
for rollout, 114–115
waiting block, 118–119
advantage of, 118–119
off-side blocking on rollout and action pass, used for, 118–119
use of modified, 119
Pass-or-run option technique, 46
Pass-or-run situations, 48
Pass-or-run skills, teaching, 47
Pass-receiver, improving, 59–60
Passer, "gun shy," 55–56
Passer practicing on his own, 10–11
Passer, selecting, 1–8
age of boy, 2–3
intelligence and eligibility for, 6–7
"football know-how," 6–7
scholastic record, 6
leader, ability as, 7–8
potential, 4–6
size, 4–5
throwing ability, 5–6
speed, 8
Passer stepping up to throw, 23–24
Passing game, 9–35
coaching situations, 9–11
group instructions, 10
individual instructions, 9–10
passers practicing on their own, 10–11 (*See*, Chap. 4)
control and accuracy of passer, 26–27
keep eyes on target, 26–27
practice, 26
select a target, 26–27
direction of throw, changing, 28–30
ability of setting up for, 28–29
drills, 29–30
fake moves, 28–29
fundamentals of, teaching, 11–15
Passing game (*cont.*)
fundamentals of (*cont.*)
moving back to pass, 12–13
control of ball by quarterback, 12–13
snap from center, 12–13
method used to improve timing, 34
in a dummy scrimmage—your ends and backfield against defensive backs and linebackers, 34
in a normal scrimmage, 34
in a one-on-one drill (receiver versus defender), 34
overhand motion, 15–19
techniques for right- and left-handed passer, 16–19
bringing ball forward, 17
drawing ball back, 16–17
follow-through, proper, 18–19
position of ball for, 16
releasing ball, proper timing when, 17–18
power behind ball, sources of, 20–23
arm, 21
drill for strengthening, 21
back, 22
shoulders, 21
strengthening, various ways of, 21
throwing motion technique, 22–23
wrist, 20–21
development, exercises for, 20
releasing ball, sense of timing when, 30–31
examples, proper release time, 30–34
set position, throwing from, 13–15
how to grip ball when, 14–15
feet position and weight of passer, 13

Passing game (*cont.*)
stepping forward to throw, 23–24
advantages, 23
disadvantage, 23–24
for greater distance, 24
into pocket, 23–24
throwing at moving targets, 27–28
drills, 27–28
for proper lead, 27–28
warming up during practice, proper, 24–25
summary, 35
Passing offense, 75–112
action passes, 105–109
cross series, 96, 106–107
fan series, 107
19–60 pass, 109
defensive adjustments and variations, 102–105
covering flat with inside linebacker, 103
covering flat with safety man, 103
defense may overshift, 105
defense may run with you, 105
loosening end, 102–103
individual pass (Roger or Louie), 93–95
moves, 94–95
rolling out on an, 94
stay, 94
offensive set-up, 78–94
"Louie" (left end), 78, 85–86, 94
"Roger" (right end), 78, 85–86, 94
"slot left," 78
offensive system, 96
numbering and play calling, 96
off-tackle pass, 98–100
27–0, against an overshifted defense, 99–100
off-tackle run, 97–98
Passing offense (*cont.*)
short pass versus long pass, 110–111
slot "T" line up compared to pro "T" lineup, 109–110
standard pass play, 75–76
advantages of, 75
disadvantages of, 75–76
pocket, 75
rollouts, short, 75
screens, 75, 89–93
standard passes, 75–76, 79–86
deep cross, 85–86
hook-go, 85
trail-in, 81–83 (*See*, Chap. 2)
trail-out, 79
standard passes, miscellaneous, 86–87
fall-off, 87
pro, 87
Roger or Louie, individual, 78, 85–86, 93–95
screen, 89–93
executing, 91
halfback technique on, 92–93
summary, 111–112
terminology, 76–78
for college level, 76–77
for high school level, 77–78
weak side off-tackle run and pass, 100–102
46–0 pass, 101–102
46–0 run, 100–101
Passing potential, 4–6
Passing practice, off-season, 49–56
accuracy, loss of, 52–53
drills, 54
underthrown pass, causes of, 52–53 (*See* Chap. 3)
underthrown pass, correcting, 52–53
"gun shy" passer, 55–56
avoid selecting, 55
courage of, 55–56
faults, 55–56
problems of, 55

Passing practice (*cont.*)
"gun shy" passer (*cont.*)
summary, 56
"heavy" ball, throwing a, 54–55
correcting, 55
lateral accuracy, loss of, 53
drills, 54
spiral, loss of, 54
cause for, 54
spring practice, 50–51
drills, 51
fundamentals of the grip, 50–51
skills of throwing from off-balance position, 50–51
spring workouts, 50
summer months, 51–52
correcting weaknesses after, 52
game films, 52
set-up for, 51–52
timing, poor, 52 (*See* Chap. 2)
winter months, during, 49–50
Passing strategy, 228
Passing technique, 20–23
Passing while moving backwards, 43–44
Passing while running forward, 42–43
Passing while running left, 39–42
Passing while running right, 38–39
Pocket protection for blocking backs, 120–121, 128, 129
Potential passer, 4–6, 15–19
Practice during spring workouts, 50
Practice during summer months, 51–52
Practice during winter months, 49–50
Practicing off-balance throwing, 36–48
Pro pass, 87
Protecting the passer, 113–140

Q

Qualities of receiver, 57–59

R

Receiver, 57–74
ability of, 57–59
catching, 57–59
running, 57
catching football, techniques for, 60–73
"giving" with the ball, 61
hands and arms of receiver, 60–61
loose hands, properly positioned, 60
with fingers, 60
characteristics of, 57–59
concentration of, 61–62
in catching ball, 62
when holding onto ball, 62
courage of, 57–58
fake moves, individual, 63–72
direction, change of, 72
double wrinkle, 65
fake block, 69–71 (*See* Chap. 13)
hook (one-on-one pattern), 68–69
pace, change of, 71–72
"wrinkle" (single), 64–65
Z-in and Z-out, 65–67
pass defense, breaking down, 73–74 (*See* Chap. 11)
films, analyzing past, 73
rules, 73
working with receivers and passers together, 73–74
pass-receiver, methods of improving poor, 59–60
by catching ball year-round, 59
by pass receiving in daily practice, 59–60
early or extra practice, 59
rules, special, 59
working with coach on catching techniques, 59
physical qualities, 57–59

Receiver (*cont.*)
physical qualities (*cont.*)
hands, good ("giving with the ball"), 58
movement, good, 58
"breaking down" defender, 58
pass patterns, with or without fakes, 58
size, 58–59
tight end needs, 59
speed, 58–59
Records, compiling and keeping, 141–155
game-by-game, 143–145
plans and defenses, 144–145
play cards of all opponent's plays and defenses, 145
scouting report and summaries, 143–145
game film analysis, 145–151
of offense, 145–149
of opponent, 149
sheet and charts, 146–149
statistics, 150
methods used for, 141–144
summary, 155
summary, seasonal, 151–153
general, 151–153
individual pass plays, 153 (*See* Chaps. 5 and 6)
Red dogging and stunting defenses, 130–131
Right end player as receiver, 58
"Right-handed factor," 37–38
Rollout right pass, 136–138
Rollout versus pocket pass, 175–177
Rose Bowl Game on TV, 46
Running pass drills, 44–46
Rushing passer, 113–114, 182–184
Rushing players, 132–134

S

Screen passes, 89–93
Selecting end as receiver, 57
Selecting passer, 1–8
Set position, 36–37
Set position, throwing from, 9–35
Short pass versus long pass, 110–111
Slot "T" line-up compared to pro "T" line-up, 109–110
Speed of passer, 8
Spiral, loss of, 54
Spring workouts, practice during, 50
Sprint series, 170–175
Standard passes, 75–76, 79–87
Stay or short pass, 94
Stepping up to throw, 23–24
Stunting and red dogging defenses, 130–131
Summaries, 35, 48, 56, 111–112, 196, 210, 229
Summer months, practice during, 51–52

T

Teamwork for pass protection, 113
Techniques for catching ball, 60–73
Terminology, 76–78
Throwing a "heavy" ball, 54–55
Throwing at moving targets, 27–28
Throwing from moving or off-balance positions, 36–48
Throwing motion technique, 22–23
Timing, poor, 52 (*See* Chap. 2)
Trail-in pass, 81–83 (*See* Chap. 2)
Trail-out pass, 79

W

Waiting block, 118–119
Weak side off-tackle run and pass, 100–102
"Wrinkle" fake move (single), 64–65

Z

Z-in and Z-out fake moves, 65–67
Zone coverage, 190–196